Killing Patton

ALSO BY BILL O'REILLY AND MARTIN DUGARD

Killing Lincoln

Killing Kennedy

Killing Jesus

Killing Reagan

Killing the Rising Sun

Killing England

Killing the SS

Killing Patton

THE STRANGE DEATH OF WORLD WAR II'S
MOST AUDACIOUS GENERAL

Bill O'Reilly

and

Martin Dugard

ST. MARTIN'S GRIFFIN ✠ NEW YORK

www.stmartins.com

Designed by Meryl Sussman Levavi

The Library of Congress has cataloged the Henry Holt edition as follows:

O'Reilly, Bill.
    Killing Patton : the strange death of World War II's most audacious general / Bill O'Reilly and Martin Dugard. — First edition.
        pages cm
    Includes bibliographical references and index.
    ISBN 978-0-8050-9668-2 (hardcover)
    ISBN 978-0-8050-9669-9 (ebook)
1. Patton, George S. (George Smith), 1885–1945—Death and burial.   I. Dugard, Martin.   II. Title.
    E745.P3O74 2014   -
    355.0092—dc23

                                                            2014019610

ISBN 978-1-250-07074-6 (trade paperback)

Our books may be purchased in bulk for promotional, educational, or business use. Please contact your local bookseller or the Macmillan Corporate and Premium Sales Department at 1-800-221-7945, extension 5442, or by email at MacmillanSpecialMarkets@macmillan.com.

First published by Henry Holt and Company

First St. Martin's Griffin Edition: September 2018

10 9 8 7 6 5

To my father, William O'Reilly,

who served his country as a naval officer in World War II,

and to my grandfather John O'Reilly,

who served in World War I

We'll win this war, but we'll win it only by fighting and showing the Germans that we've got more guts than they have; or ever will have. We're not just going to shoot the sons-of-bitches, we're going to rip out their living Goddamned guts and use them to grease the treads of our tanks.

GEN. GEORGE S. PATTON JR.
JUNE 5, 1944

Map Legend

Allied

→ Advance

⇒ Highlighted movement

┈┈► Retreat

🪖 Infantry

🛡 Armor/
U.S./U.K.

🛡 mechanized*
U.S.S.R.

*On some maps, only tank symbols are used. In these cases, tanks represent armies or army groups that also include infantry.

White symbols are used periodically to highlight Allied units and their movements.

Axis

← Advance

⬅ Highlighted movement

◄┈┈ Retreat

🪖 Infantry

🚙 Armor/ mechanized*

Military features

〜 Front line

〜 Defensive position

〜 West wall

✳ Clash/event

●●● Battery

↔ Machine-gun emplacement

▨ Barbwire

Physical features

〜 Major roads

〜 Minor roads

〜 Railroads

〜 Rivers

Terrain

Forest

City/town with urban area

Combatant nationalities

🇺🇸 United States

🇬🇧 United Kingdom

Canada

🇫🇷 France

U.S.S.R.

Germany

Killing Patton

Prologue

———◆———

Room 110
U.S. Army 130th Station Hospital
Heidelberg, Germany
December 21, 1945
5:00 p.m.

The man with forty-five minutes to live cannot defend himself.

Gen. George S. Patton Jr. fears no one. But now he sleeps flat on his back in a hospital bed. His upper body is encased in plaster, the result of a car accident twelve days ago. Room 110 is a former utility closet, just fourteen feet by sixteen feet. There are no decorations, pictures on the walls, or elaborate furnishings—just the narrow bed, white walls, and a single high window. A chair has been brought in for Patton's wife, Beatrice, who endured a long, white-knuckle flight over the North Atlantic from the family home in Boston to be at his bedside. She sits there now, crochet hook moving silently back and forth, raising her eyes every few moments to see if her husband has awakened.

Patton is fond of the finer things in life, and during the course of the Second World War, he made his battlefield headquarters in mansions, palaces, castles, and five-star hotels. But right now the sole concession to luxury is that, as a four-star general, Patton does not have to share his room with another patient.

"Old Blood and Guts," as his soldiers refer to the sixty-year-old legend, is a man both revered and feared. He has many enemies. Thus the need for the white-helmeted armed guards posted directly outside his door, at the end of the long hallway leading to the hospital lobby, and at every entrance and exit of the building. Nicknamed for their helmets, these "Snowdrops" protect Patton from the American journalists who have descended on this quiet former cavalry barracks in a great pack, ignoring the ongoing Nuremberg war crime trials so that they might write about Patton's accident and expected recovery. General Patton "is getting well like a house afire," the Associated Press reported four days ago, basing its information on the army's daily 6:00 p.m. briefing about his condition. The story also reported that Patton sat up in bed, throwing off his injury "with a speed reminiscent of his wartime advances."

The truth, however, is far different. Gen. George S. Patton Jr. is paralyzed from the neck down. Bones in his spine were dislocated when his car collided with an army truck full of drunken joyriding soldiers. Patton's number three cervical vertebra was shattered, badly bruising his spinal cord. The good news is that he has recovered some movement in his extremities. The bad news is that his doctors believe it is highly unlikely he will walk again.

The reporters don't know this, and so they work overtime to invade Patton's privacy to see his amazing recovery for themselves. Some have tried to sneak into Room 110 dressed as nurses or orderlies. Others have bribed hospital staff with Hershey bars and nylons. Thanks to the sentries, however, all of them have failed. The closest call was when Richard H. O'Regan, the same reporter from the Associated Press who wrote of Patton's remarkable recovery, cadged an interview with Patton's nurse by pretending to be a patient. For his troubles, O'Regan was able to reveal to the world that doctors were allowing Patton to sip a thimbleful of whisky each night with dinner.

But reporters are the least of Patton's worries. Throughout the course of the Second World War, he made many high-ranking enemies in Moscow, Berlin, London, and even Washington, DC. Patton's fiery determination to speak the truth had many powerful men squirming not only during the war, but also afterward. He recently went on the record praising his former German enemies for their skills as soldiers, while also criticizing the Soviet Union as being a foe rather than an ally of the United States. Some have come to see Patton as a roadblock to world peace. And now Patton is at his most vulnerable, an easy target for any of those enemies.

A year ago to this day, Patton was in the midst of the most glorious battle of his career, racing across France with his beloved Third Army to rescue American forces pinned down at the crossroads in Bastogne, Belgium. The German army had long considered Patton to be the Allies' greatest general, but the Battle of the Bulge, as it would become known, elevated him to legendary status throughout the world.

Now the swaggering, fearless renegade who prowled the front lines in a specially modified Dodge WC57 command car outfitted with a .50-caliber machine gun, siren, and two air horns to announce his arrival is hidden from the public. The George S. Patton who sleeps fitfully as Friday evening descends upon Heidelberg has a low pulse and a high fever. He drank eggnog for lunch and for a time felt upbeat, but his energy sagged before he finally fell asleep. A blood clot in his lungs made his face turn blue yesterday, and there are fears that another embolism might soon give him more trouble breathing.

The auto accident was brutal. Stitches and bruising cover Patton's head from the bridge of his nose to the top of his scalp, marking the line where doctors sewed a Y-shaped flap of skin back onto his head. His face is gaunt from weight loss, and there are open holes in his cheekbones where doctors drilled into his face to insert steel fish hooks to hold his head in traction. But the general has a high pain threshold and has endured his sufferings with a smile and his usual blue humor. He banters with the nurses, who find him "cute." Despite the fact that he has taken a sudden and unexpected turn for the worse in the past few days, the general still expects to be flown to Beverly General Hospital in Boston to further his recovery.

Beatrice has been with him around the clock, reading to him and calling for the doctors when he has a hard time catching his breath. She has a small room of her own down the hall, but is rarely there. The former heiress is a plain woman with a charismatic personality who wed Patton just a year after he graduated from West Point. Throughout their thirty-five-year marriage, Beatrice has braved the many hardships of military life for her beloved "Georgie," never wavering in her love and support.

Suddenly Patton wakes up. His dark blue eyes flick back and forth, searching for signs of Beatrice.

There she is.

"Are you all right, Georgie?" Beatrice asks. She is every bit as fiery as her husband, a fearless equestrienne and accomplished sailor.

Patton gazes intently at his wife. She is the only woman he ever truly loved, and the mother of his three children. Beatrice leans forward to pat her husband's hand.

"It's so dark," Patton says. "So late." He closes his eyes and falls back to sleep.

Beatrice soon leaves for the hospital mess, where she hopes to grab a quick dinner before returning to the bedside, not knowing that her husband has just spoken his last words.

At 6:00 p.m. the urgent news is delivered for Beatrice to return immediately to Room 110.

But she is too late.

The general whom Nazi Germany feared more than any other, the former Olympic pentathlete, the cavalry officer who once hunted the infamous Pancho Villa across the desert plains of Mexico, and the warrior who publicly stated that he wanted one day to be killed "by the last bullet, in the last battle, of the last war," is already dead.

★   ★   ★   ★

The official military report states that Gen. George S. Patton Jr. "died at 1745, 21 December 1945." A pulmonary embolism, brought on by his twelve days lying immobile, had weakened his heart. The official causes of death, as listed in the army adjutant general's report, are "traumatic myelitis, transverse fourth cervical segment, pulmonary infarction, and myocardial failure, acute."

There is no autopsy. His body is immediately taken to the hospital basement and placed inside what was once a horse stall, where his personal four-star flag is laid over the corpse. At Beatrice's request, Patton is laid to rest at the American Cemetery in Hamm, Luxembourg, near the scene of his greatest battlefield triumph. Years later, when Beatrice falls from a horse and dies, she will be denied burial next to her husband, so her children will secretly smuggle her ashes into Europe and sprinkle them atop the grave.

It is a grave that may hold even deeper secrets.

★   ★   ★   ★

The truth is, some do not believe Patton's death was accidental. He had already survived several "accidents," including the time his personal airplane was almost shot down by a British Spitfire fighter plane in April 1945—almost miraculously, Patton escaped injury.

But the auto crash that paralyzed Patton on December 9, 1945, was a far different story. The two-and-a-half-ton GMC army truck that collided with the general's touring car suddenly and inexplicably veered from the opposite lane and into Patton—as if intentionally trying to injure the general. Both the man driving the truck and his two passengers quickly vanished after the incident. No criminal charges were ever filed. No accountability was ever recorded.

Also, both the official accident report and several key witnesses soon went missing. And most ominous of all, a former American intelligence operative confessed in October 1979 that he had planned and participated in the assassination of Gen. George S. Patton Jr.

It was a shocking assertion that was mostly ignored.

And so it was that a man who saw so much death on the battlefields of Europe and Africa officially died in a most pedestrian way.

Officially.

United States Third Army (October 1944)

LT. GENERAL GEORGE S. PATTON JR.

XII CORPS
MAJ. GEN. MANTON EDDY

XX CORPS
MAJ. GEN. WALTON WALKER

26th Division
MAJ. GEN. WILLARD PAUL
101 Infantry Regiment
104 IR
328 IR

5th Infantry Division
MAJ. GEN. LEROY IRVIN
2 Infantry Regiment
10 IR
11 IR

35th Division
MAJ. GEN. PAUL BAADE
134 IR
137 IR
320 IR

90th Division
MAJ. GEN. RAYMOND McCLAIN
357 IR
358 IR
359 IR

80th Division
MAJ. GEN. HORACE McBRIDE
317 IR
318 IR
319 IR

95th Division
MAJ. GEN. HARRY TWADDLE
377 IR
378 IR
379 IR

4th Armored Division
MAJ. GEN. JOHN WOOD
8 Tank Battalion
35 TB
37 TB
10 Armored Infantry Battalion
51 AIB
53 AIB

10th Armored Division
MAJ. GEN. WILLIAM MORRIS
3 Tank Battalion
11 TB
21 TB
21 Armored Infantry Battalion
54 AIB
61 AIB

6th Armored Division
MAJ. GEN. ROBERT GROW
15 TB
68 TB
69 TB
9 AIB
44 AIB
50 AIB

1

———◆———

THE HILLS ABOVE METZ, FRANCE
OCTOBER 3, 1944
12:02 P.M.

Private First Class Robert W. Holmlund is scared. He believes his life may be over at age twenty-one. The American assault is just two minutes old—two minutes that feel like twenty. The private serves as an explosives expert in the Third Army, Company B, Eleventh Infantry Regiment, Fifth Infantry Division. Holmlund is a student from the American heartland who left trade school to join the war. His senior commander is the most ferocious general on the Allied side, George S. Patton Jr. But unlike Patton, who now oversees his vast army from the safety of his headquarters twenty-five miles behind the front, Holmlund and the men of Baker Company are in grave danger as they sprint toward the heavily defended German fort known as Driant.

German machine-gun bullets whiz past Holmlund's helmet at twice the speed of sound. Heads and torsos shatter all around him. U.S. artillery thunders in the distance behind them, laying down cover fire. The forest air smells of gunpowder, rain, and the sharp tang of cordite. The ground is nothing but mud and a thick carpet of wet leaves. Here and there a bramble vine reaches out to snag his uniform and trip his feet. Over his broad shoulders, Holmlund wears a block of TNT known as a satchel charge. Grenades dangle from his cartridge belt like grapes on a vine. And in his arms, rather than carrying it by the wooden handle atop the stock, Holmlund cradles his fifteen-pound, four-foot-long Browning Automatic Rifle, or BAR, as he would an infant. Only, this baby is a killing machine, capable of firing 650 three-inch bullets per minute.

Though he doesn't show it, Robert W. Holmlund is scared, despite all that firepower, just like every single man in this lethal forest.

But there is no time to indulge his fear right now. No time for homesickness or doubt. Fort Driant looms four hundred yards distant. Everything about the fortress is a mystery, from the location of its big 150 mm howitzers to the maze of tunnels deep underground where its Wehrmacht inhabitants eat, sleep, pray, clean their rifles, plan their battles, and then suddenly poke their heads out of secret openings to kill.

Patton has ordered Baker Company to get inside Driant. The best way to do that is to climb on the roof, which is concealed by mounds of earth. From there, it's a matter of finding a doorway or some other hidden opening that will allow Baker to descend and wage war in the tunnels.

Baker is part of a two-pronged assault. On the opposite side of the fort, the men of Easy Company are also on the attack. But they do so warily, for Driant has already bloodied them once.

It happened six days ago. Skies were clear. P-47 fighter-bombers screamed in low on the morning of the assault, dropping napalm and thousand-pound bombs. American artillery then pounded Driant, shelling the Germans with deadly accuracy.

Easy Company launched their attack alongside the men of George Company at 1415 hours under a heavy smoke screen. They had no way of knowing that the aerial bombing and ground artillery had no effect on the Wehrmacht fighters, nor that the enemy was snug and secure within Driant's fifteen-foot-thick walls and in hidden forest pillboxes.

Step by step, thinking themselves unseen, the U.S. soldiers advanced. Fingers were on triggers as the men scanned the forest, waiting for the muzzle flashes that would expose the enemy. But the Germans did not shoot. Not yet. So Easy and George crept closer to Driant. With each passing moment, they became more convinced that the smoke screen had completely concealed them. They marched closer and closer, and still no German gunshots. Soon a thick tangle of barbwire loomed before the Americans, marking the outer perimeter of Driant's defenses. There was no way through the razor-sharp coils. The advance ground to a halt.

The Germans opened fire.

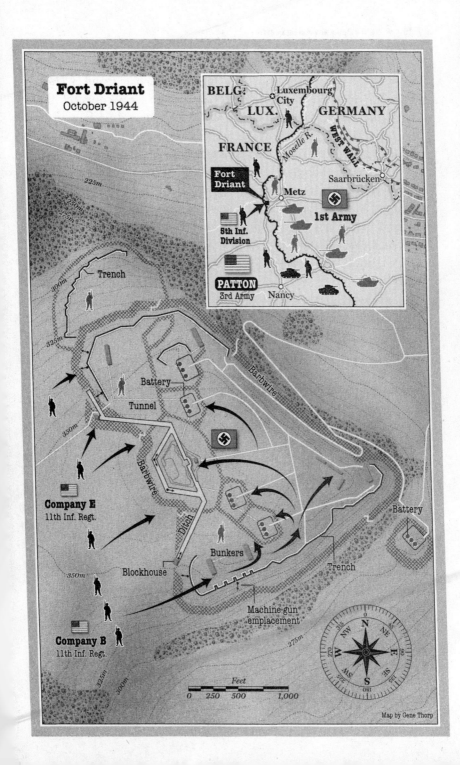

Fort Driant
October 1944

BELG.
Luxembourg City
LUX.
GERMANY
FRANCE
Moselle R.
WEST WALL
Fort Driant
Metz
Saarbrücken
5th Inf. Division
1st Army
PATTON
3rd Army
Nancy

225m
300m
325m
350m
350m
325m
300m
275m

Trench

Battery
Tunnel

Barbwire

Company E
11th Inf. Regt.

Barbwire

Ditch

Blockhouse
Bunkers

Machine-gun emplacement

Trench

Battery

Company B
11th Inf. Regt.

Feet
0   250   500   1,000

N
NW   NE
W   E
SW   SE
S

Map by Gene Thorp

The autumn afternoon was rent by a terrifying sound the Americans knew all too well. Their slang for the high-speed ripping sound of a German MG-42 machine gun is "Hitler's Zipper." To the Wehrmacht, this killing tone is simply the "Bone Saw." MG-42s opened up from every direction. Bullets tore through the woods at twelve hundred rounds per minute, capable of killing a man from more than a half mile away.

But the machine guns were just the beginning. Soon mortars, rifles, and even heavy artillery pounded the Americans from every direction. And just like that, the American attack was over. Soldiers hugged the ground for four long hours as German gunners pinpointed their positions and took slow, deliberate aim. It was only after darkness fell that the men of Company E and Company G crawled back to the safety of the American lines.

September 27 was a bad day for the men of Easy. By the end of the fight, eighteen soldiers had been either killed or wounded.

Today will be even worse.

★   ★   ★

Private Holmlund can go no farther. Nor can the rest of Baker Company. The mountain of barbwire surrounding Driant blocks their path. Thirty feet tall and just as thick, the impenetrable tangle waits to trap any man unlucky enough to snag his uniform or his body within its tendrils. Clipping at it with hand cutters will take days—which is why Holmlund's company commander, Capt. Harry Anderson, has given the order: blow the wire to hell.

Behind him, Holmlund hears the low rumble of a Continental R-975 air-cooled engine. The telltale crunch of steel treads soon follows, announcing the arrival of an M-4 Sherman tank. Even as the German machine gunners continue to fire on Baker, the Sherman weaves through the trees and takes aim. Its 75 mm gun belches smoke as it fires a round of M-48 high explosive into the wire. A direct hit is soon followed by another, and then another. Within moments, the barbwire parts just enough for Baker Company to sprint through.

Captain Anderson splits the soldiers into three groups. Holmlund's squad continues toward Driant in a straight line, while the other two squads flank to the right. The landscape is pocked with shell craters, like a man-made lunar surface. Trees and shrubs grow randomly, offering just the slightest bit of camouflage from the German defenders.

The private is in the first wave of American attackers. He dives into a shell crater, presses himself flat against the lip, then pokes his head over the top and fires his BAR at the enemy. Holmlund then sprints forward to a row of small elm trees, where he once again takes cover and seeks out a target. The ground is cool and damp, moisture seeping through his uniform. He fires and moves forward, always forward, never taking his focus off the flat roof of Driant. Despite the cool October temperature, Holmlund is now drenched in sweat. His face and hands are flecked with mud. He hurls himself into another shell crater and hugs the earth. This close to the ground, he is eye level with the fungus and bright green mold sprouting up through the fallen leaves. Bullets whiz low over his head. He reloads and listens, waiting for the chance to fire.

The sounds of the battlefield are familiar: the chatter of machine guns, the screams of the mortally wounded, the concussive thud of hand grenades, orders barked in short, terse sentences. Screams for "Medic" fill the air.

Holmlund fires a burst from his rifle and then runs forward. He races past fallen comrades. He knows them all. They did push-ups side by side during basic training in Alabama. They sailed together for Europe in the hold of a troopship. They sat in an English pasture just hours before D-day, listening to General Patton deliver the greatest speech any of them had ever heard. And then, after D-day, Holmlund and Baker fought their way across France, rejoicing as they captured one small village after another, following Patton's order that they kill Germans in brutal and relentless fashion—lest they themselves be killed first.

Now many of Holmlund's buddies lie dead or dying. And so ends the sound of their laughter, their rage, their boasts, their tales about that special girl back home, and all that talk about what they're going to do with their lives once the war ends.

Holmlund doesn't even give them a second glance.

And he doesn't stop moving forward. To stop is to become a target. Holmlund's fighting squad dwindles from twelve men down to six. The squad leader is hit, and Holmlund takes command without thinking twice about it. Slowly, in a form of progress that is measured in feet and inches instead of yards, Baker Company moves closer and closer to the German fortress.

Two hours into the battle, PFC Robert W. Holmlund of Delavan City, Wisconsin, finds himself standing atop Fort Driant.

★　★　★

"The real hero," Holmlund heard George S. Patton say just four months ago, "is the man who fights even though he's scared. Some men get over their fright in a minute under fire. For some, it takes days. But a real man will never let his fear of death overwhelm his honor, his sense of duty to his country, and his innate manhood."

As Holmlund watched, General Patton drew himself up to his full six-foot-two-inch height. His shoulders were broad and his face ruddy, with a strong chin and an aquiline nose. His uniform was a marvel, with four rows of ribbons, four shiny brass buttons, a polished helmet bearing his three general's stars, tan riding pants, and knee-high cavalry boots. Most vividly, a Colt .45-caliber pistol with an ivory grip was holstered on his hip, sending a strong signal that Patton is no bureaucrat. He's a warrior, and everybody had better know it.

Patton continued: "Battle is the most magnificent competition in which a human being can indulge. It brings out all that is best, and it removes all that is base. Americans pride themselves on being He Men— and they *are* He Men. Remember that the enemy is just as frightened as you are, and that they are not supermen."

George Patton delivered "the Speech" in the British countryside, to the men of his Third Army, on June 5, 1944. Some of the soldiers watching were combat veterans. Most, like Holmlund, were brand new to the war. They found hope in Patton's words. They found a belief in their own courage. And most of all, each man sitting in that pasture under a glorious blue English sky found strength in the knowledge that he was being commanded by the most audacious, forthright, and brilliant general on either side of the war.

Until that day, Holmlund had never seen Patton in the flesh, and had only heard stories about the legendary general—the man who'd never lost a battle, hero of North Africa and Sicily, but who was temporarily relieved of his command for slapping two privates convalescing in a military hospital whom he considered cowardly.

Neither Holmlund nor any of the thousands of other soldiers seated in this pasture had any idea that their feelings for the general would come to vacillate between love and hate. In fact, Patton's nickname is "Old Blood and Guts," with the understanding that the guts of Patton rode on the blood of his soldiers.

"You are not all going to die," Patton reassured the men whom he would soon lead into combat. His voice was high instead of gruff, which came as a surprise to Holmlund. "Only two percent of you right here today will die in a major battle. Death must not be feared. Death, in time, comes to all men."

★ ★ ★

One half mile north of where Private Holmlund and the men of Company B are making their stand atop Fort Driant, death, as predicted, is coming to their fellow soldiers in Easy Company. The hope of Patton's speech is long forgotten.

Unlike their first attack on Driant six days ago, Company E made it through the barbwire this time. But the Germans turned that into a fatal accomplishment, for once inside Easy was pinned down with precision mortar fire. Going forward has become impossible. Even worse, enemy shells are exploding to their rear, meaning that retreating back through the wire is also out of the question. Easy Company tries to solve the problem by calling in an artillery strike on their position, but this "Danger Close" barrage does nothing to stop the dug-in German gunners. Instead, friendly fire kills one of their own in a most gruesome fashion: the soldier's head is sliced cleanly from his body by a piece of flying explosive.

Easy Company digs in. They have no choice. Two-foot-long portable shovels scrape troughs in the earth as German machine gunners continue to rake Easy's position. It is every man for himself.

The terror continues. The Germans of Kampfgruppe Petersen take aim with 8 cm Granatwerfer 34 mortar fire and MG-42 machine guns. The Americans are defenseless. Killing them is as easy as finding the target and patiently squeezing the trigger. The Germans are in no hurry. The

Americans are going nowhere. One after another, the young men who comprise Easy Company are cut down in the prime of their life. The company medics race from foxhole to foxhole to tend the wounded. But soon, one after another, they die, too.

Hours pass. Rain drizzles down. The nightmare chatter of the *Maschinengewehr* accompanies the sounds of Company E digging their trenches deeper and deeper. Each man squats as low as possible, careful not to lift his head above ground level. Doing so would be an act of suicide. Easy's foxholes become filled with water, mud, blood, and each man's personal filth. Trench foot, from prolonged exposure to cold and wet, has become so common since the autumn rains arrived that it makes standing in yet another puddle a time of agony. But the men are beyond caring about the stench and squalor of their fighting holes.

All they want to do is stay alive.

⋆ ⋆ ⋆

"Americans despise cowards," Patton continued all those months ago, putting his own spin on U.S. history. "Americans play to win all the time. I wouldn't give a hoot in hell for a man who lost and laughed. That's why Americans have never lost nor will ever lose a war; for the very idea of losing is hateful to an American.

"All through your Army careers, you men have bitched about what you call 'chickenshit drilling.' That, like everything else in this Army, has a definite purpose. That purpose is alertness. Alertness must be bred into every soldier. I don't give a f-ck for a man who's not always on his toes. You men are veterans or you wouldn't be here. You are ready for what's to come. A man must be alert at all times if he expects to stay alive. If you're not alert, sometime, a German son-of-an-asshole-bitch is going to sneak up behind you and beat you to death with a sock full of shit!"

A handful of the senior officers listening to the speech disapproved of Patton's coarse language. Patton could not care less. He believes that profanity is the language of the soldier, and that to speak to soldiers one must use words that will have the most impact.

Few can deny that George Patton is entitled to this belief, nor that he is the consummate soldier. He is descended from a Civil War Confederate colonel, and has himself been in the military since graduating from the U.S. Military Academy at West Point in 1909. Soon after, he fought in Mexico against Pancho Villa. He then fought in the First World War at Saint-Mihiel, the legendary battlefield west of Metz where he walks now. Patton was the very first officer ever assigned to the U.S. Army tank corps, and is renowned for his tactical brilliance on the battlefield. He lives by the words of the great French general Napoléon, "L'audace, l'audace, toujours l'audace"—"Audacity, audacity, always audacity"—a motto that works well on the field of battle, but not so well in diplomatic situations. Patton has damaged his career again and again by saying and doing the sort of impulsive things that would see a lesser man relieved of his command for good.

"An Army is a team," he continues; "it lives, sleeps, eats, and fights as a team. This individual heroic stuff is pure horse shit. The bilious bastards who write that kind of stuff for the *Saturday Evening Post* don't know anything more about real fighting under fire than they know about f-cking!"

Patton was forced to pause, as he knew he would be. The waves of laughter rolling toward the stage were deafening.

★ ★ ★

Four months later, Patton knows the battle for Metz is failing, and that Easy Company is being decimated. Even more galling, his intelligence briefing about the defenders of Fort Driant was wrong. These are not the cooks, clerks, and new recruits he was led to expect. These are hardened German veterans, willing to die for their Nazi führer, Adolf Hitler. They are not about to surrender. Word is arriving from the battlefield that the attack has stalled. For the second time in six days, an assault on Driant teeters on the brink of failure.

Normally in such a situation, Patton might jump in his staff car and race to the battlefield to direct the action. More than one soldier has been shocked to see the general himself barking orders at the front lines. But that is clearly impossible now. The risk would be too great. So Patton can only pace in his headquarters and fret, swear loudly, and quietly seethe about the lack of gasoline and bullets that are limiting his ability to assault Driant with a massive, full-blown attack. Due to a shortage of supplies, Patton has been capable of sending only two companies, numbering a total of just three hundred men, to capture this citadel. It is madness. He should have far more firepower at his disposal.

George S. Patton wants to defeat the Germans at Driant for any number of reasons, but the deep desire to wage war is at the top of the list. Decisions above his pay grade and logistical difficulties have forced the Third Army to a screeching halt after six weeks of nonstop running battle. He hoped that his rush from one side of France to the other would continue all the way across Germany to Berlin, where he planned on winning the war single-handedly. "We shall attack and attack until we are exhausted, and then we shall attack again," he boldly ordered his troops. And they did. Patton's aggressive tactics have placed the Third Army far in advance of the British forces, who are approaching Germany to the north. But now the supreme commander of Allied forces in Europe, Gen. Dwight Eisenhower, has ordered Patton to go on the defensive, while allocating precious supplies of gasoline and bullets to the armies of British field marshal Bernard Law Montgomery. It is Monty, a finicky and self-important Englishman who considers himself a far superior general to Patton, who has been given the go-ahead to launch a decisive offensive toward Germany's Rhine River. For the time being, there will be no more forward movement by the Third Army.

Patton feels that the decision was Ike's call, based on his incorrect assessment of the battlefield. Allied politics also played a role. The British have suffered grievously for five years, with London being devastated by German bombing. Tens of thousands of British subjects have died in the streets. Winston Churchill and his government want to deliver their vengeance.

The Nazi dictator Hitler was on the verge of victory, and might even have forced Great Britain to its knees, had it not invaded Russia. By opening a two-front war, Hitler put too much pressure on his ferocious military machine. The ten-million-man Wehrmacht could not possibly control all the hundreds of thousands of square miles it conquered. And so began the inevitable Nazi retreat, which is now in its final stages.

But the Germans are fiercely defending their homeland as Allied forces push toward the Rhine River border. The fighting is hard and personal, and Patton wants a piece of it. Nevertheless, Eisenhower has reduced Patton's fuel and supply line to a trickle.

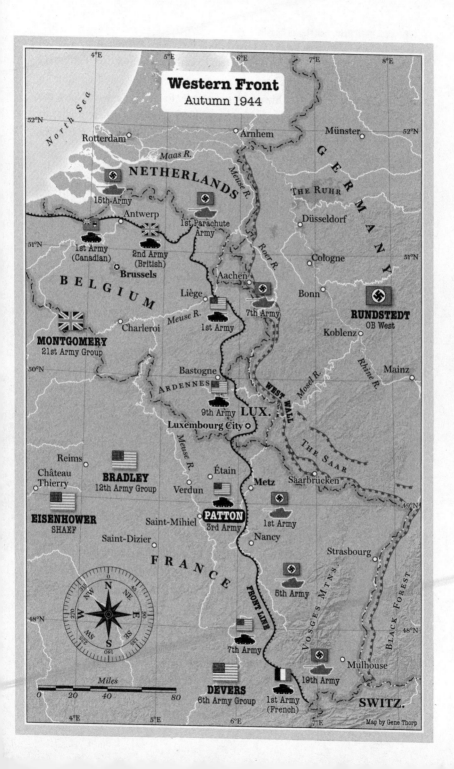

Western Front
Autumn 1944

North Sea

Rotterdam

NETHERLANDS

Maas R.

Arnhem

Münster

GERMANY

THE RUHR

Düsseldorf

15th Army

Antwerp

1st Parachute Army

Meuse R.

Roer R.

Cologne

1st Army (Canadian)

2nd Army (British)

Brussels

BELGIUM

Aachen

Liège

7th Army

Bonn

RUNDSTEDT
OB West

Koblenz

Charleroi

Meuse R.

1st Army

MONTGOMERY
21st Army Group

Bastogne

ARDENNES

9th Army

LUX.

WEST WALL

Mosel R.

Rhine R.

Mainz

Luxembourg City

Meuse R.

THE SAAR

Reims

Château Thierry

BRADLEY
12th Army Group

Étain

Verdun

Metz

Saarbrücken

EISENHOWER
SHAEF

Saint-Mihiel

PATTON
3rd Army

1st Army

Saint-Dizier

Nancy

Strasbourg

FRANCE

5th Army

VOSGES MTNS.

BLACK FOREST

FRONT LINE

7th Army

DEVERS
6th Army Group

1st Army (French)

19th Army

Mulhouse

SWITZ.

Miles

0   20   40   80

Map by Gene Thorp

But rather than simply sit still, per Eisenhower's directive, Patton has chosen to "adjust his lines" by crossing the Moselle River and conquering the ancient city of Metz. One problem: in order to take the city, he must first conquer Fort Driant, with its big guns capable of lobbing artillery shells into the town square. Only then will Patton accept Eisenhower's order that the Third Army stand down.

Right now, that moment seems far away.

In fact, what Patton desperately needs is one of his soldiers to do something audacious that will turn the tide in this desperate battle.

That man, unbeknownst to anyone, is PFC Robert W. Holmlund.

★ ★ ★

The Germans are doing the unthinkable: they are calling in friendly fire on their own positions.

Private Holmlund presses his body flat against the ground as shell after artillery shell explodes on the roof of Fort Driant. The concussion of each blast feels like a sharp kick in the stomach. A wave of nausea washes over him, and his eardrums feel as if they are about to burst.

No longer are the Germans content to wage a defensive gun battle with Company B. Instead, they have radioed to nearby German gun batteries and requested that they fire artillery onto the top of the fort to dislodge the Americans. Exposed and vulnerable, the men of Baker can do nothing to fight back.

From his vantage point on the roof, Private Holmlund sees an odd sight among the tangle of shrubs and dead grass atop the fort. It appears to be some sort of conical grate. Holmlund kicks at it. The grate flies to one side, revealing a narrow pipe leading straight down into the fort. It has never occurred to Holmlund, or any of the other men from Baker Company, that such a pipe would exist. But it is logical, because the Germans hunkered down inside Fort Driant need some form of ventilation. The conical shape lets in air but keeps out rain.

Holmlund considers dropping his satchel charge down into the pipe. But it would never fit. The canvas cover holding the charge is too bulky, and likely to get stuck before falling more than a few inches in. Instead, he calls out for a Bangalore torpedo. Five feet long, two inches wide, and packed with nine pounds of dynamite, the slender tube of explosive is the perfect solution.

A soldier in Holmlund's squad hands one over.

Holmlund sets his BAR on the rooftop, then pulls a blasting cap out of one cartridge pocket. He inserts the primary explosive device into the recessed tail end of the Bangalore. When the blasting cap explodes, it will force a much larger, secondary explosion from the TNT within the torpedo.

Holmlund lights the time-delayed fuse, measured to ensure that the Bangalore will fall the length of the ventilation shaft before exploding. Then he drops the torpedo down and rolls away from the shaft.

The Bangalore clatters against the side of the metal pipe as it falls. There is a quiet moment just before it hits the bottom. Then comes the explosion. The thunder is enormous, rocketing back up the ventilation shaft. Holmlund soon hears confused Germans screaming at one another. He preps another Bangalore and drops it inside. The second explosion elicits even more chaos among the Germans. "They're trampling over one another, trying to get out," Holmlund exclaims to a member of his fighting squad.

The building turns out to be a barracks. Holmlund calmly leads the rest of the men off the roof and down to a locked fort entrance.

It takes time, several rounds of well-placed explosives, and a direct shot from a nearby self-propelled howitzer, but the massive steel door gives way.

Thanks to the quick thinking of PFC Robert W. Holmlund, Company B soon enters Fort Driant. The tide of the battle has shifted. Capt. Harry Anderson leads the charge into the subterranean world. Now winning the battle is a bloody but simple matter of going from tunnel to tunnel to flush out the defenders—or so Anderson believes.

Baker is joined in the tunnels by Company G, a group of reinforcements led by Capt. Jack Gerrie, a man whose bravery under fire is well known within the Eleventh Infantry Regiment.

The Germans and Americans soon fight in close quarters, the deafening clamor of explosives and gunshots thundering down the narrow corridors. Death comes from all angles as bullets ricochet off the thick concrete walls. Companies B and G make their way deeper and deeper into the fort, but the Wehrmacht soldiers thwart their advance by filling the tunnels from floor to ceiling with debris as they retreat. Clearing a path is both time-consuming and dangerous for the Americans, for they take fire the minute they blast a hole in the blockades.

With night about to fall, an exhausted PFC Robert W. Holmlund and his squad leave the tunnels. They are needed on the roof, where they will set up a defensive position to guard against a German counterattack. The plan is for Holmlund and his men to return to the tunnels tomorrow, to continue the slow and deliberate underground battle.

Once on the roof, Holmlund hears the telltale radial-engine drone of American P-47 Thunderbolt fighter-bomber aircraft. After a full day without airpower, the skies have cleared up enough to get the planes airborne. But the timing is odd. With American forces out in the open, it is not the right time to drop bombs.

That's when Holmlund notices that the planes aren't flying toward Baker's position. They're headed for the opposite side of the fort—and a very exposed Easy Company.

★ ★ ★

Kampfgruppe Petersen—the German fighting force that has toyed with Easy Company all afternoon—is counterattacking, leaving their dug-in positions to confront the Americans directly. The aim of the Wehrmacht is to kill the Americans in their fighting holes.

The Americans are exhausted. The corpses of their dead reek of decomposition, and infection is setting in among the wounded. But the P-47 pilots save the day, strafing the Wehrmacht positions with their eight wing-mounted .50-caliber machine guns and dropping five-hundred-pound bombs down on top of the advancing Germans.

Within moments, Kampfgruppe Petersen falls back to the underground tunnels.

But the Germans don't go away. Soon enough they return to harassing Easy Company from the distant safety of bunkers and the fort, firing on them with mortars and machine guns.

Night falls, and when the Thunderbolt pilots can no longer see their targets, they fly the one hundred miles back to the safety of their base in Saint-Dizier, and the warmth of a hot shower and a clean bed before taking to the skies in the morning, leaving the men of Easy Company to do their best to survive in their foxholes overnight. Thanks to the possibility of yet another German counterattack, sleep is not an option.

★　★　★

Private Holmlund is exhausted. The German counterattack came, just as expected. Holmlund once again displayed the sort of selfless courage that George Patton spoke about in England.

As the German forces swept across the roof of Driant, trying to push back Company B and Company G, Holmlund ignored the hail of bullets. Knowing that his Browning Automatic Rifle had the sort of rapid-shot firepower that could effectively halt the German attack, he raced from a safe defensive position to a new fighting spot, one that was completely exposed to enemy fire. After only a short time in the army, Holmlund had developed a strategic intuition similar to that of the great Patton himself. In an act of courage that Patton will one day personally reward with the Distinguished Service Cross, Holmlund poured fire directly at the Germans. All by himself, Private Holmlund scattered an entire German unit and ended their counterattack.

The retreat accomplished, Holmlund finds a quiet corner on the roof. But before he can rest, he double-checks that each man in his squad has chosen a solid defensive position. A second counterattack is likely, and he wants Baker to be ready.

There are just four men left in the squad. Eight have been killed or wounded. Holmlund crouches low as he studies his men's locations and inquires about ammo and water to last the night. It's not a selfless act. Great leaders take care of their men first, and then worry about their own needs.

Suddenly a shot rings out. A German sniper's rifle has spoken.

PFC Robert W. Holmlund from Wisconsin drops to the ground.

Dead.

★　★　★

"Things going very badly at Fort Driant," George Patton writes in his journal. It is nighttime in his headquarters. The Third Army lost 110 men in the first day of fighting, and the toll continues to rise. He has spent the evening pacing, fretting, and resisting the urge to smoke a cigar, a habit he is forever trying to quit. "We may have to abandon the attack, because it is not worth the cost. I was over optimistic."

Days have passed since PFC Robert Holmlund dropped that Bangalore down into the German barracks. The battle for Driant has become a bloody stalemate. It is quiet far behind the lines at Patton's château in the small town of Étain, but he can envision the chaos at Driant. Reports from the battlefield have been grim, with casualties mounting and no forward progress being made.

Easy can go nowhere. The men are dazed and drained by more than three days without sleep, food, or water. The Germans are so well hidden, and have zeroed in on the American positions so accurately, that any attempt to reinforce or rescue Easy is tantamount to a suicide mission. The number of dead in the unit is more than thirty—and rising by the hour. But enemy fire is so intense that no bodies can be removed.

In the words of one fellow general, Patton paces like a "caged tiger." He is in no mood to lose a battle, particularly when Montgomery and the British have been given the green light (and the gasoline) to attack deep into Germany.

Patton knows his reputation could be damaged by any defeat. He is also aware that the nature of warfare is that many men will lose their lives for the sake of a common objective. Capturing Fort Driant, the lone obstacle standing between Patton's army and the invasion of the German homeland, is such an objective. So it is that Patton orders his old friend Gen. Walton Walker, who serves as commander of the Third Army's Twentieth Corps, to press the attack on Driant. Patton tells the burly Texan that the battle must be won "even if it takes every man."

★ ★ ★

Capt. Jack Gerrie hasn't slept in two days. He has just spent another endless night atop Fort Driant, and now presses his body flat against the curve of a shell crater as the constant rip of the German Bone Saw cuts through the morning air.

It seems impossible to escape that lightning-fast death spray. And Captain Gerrie has had enough of it. With many of his men dead,

Gerrie finds a piece of paper and prepares to scratch out a letter to none other than Gen. George S. Patton.

There isn't a man on the battlefield who would consider Gerrie a coward. Just last month, he single-handedly changed the course of a battle by paddling a canoe across the Seine River under heavy fire to better observe enemy positions. Once ashore, he shot the first German he encountered, did his reconnaissance while under further enemy fire, and then, staying underwater as much as possible, swam the two hundred yards back across the river to direct the U.S. attack.

And one week ago, Gerrie and his men of Company G were with Easy Company on that first ill-fated probe into Driant. He was pinned down for four hours with MG-42 bullets whizzing over his head, waiting for night to fall before he and his men could retreat.

So Capt. Jack Gerrie knows something about hopelessness. But this is different. He and his men are now completely stuck. His faith in Patton's attack has vanished. Meanwhile, the majority of the German soldiers concealed within Fort Driant are completely safe. They have taken almost no casualties. As a company commander, Gerrie feels it is his duty to get the word about this dire situation back to General Patton.

He thinks carefully about what he is about to write. There is so much to tell. Only those with him on the battlefield can truly appreciate the futility of the U.S. position.

Gerrie has fought in the tunnels and on the roof over the past two days. He knows firsthand that the passages below Driant are a warren of steel doors, rubble, and other obstacles that will take weeks to get through. The tunnels are three feet wide and seven feet tall, and the Germans can block the American advance simply by throwing up new barriers of debris along their lengths. The fighting is accomplished through machine-gun fire and lobbed grenades. The acoustics amplify even the slightest explosion, rendering each man deaf for the length of any firefight. And of course there's the odor. Soldiers fighting inside the fort on both sides have no choice but to relieve themselves in the tunnels. The foul aroma mixes with the smell of gunpowder, the thick haze of TNT, and the many pools of blood to form a horrific bouquet that Captain Gerrie will never forget.

The rooftop is equally terrifying. The German snipers are selective, focusing their bullets on Americans carrying flamethrowers or Bangalore torpedoes. When Gerrie and Company G moved in to reinforce Baker Company two days ago, a column of tanks followed them. Those Shermans are now just rusting hulks. The Germans knocked them out, one after the other, with precision firing from a Jagdpanzer IV tank destroyer.

Now the American forces atop Fort Driant are in a state of chaos. The soldiers hide from snipers anywhere they can—in abandoned pillboxes, shell craters, empty bunkers. Any movement outside these shelters during daylight is pure folly. Many of these men are brand-new soldiers, rushed from a replacement depot and into the front lines. Most are no more than boys, eighteen to twenty years old, with no combat experience. They don't understand military tactics, and until now they have never heard a shot fired in battle. These bewildered young men do the only things they can to stay alive: take cover, hug the earth, and pray.

But that only gets them through the day. The nights atop Fort Driant are far deadlier. The Germans sneak out of their holes in the ground and silently prowl the battlefield. The Wehrmacht soldiers have the advantage of surprise and know this terrain far better than their enemies do. They slaughter the men of the Third Army where they lie hiding, killing them one by one. The last words many of the Americans will ever hear are spoken in German, in the quiet whisper of an assassin.

Last night, Gerrie tried to turn the tables by venturing into the killing zone to locate the men of Company G and organize them into a cohesive fighting unit. But he could find only half his soldiers. The rest are either missing or dead; the rooftop is not a place for taking prisoners. The time has come for Jack Gerrie to dispel once and for all any delusions that this battle is winnable.

"The situation is critical," Gerrie tells Patton in writing. He uses a pencil, trying to be legible even as the fatigue and the need to remain battle-ready muddy his thoughts. This letter will become, quite possibly, one of the most brutally honest communiqués ever posted from the field of battle. "A couple more barrages and a counterattack and we are sunk. We have no men, our equipment is shot, and we just can't go on. The troops in Company G are done. They are just there, what's left of them. Enemy has infiltrated and pinned what is here down. We cannot advance . . . We cannot delay any longer in replacement. We may be able to hold till dark but if anything happens this afternoon I can make no predictions."

All around Gerrie's shell hole, American corpses sprawl where they died, the bodies already fleeced for additional ammunition and explosives by the surviving GIs.

Gerrie continues his letter: "There is only one answer, the way things stand. First, either to withdraw and saturate [the fort] with heavy bombers or reinforce with a hell of a strong force. This strong force might hold here, but eventually they'll get it by artillery fire. They have all these places zeroed in by artillery. The forts have 5–6 feet walls inside and 15-foot roofs of reinforced concrete. All our charges have been useless against this stuff. The few leaders are trying to keep left what is intact and that's all they can do. The troops are just not sufficiently trained and what is more they have no training in even basic infantry. Everything is committed and we cannot follow attack plan. This is just a suggestion, but if we want this damned fort let's get the stuff required to take it and then go."

"Right now," Gerrie concludes, aiming his words directly at Third Army commander George S. Patton, "you haven't got it."

★ ★ ★

Patton ignores Captain Gerrie's letter—but only for a time. A week after the attack began, Patton admits that this battle cannot be won. He makes the decision to call off the assault on Fort Driant. On the night of October 12, American combat engineers booby-trap an escape route that will successfully take American troops back out of Fort Driant. They lay three tons of explosives, with fuses timed to go off at irregular intervals, in order to discourage the Germans from following for up to six hours.

Capt. Jack Gerrie survives the battle, and receives the Distinguished Service Cross a week later for his exploits crossing the Seine in August.

Thanks to his quick action with the Bangalore torpedo, PFC Robert W. Holmlund is also awarded the army's second-highest award for valor—albeit posthumously.

After four days under fire, the men of Easy Company crawl out of their foxholes and make it back to the safety of the American lines. Of the 140 men who began the offensive, just 85 are physically unscathed.

The emotional toll of Easy's harrowing time under fire, however, will not be counted for many years to come.

★   ★   ★

George S. Patton walks the battlefields of his youth, even as the time has come to admit defeat at Fort Driant. Just hours before the retreat is to begin, he visits the World War I battlefields at Saint-Mihiel and Meuse-Argonne, where he fought as a young tank commander. Now these rolling fields are peaceful and still. Death seems so far away. But it was here, on the muddy pastures of eastern France, that the final Allied offensive began in the summer of 1918. Almost thirty thousand Americans died in a hail of German machine-gun bullets and deadly mustard gas, but the battle (and the war) was ultimately won.

That the Battle of Meuse-Argonne was launched on September 26, almost twenty-six years to the day that Patton ordered elements of the Third Army to take Fort Driant, is an irony not lost on a man who is deeply steeped in history, and the history of war in particular. Now, instead of launching the final drive into Germany that would end the Second World War, he commands an army that is going nowhere.

That irony is not lost on Patton, either.

In all, he has just suffered nearly 800 casualties. Almost half the men who took part in the Battle of Fort Driant are dead or wounded. Some 187 men are classified as "missing," a vague euphemism that defines a prisoner of war, a deserter, or a man whose body has been completely obliterated by an artillery shell.

Patton studies the topography of Meuse-Argonne alongside a visiting political dignitary, J. F. Byrnes of South Carolina. Byrnes is a close confidant of U.S. president Franklin D. Roosevelt, so Patton must rein in his tongue at a time when he would most like to lash out. The two men, however, have become quick friends, and walking the battlefield with him is a form of solace for Patton.

But beneath his external calm, Patton is furious. He seethes about the politics that saw his army halted in its tracks, and that then deprived him of the manpower and firepower he needed to win at Driant. Field Marshal Montgomery, his British rival who was the recipient of the scarce fuel and ammunition, chose to call off his assault on Germany at the height of the

Driant assault. If Patton and his men had the supplies Montgomery is now hoarding, there would have been no defeat. By the end of the Driant attack, Patton's big guns possess so little ammunition that they can fire only seven rounds per day. Patton believes his army is unbeatable if given enough gas, guns, and ammo.

Since arriving in France in early August, his army has killed more enemy, gained more ground, and lost fewer men than any command in Europe. The Third Army has been unstoppable, pressing the attack from one side of France to the other without losing a battle. But Patton has now failed miserably. The U.S. newsreel cameras that filmed Patton meeting with Eisenhower on the eve of the Metz offensive, sensing yet another great victory for America's best general, must now report back to the American public that the great George Patton is not invincible after all.

On October 13, Patton moves his headquarters south to the French city of Nancy, where he finally follows Eisenhower's order to stop his army and regroup. And so begins the "October Pause." The lull in the action is a foolish move on the part of Eisenhower. The American army might be using the lull to reinforce, but so are the Germans. Unbeknownst to the Americans, Adolf Hitler is planning a major attack of his own.

And while the Führer has a deep hatred for the Americans, he also fears and respects George S. Patton, who has laid waste to so many German soldiers. These plans are designed to make sure that Old Blood and Guts is kept off the battlefield at all costs.

2

THE WOLF'S LAIR
EAST PRUSSIA
OCTOBER 21, 1944
9:30 A.M.

The Wolf limps through the woods.

The autumn air is chill and damp. As he does each morning at just about this time, Adolf Hitler emerges from the artificial light of his concrete bunker into the morning sun. He holds his two-year-old German shepherd Blondi on a short leash for their daily walk through the thick birch forest. A fussy man of modest height and weight who is prone to emotional outbursts, Hitler wears his dark brown hair parted on the right and keeps his Charlie Chaplin mustache carefully combed and trimmed.

Hitler spends more time at the Wolf's Lair than in Berlin—some eight hundred days in the last three years alone. The Führer is fond of saying that his military planners chose the "most marshy, mosquito-ridden, and climatically unpleasant place possible" for this hidden headquarters. On humid summer days, the air is so heavy and thick with clouds of mosquitoes that Hitler remains in the cool confines of his bunker all day long.

But autumn is different. The forests of East Prussia have a charm all their own this time of year, and Hitler needs no convincing to venture outside for his daily walk. These long morning strolls offer him a chance to compose his thoughts before long afternoons of war strategizing and policy meetings. Sometimes he amuses himself by teaching Blondi tricks, such as climbing a ladder or balancing on a narrow pole. While frivolous on the surface, Hitler's time alone with his beloved Blondi is actually a

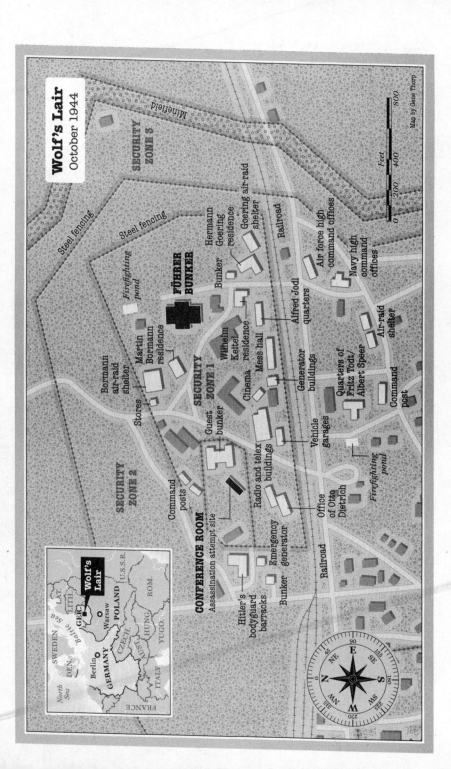

Wolf's Lair
October 1944

SECURITY ZONE 3

Minefield

Steel fencing

Steel fencing

Firefighting pond

SECURITY ZONE 2

SECURITY ZONE 1

Command posts

Stores

Bormann air-raid shelter

Martin Bormann residence

FÜHRER BUNKER

Bunker

Hermann Goering residence

Goering air-raid shelter

Railroad

Wilhelm Keitel residence

Mess hall

Alfred Jodl quarters

Air force high command offices

Navy high command offices

Cinema

Generator buildings

Air-raid shelter

Guest bunker

Vehicle garages

Quarters of Fritz Todt/ Albert Speer

Command post

Radio and telex buildings

Office of Otto Dietrich

Firefighting pond

CONFERENCE ROOM
Assassination attempt site

Emergency generator

Bunker

Hitler's bodyguard barracks

Railroad

Feet
0   200   400   800

Map by Gene Thorp

North Sea

SWEDEN

DEN.

Baltic Sea

LAT.
LITH.

GER.

Wolf's Lair

Warsaw

GERMANY

Berlin

POLAND

U.S.S.R.

FRANCE

CZECH.

AUST.

HUNG.

ROM.

ITALY

YUGO.

N NE E SE S SW W NW
90 135 180 225 270 315

Adolf Hitler in 1944

vital part of his day. The Führer suffers from a condition known as mete-orism, the primary symptom of which is uncontrollable flatulence. Time alone in the fresh air allows him to manage the discomfort without wrin-kling the noses of his staff, which would be an acute embarrassment to the exalted leader.

The journey through the dictator's six-hundred-acre wooded hide-away takes Hitler and Blondi past concrete bunkers, personal residences, soldiers' barracks, a power plant, and even the demolished conference room where, just three short months ago, Hitler was almost killed by an assassin's bomb. But despite all these visible reminders that the Wolf's Lair is in fact a military headquarters, the fifty-five-year-old Nazi dictator who likes the nickname Wolf strolls with an outward air of contentment, utterly lost in thought.

But Hitler is not tranquil. His right eardrum was ruptured in the bomb blast during the assassination attempt and has only recently stopped bleeding. That same blast hurled him to a concrete floor, bruising his but-tocks "as blue as a baboon's behind" and filling his legs with wooden splinters as it ripped his black uniform pants to shreds.

However, the failed assassination plot, engineered by members of the German military who no longer believed that Hitler was fit to rule Germany, did not cause all the Führer's health issues. His hands and left leg have long trembled from anxiety. He is prone to dizziness, high blood pressure, and stomach cramps. The skin beneath his uniform is the whitest white, thanks to his fondness for remaining indoors and keeping a nocturnal schedule. And his energy is often so low that his longtime personal physician, the extremely obese and medically unorthodox Dr. Theodor Morell, makes it a practice to inject Hitler each day with methamphetamines. A second doctor, Dr. Erwin Geising, also places drops containing cocaine in each of the Führer's dark blue eyes, in order to give the dictator a daily rush of euphoria.

Despite recent German setbacks on the battlefield, the Wolf still has hope that his plans for global domination will yet be realized. His greatest goal is the eradication of the Jewish people, with whom he is obsessed, despite not having had any intentional contact with a Jew in twenty years. "This war can end two ways," he said in a January 30, 1942, address to the German parliament. "Either the extermination of the Aryan peoples or the disappearance of Jewry from Europe."

Prior to the war, Hitler's anti-Semitic policies led hundreds of thousands of Jewish citizens to emigrate from Germany, a number that includes 83 percent of all German Jews under the age of twenty-one. But no more were allowed to leave once the war began. Now, trapped within Germany and each of the countries that the Nazis have conquered, the remaining Europeans of Jewish ancestry are being systematically rounded up and murdered.

Hitler fancies himself a military strategist, despite no formal training in field tactics. He takes full credit for Patton's defeat at Fort Driant, because it was his decision to send reinforcements to Metz rather than let the city fall. He is also cheered by the news that Nazi scientists are developing a bomb with nuclear capacity, a weapon that would allow Hitler to wipe his enemies off the face of the earth. In addition, Hitler is quite sure that the audacious surprise attack he will unveil to his top commanders in a few hours will push the Allied armies back across France, and allow Germany to regain control of the European Theater.

And most encouraging of all, Adolf Hitler is finally rid of those top generals who have long despised him. SS death squads were relentless in discovering the identities of each of the men who took part in the July 20 assassination plot, then hunting them down and taking them into custody.

Some were shot immediately, which infuriated Hitler, because such a death was far too quick. On his orders, the others were hanged. The executions were done individually, with each man marched into a small room. They entered stripped to the waist, wearing handcuffs. The hangman's noose was then draped over the condemned man's shoulders and slowly pulled tight. The other end of the rope was thrown over a hook affixed high up on the wall and left to dangle. A cameraman filmed the event for Hitler's enjoyment. To ensure maximum embarrassment when the graphic movie was shown, each man's pants were yanked down to his ankles.

Hitler originally suggested that the assassins be impaled on the hook, to be "hanged like cattle." But that sort of death would not have allowed the plotters to suffer sufficiently. Instead, the hangman picked up the loose end of the rope and pulled it taut, using the hook as a pulley to lift the condemned man slowly off the ground. The executioner was in no hurry, and very often the hangings lasted fifteen minutes or more, with the victim's airflow cut off and restored multiple times. Before dying, the accused had plenty of time to memorize the interior of the room: the whitewashed walls, the cognac bottle on the simple wooden table, the door through which he entered alive and would exit quite dead.

Each execution was brutal, but the suffering was not enough for Adolf Hitler. He wanted even more revenge. Hitler then ordered the conspirators' immediate families and other relatives rounded up. More than seven thousand innocent men, women, and children were arrested—and almost five thousand of them executed.

The most significant of these murders took place just seven days ago, and it means that Adolf Hitler will have to launch his major new offensive, code-named Operation Watch on the Rhine, without the only German general who can even remotely compare with George S. Patton.

The Wolf could have waited until after Operation Watch on the Rhine was completed to pass judgment on his favorite field marshal. From a tactical perspective, it would have been the smart thing to do. But Adolf Hitler needed his revenge. Nothing, not even winning the war, matters more.

Hitler and Blondi finish their walk and reenter the massive concrete fortress that serves as the Führer's home away from Berlin. It is almost time for lunch—and the unveiling of his brilliant new campaign.

Or, as it will soon become known around the world, the Battle of the Bulge.

★ ★ ★

George S. Patton thinks so highly of Field Marshal Erwin Rommel that he keeps a copy of Rommel's book on infantry tactics near his bedside. Often at night, when he is unable to sleep, Patton opens it to reread a chapter or two. But while the armies of the two great generals collided in the North African desert two years ago, engaging in the sort of epic tank warfare that only the wide open desert spaces can allow, they have not fought one another since. Patton's Third Army did not become active in Europe until early August, nearly three weeks after Rommel's skull was fractured in three places when a Royal Air Force Spitfire fighter plane strafed his car.

Now, as Patton's retreat from Fort Driant brings the attack to a bitter end, Rommel is just 230 miles away, convalescing from his wounds at home in Herrlingen. On the evening of October 13, a phone call from the Wolf's Lair informs Rommel that he will be visited by Generals Wilhelm Burgdorf and Ernst Maisel the next morning. They will bring news from the Führer about Rommel's next assignment.

This can mean only one of two things: a new command or a death sentence. Rommel knew of the assassination plot in advance, but said nothing. By proxy, this makes him as guilty as the men who concealed the bomb in the briefcase and hand-carried it into Hitler's conference room.

But Rommel is not sure whether Hitler knows of his betrayal. He is Germany's most famous general, a man who has shown his loyalty to the Führer through extraordinary service on the field of battle, and a man the Führer holds in high esteem. Until recently, that feeling was mutual. But Hitler will never sue for peace, and this could lead to the complete destruction of Germany. Rommel now has grave doubts about Hitler's ability to lead the war effort, and is in favor of negotiating with the Allies rather than continuing to fight. But he has never voiced this opinion publicly.

Rommel is restless as he tries to sleep through the night. If his awareness of the assassination plot has been made known to the SS interrogators

Erwin Rommel outside Hitler's headquarters in Berlin

who have tortured those implicated in the bombing, then General Burgdorf is most likely coming to take Rommel away to be publicly tried before a people's court; if not, there is a very good chance that Burgdorf is coming to offer him a new army.

Morning arrives. Rommel's fifteen-year-old son, Manfred, who serves as a soldier in a nearby antiaircraft battery, returns home for two days' leave. When he walks in the door, he finds the field marshal dressed in riding pants, a brown jacket, and a tie. Rommel asks Manfred to join him for breakfast.

"At twelve o'clock today two generals are coming to see me to discuss my future employment," Rommel tells his son. "So today will decide what is planned for me: whether a people's court or a new command in the east."

"Would you accept such a command?" Manfred asks.

"My dear boy," Rommel responds, grabbing his son by the arm. "Our enemy in the east is so terrible that every other thought has to give way before it. If he succeeds in overrunning Europe, it will be the end of everything that has made life worth living. Of course I would go."

Shortly before noon Rommel walks to his room on the first floor and changes into his favorite uniform, a tan tunic that he wore in the North African campaign. Soon a dark green Opel pulls up the gravel driveway. The driver wears the black uniform of the Waffen SS, Hitler's most feared and loyal fighters, who swear a personal oath of loyalty to the Führer. In the backseat sit the round-faced Burgdorf and the wiry Maisel, who themselves fear the SS.

The two men enter the home and treat Rommel with the utmost respect and courtesy. When they ask the field marshal if they might speak with him alone, their deference is so overwhelming that Manfred is sure his father will not be made to appear before a people's court. He calmly walks upstairs to look for a book to read.

But unbeknownst to Manfred Rommel, Burgdorf and Maisel are giving his father the worst possible news: SS troopers have surrounded the house and have orders to kill everyone inside should Rommel attempt to flee.

Erwin Rommel, the famous Desert Fox, is being accused of high treason by Adolf Hitler. If only out of respect for the field marshal's bravery, and the devastating effects a public trial would have on the morale of German citizens, he is being offered the option of committing suicide.

Manfred Rommel hears his father walk upstairs and enter his wife's bedroom. Curious, the younger Rommel follows his father into the room.

Lucie Rommel is lying on the bed, the picture of utter sorrow. Erwin Rommel stands and leads his son back to his bedroom. When the field marshal finally speaks, his voice is pinched in grief.

"I shall be dead in a quarter of an hour," he tells Manfred in a level voice. "The house is surrounded, and Hitler is charging me with high treason."

Now Rommel's voice turns sarcastic. "In view of my services in Africa, I am to have the chance of dying by poison. The two generals have brought it with them. It's fatal in three seconds. If I accept, none of the usual steps will be taken against my family—that is, against you."

"Can't we defend ourselves?" Manfred asks, ready to die for his father.

Rommel cuts him off. "It's better for one to die than for all of us to be killed in a shooting affray.

"Anyway," Erwin Rommel adds, a soldier to the end, "we've practically no ammunition."

Rommel dons his long leather jacket and walks to the Opel with his son. His face is without emotion. Manfred will always remember that "the crunch of gravel seemed unusually loud." The two shake hands when it comes time to say farewell. There are no tears, no final orders, and no mention of the horrible event that will take place in just a few minutes. A crowd of local villagers has seen the Opel and now gathers to watch Rommel be driven away, not having any idea about his fate. The general reaches into his jacket pocket and discovers his house keys and wallet. "I don't need these anymore," he says, handing them to Manfred.

The SS driver salutes and stands stiffly at attention as Erwin Rommel steps toward the car, his field marshal's baton tucked precisely against his elbow. Rommel sits in back. Burgdorf and Maisel slide in beside him. The bodies of the three generals press snugly against one another on the very small seat.

The Opel drives away, leaving Manfred Rommel to watch the back of his father's head through the back window as the car disappears into the distance. His father does not turn for one last look.

After a few minutes, the car pulls off the road and into a forest clearing. A squad of SS troopers form a perimeter ring, with orders to shoot should the field marshal make a run for it.

Rommel has no such plans.

General Burgdorf tells the driver to go for a walk. Rommel never even gets out of the car. He is handed the suicide pill.

Fifteen minutes later, as predicted, Field Marshal Erwin Rommel is dead.

The official cause of death is not the cyanide that he was forced to swallow, turning his mucous a dark brown as his body lost its ability to breathe. Instead, the good people of Nazi Germany will be saddened to read that Rommel endured "death as a result of a heart attack suffered while in service of the Reich in the west."

★ ★ ★

One week later, on October 21, SS officer Otto Skorzeny snaps to attention in Adolf Hitler's Wolf's Lair bunker. At six foot four, the legendary

Otto Skorzeny

commando stands a half foot taller than the Führer. His enormous hands dwarf Hitler's as he accepts the jewelry case containing his newest in a long line of decorations, the vaunted German Cross in Gold.

British Intelligence considers Skorzeny the most dangerous man in Europe. He is thick across the chest like a heavyweight fighter, and the epaulets on his powerful shoulders display the rank of Sturmbannführer—or, in the American equivalence, major. He sports a stylish mustache that lends him a passing resemblance to the swashbuckling American movie star Errol Flynn. And while Hitler's face is lined only by weariness, a scar creases Skorzeny's left cheek from ear to mouth, a memento from a saber duel he fought for the love of a ballerina back in his college days.

But as esteemed as the Cross in Gold might be—and to be sure, it is one of Germany's highest honors, awarded only to men exhibiting repeated bravery in battle—Hitler and Skorzeny both know that the strapping warrior is deserving of so much more. If Erwin Rommel was once Hitler's favorite general, then the "Long Jumper," as Skorzeny is nicknamed, is Hitler's favorite commando. Time and again, the gruff Austrian has shown his loyalty to the Führer by accepting missions that other men would have refused on the grounds that they were impossible or suicidal. Most famously, it was Skorzeny and his crack team of SS troopers who discovered where the deposed Italian dictator Benito Mussolini was being held prisoner by partisan forces loyal to the Allies in the summer and fall of 1943. After months of deceit and intrigue as Mussolini was ferried from hiding place to hiding place, Skorzeny learned that the Fascist leader was being held at the Campo Imperatore Hotel, high atop the tallest peak in the central Italian Apennine Mountains. Gran Sasso, as the rugged and rocky summit is known, was accessible only by a single cable car.

Skorzeny was undeterred. He devised an ingenious plan that involved landing his commando team atop the peak in a glider. Not only did Skorzeny and his men rescue Mussolini, but they did so without firing a single shot.

And just last week, the great Skorzeny trumped even that bold raid.

Six days ago, anticipating that the Hungarian government would switch its allegiance to Germany's enemy Russia, Hitler ordered Skorzeny to make sure this betrayal did not occur. In less than twenty-four hours, "Operation Mickey Mouse"* netted the son of Hungarian regent Miklós Horthy. The thirty-seven-year-old was lured into a trap, beaten unconscious, rolled up in a carpet, and smuggled through the city streets to the airport, where he was flown to Vienna and placed under Gestapo detention.

There was no request for monetary ransom. Instead, Skorzeny demanded Hungary's enduring loyalty. When that pledge didn't materialize, he sent shock troops into the heart of Budapest to take control of the city. An armistice was soon secured, and Miklós hoped his son would be returned to him unharmed. This was not to be. Even now, as Skorzeny and Hitler exchange pleasantries, Miklós Horthy Jr. is on his way to the

---

*Operation Panzerfaust, a.k.a. Operation Mickey Mouse, was launched on October 15, 1944, in response to Miklós Horthy's public declaration of alliance with the Soviet Union. Adolf Hitler's security forces had advanced knowledge of Horthy's plans, and Skorzeny was already in place in Budapest to remove Horthy from power. The name "Mickey Mouse" was based on the nickname of Horthy's son, Miki. In addition to capturing the younger Horthy, the Germans also took the regent prisoner. Miklós Horthy was taken to Bavaria by Skorzeny, where he lived out the war under round-the-clock SS guard.

Dachau concentration camp, a prison from which few men, women, or children ever come back.

In the Wolf's Lair, Skorzeny and Hitler finish their small talk. The moment is warm. Hitler laughs frequently as Skorzeny recounts his escapades in Hungary. Skorzeny served as Hitler's personal bodyguard many years ago, and the two men are well acquainted. But Skorzeny knows his place, and he turns to leave before overstaying his welcome.

"Don't go, Skorzeny," Hitler orders him.

Skorzeny turns around, puzzled. Clearly, the Führer has something else he would like to discuss. From the sound of it, perhaps there is another pressing issue that requires Skorzeny's expertise.

"In December, Germany will start a great offensive which may well decide her fate," Hitler continues. "The world thinks Germany is finished, with only the day and the hour of the funeral to be named. I am going to show them how wrong they are. The corpse will rise and throw itself at the West."

The Führer has done away with those who might be disloyal to him and is building his battle plans around loyal worshippers such as Otto Skorzeny. So even without Erwin Rommel and his unmatched prowess as a battlefield commander, Hitler is confident of success. The goal of the offensive is to split the British and American armies. It helps that his tank commanders will not have to face George S. Patton and his Third Army, because the secret offensive is deliberately being launched too far north for Patton and his sharp tactical mind to reach the battlefield in time to engage.

Hitler then tells his fellow Austrian the details of the coming offensive. Skorzeny and his men are more than capable of playing a pivotal role in this surprise attack known as Operation Watch on the Rhine, but that is not how Hitler intends to use them.

The coup de grâce will be another operation that will demonstrate to the world that the Nazis have indeed regained the upper hand. That will take place far from the bloody battlefields. Hitler's orders are quite simple: "Operation Greif"* will see Skorzeny and his men infiltrate enemy lines

---

*"Greif" refers to the griffin, a mythological beast with the body of a lion and the head of an eagle. In Greek antiquity, it was considered the most powerful of all creatures.

by dressing in American uniforms and pretending to be U.S. soldiers. They will speak English and will sow confusion by spreading false rumors, capturing vital bridges, and killing Americans caught by surprise. Chief among the rumors is one that is meant to cause fear and distraction at the highest levels of Allied leadership: that Skorzeny is en route to Paris to kidnap Gen. Dwight D. Eisenhower, supreme commander of the Allied forces in Europe.

"I am giving you unlimited power to set up your brigade. Use it, colonel!" Hitler says triumphantly.

Skorzeny's face breaks into a broad smile as he realizes that he has just risen in rank.

"Yes," Hitler beams. "I have promoted you to Obertsturmbannführer!"

Hitler extends his hand. Once again Skorzeny's meaty paw envelops the Führer's.

"Good-bye, Skorzeny," Hitler says. "I expect to hear great things of Operation Greif."

Otto Skorzeny's eyes shine. He is only too happy to accept the challenge.

3

TRIANON PALACE HOTEL
VERSAILLES, FRANCE
OCTOBER 21, 1944
EARLY AFTERNOON

Just as Hitler is briefing Skorzeny, Gen. Dwight D. Eisenhower lights a cigarette in his first-floor office. His headquarters, a white stone French château one thousand miles west of the Wolf's Lair, is spotless and regal. The only challenge Eisenhower should be facing right now is how best to celebrate a major turning point in the war. The American army has spent weeks leveling the city of Aachen. At 10 a.m. this morning the famous resort town became the first German municipality to fall into Allied hands. There is widespread hope that this marks the beginning of the end for the Nazi war machine, and that the fighting will end by New Year's Eve.

Eisenhower smokes and paces. The fifty-four-year-old general played football back in his West Point days, but now he carries a small paunch and walks with his shoulders rolled forward. For security purposes, there is not a situation map tacked to the plywood partition in his office. Instead, he carries details of the German, British, and American armies in his head.

Eisenhower endures a daily barrage of worries. If anything, his life since becoming supreme commander of the Allied forces in Europe has been one headache after another, punctuated by moments of world-changing success. But new expectations torment Ike. His boss, the four-star general George Marshall, has set in stone New Year's Eve as the last day of the war. Ike believes that the proposed deadline will be impossible. Hence the deep frown lines on his high forehead.

General Dwight D. Eisenhower and his generals,
including Omar Bradley (far left)

Marshall is back in Washington, thirty-five hundred miles from the front. He is chief of staff of the army and chief military adviser to President Roosevelt. No other officer in the combined Allied armies has more power and influence than this lean, tough-talking Pennsylvanian.

Marshall's return to the United States came after a weeklong tour of the European Theater of operations. Now he has cabled Eisenhower his great displeasure about the strategic situation. The "October Pause" that enrages George Patton infuriates Marshall, too. He is demanding an end to the stalemate. Everything possible must be done to attack deep into Germany and end the war by January 1.

Per Marshall's orders, this is to include the use of weapons currently considered top secret, and the placement of every single available American, British, and Canadian soldier onto the front lines. Nothing must be held back.

Eisenhower must find a way. Orders are orders, and his success has been largely based on obeying them—unlike George Patton's. So Ike smokes one cigarette after another. A few top American generals are coming over for dinner tonight. The celebration of the victory at Aachen can wait until then.

Across the hall, pale autumn light floods the glass-walled foyer, where a bronze bust of German air force commander Hermann Goering has been turned to face the wall. Eisenhower smokes another cigarette. He doesn't have a favorite brand, and doesn't know how many packs he smokes each day. The number is actually four, as evidenced by his yellow-stained fingertips and the nicotine stench from his trademark waist-length "Ike" jacket. His breath reeks of cigarettes and the countless pots of coffee he drinks each day.

Nicotine and caffeine are the only ways Eisenhower can manage the stress. He certainly can't play golf in the midst of war. And right now, it's still several hours too early for either a weak scotch and water, time alone in his upstairs apartment with a dime-store cowboy novel, or perhaps even a furtive romantic liaison with Kay Summersby, his personal chauffeur. At age thirty-six, the divorced Irish brunette who wears a captain's rank has been assigned to Ike for two years.

At first she was merely his driver, a member of Britain's all-volunteer Mechanised Transport Corps assigned to guide Eisenhower's official Packard sedan through the blacked-out streets of London. Eisenhower admired her confidence behind the wheel and arranged for Summersby to be transferred permanently to the U.S. military's Women's Army Corps, where she was commissioned as an officer.

The turning point in their relationship came in June 1943, when the American colonel to whom Summersby was engaged got blown up by a land mine in Tunisia. It was Eisenhower who held Kay in his arms as she sobbed in grief. A spark passed between them in that moment, and the relationship deepened. Now the former fashion model has become Eisenhower's chief confidante. She travels with him everywhere, and even sits in on high-level meetings, which makes her privy to top-secret war strategy. The two chatter and laugh constantly, passing the rare moments away from the pressure of the war by riding horses or playing bridge. Summersby has even gotten Eisenhower in the habit of taking tea each afternoon at 4:00 p.m., just like the British. He is so used to her constant presence that

Kay Summersby

recently, while back in America for a short leave, Ike infuriated his wife, Mamie, by calling her "Kay" on two different occasions.

The close relationship between Summersby and Eisenhower goes on in secret—most of the time. But as John Thompson of the *Chicago Tribune* noted, their fondness for each other surfaces publicly now and then. "I have never before seen a chauffeur get out of a car and kiss the General good morning," Thompson told American major general James M. Gavin when asked if the rumors were true.

No less than President Franklin Delano Roosevelt can see the sparks between Summersby and Ike. After the landmark Tehran Conference*

---

*The first meeting of the Big Three (Roosevelt, Stalin, and Churchill) in which it was agreed that the Americans and British would open a second front in Europe. This strategy was designed to take the pressure off the Russians, who had been battling the Nazis on Soviet soil for more than two years, at the cost of more than twenty million dead, wounded, or missing Soviet soldiers and citizens. The meeting was held at the Soviet embassy in Tehran, Iran. Eisenhower and other top military commanders were also in attendance, along with their personal staff.

in 1943, FDR confided to his daughter, Anna, that he thought Eisenhower and his chauffeur were sleeping together.

In many ways, Eisenhower is a victim of his own success. Even though he has never once fought in battle, he has risen through the ranks and accrued power through intellect, shrewd diplomacy, and, most of all, finding ingenious ways of turning the outrageous demands of men such as George Marshall into reality.

The problem is his forces are as stuck and immobile now as they were a month ago. The shortage of gasoline, guns, and bullets that ground George S. Patton to a halt outside Metz still afflicts all the Allied forces up and down their five-hundred-mile front lines.

If there is one positive about the situation, it is that for the first time in ages, George S. Patton is not at the top of Eisenhower's long list of problems in need of solving.

★　★　★

August 3, 1943, more than a year prior. Patton is visiting the Fifteenth Evacuation Hospital near the Sicilian city of Nicosia. He is exhausted after three straight weeks of managing the American attack on Italy, pushing his army past the unharvested fields of grain and the vineyards where ripened grapes dangle in enormous bunches. American and British forces are racing from the southern shores of Sicily to Messina, in the island's north, where they hope to trap and capture the German army before its soldiers can flee to the Italian mainland. The fighting has been tough, with thousands killed on both sides. Patton's army has captured more than twenty thousand German and Italian soldiers, as well as thousands of Sicilian peasants forced to fight for the Nazi cause. Always determined to win, Patton is more driven than ever because operational priority has been assigned to his archrival, British general Bernard Law Montgomery.*

Monty was given a plum landing spot in Sicily, on the coastal plains near Syracuse. British leadership, who had operational control of the battlefield, ordered Patton's army to slug it out with the Axis defenders in the rugged Sicilian mountains.

This, Patton cannot allow. Nor can he stand to hear any more British

---

*Montgomery was not promoted to field marshal until September 1, 1944.

General Bernard Law Montgomery

gossip about Americans being inferior soldiers. He is determined to beat Monty into Messina and win glory for his army, despite the obstacles thrown in his way. "This is a horse race in which the prestige of the U.S. Army is at stake. We must take Messina before the British," he writes to one of his commanding generals. "Please use your best efforts to facilitate the success of our race."

The end of the race is still two weeks away as Patton visits a small field hospital in the crags of Sicily's central highlands. His love of the fighting man is profound, and extends to the aftermath of battle, where he is fond of personally presenting the wounded with their Purple Heart, a medal that recognizes injury during the course of combat.

The air smells of antiseptic and dust. Men lie on litters and improvised beds, their eyes glassy from sedatives. Many have their hands, faces, and torsos wrapped in gauze, speckled here and there with blood that has soaked through the dressings. Nurses and doctors weave through this sea of men, managing their pain the best they can before determining who will be sent back to the front and who will be transferred to a hospital far behind the lines for further treatment. "All," Patton will write in his journal tonight, "were brave and cheerful."

Except one soldier.

Pvt. Charles H. Kuhl of the First Infantry Division sits on the edge of a stool. He is being treated for exhaustion and anxiety. This is his third trip to a field hospital for this diagnosis in his eight short months in the army.

The general spots him.

"Why are you here?" Patton demands. His nerves are on edge. The race to Messina has him taking dangerous tactical chances. The ego that has so often defined him has pushed him to his emotional limits.

"I guess I can't take it, sir."

Patton seethes. "You coward," he bellows. "Leave this tent at once."

Kuhl remains motionless, sitting straight up at attention. The silence so unnerves Patton that he explodes. The general slaps Kuhl hard across the face with the gloves he is holding. He then lifts Kuhl off the stool by the collar of his uniform, shoves him toward the exit, and kicks him hard in the rear end. "You hear me, you yellow bastard. You're going back to the front," Patton screams at him.

The doctors and nurses working in the small field hospital are horrified, yet, surprisingly, they soon move on from the incident. As a professional soldier, Patton thinks nothing of it. Indeed, when news of the confrontation starts to spread, and eventually reaches his German counterparts, they are mystified that anyone would be bothered in the slightest by Patton's treatment of Kuhl. In the German army, such men are not slapped. They are forced to their knees and a bullet is shot through their brain.

Patton writes as much in his journal that night: "Companies should deal with such men, and if they shirk their duty they should be tried for cowardice and shot."

The press knows Patton's arrogance. The British understand his competitive nature. The Germans believe him to be America's top general. But now he is battling his own generals, who despite the rapid American advance toward Messina are appalled by his willingness to embrace unnecessary danger. But only those close to him understand how emotional he becomes at the sight of wounded American soldiers. He is deeply moved by their bravery, and thus cannot stand the sight of those he considers cowards.

Two days after slapping Kuhl, he writes a memo to each of his commanders, ordering them not to allow men suffering from combat fatigue to receive medical care. "Such men are cowards and bring disgrace to their comrades," he writes, "whom they heartlessly leave to endure the danger of battle while they themselves use the hospital as a means of escape. You will see that such cases are not sent to the hospital."

On August 10, as Allied troops approach Messina, and Nazi soldiers begin evacuating to the Italian mainland, Patton visits the Ninety-Third Evacuation Hospital in Santo Stefano, a city nestled in a long green valley. Patton steps from his staff car after a long drive through the twisting mountain roads and is surprised to see a soldier without battle dressings or a splint sitting among the litters.

"And what's happened to you?" Patton asks the young man. His name is Pvt. Paul Bennett. He has been in the army four years, serving with C Battery of the Seventeenth Field Artillery Regiment. He is just twenty-one years old. Until a friend died in combat, he had never once complained about battle. But he now shakes from convulsions. His red-rimmed eyes brim with tears.

"It's my nerves, sir. I can't stand the shelling anymore."

"Your nerves, hell. You're just a goddamned coward."

Bennett begins sobbing. Patton slaps him. "Shut up," he orders, his voice rising. "I won't have these brave men here who've been shot see a yellow bastard sitting here crying."

Patton hits him again, knocking off Bennett's helmet, which falls to the dirt floor. "You're a disgrace to the army and you're going back to the front to fight," he screams. "You ought to be lined up against a wall and shot. In fact, I ought to shoot you right now."

Patton pulls his ivory-handled pistol from its holster with his right hand. With his left, he backhands Bennett across the face with such force that nearby doctors rush to intervene.

The medical staff is disturbed by Patton's actions and file a report. Word of the incidents soon reaches Eisenhower. "I must so seriously question," Ike writes to Patton on August 16, "your good judgment and your self-discipline as to raise serious doubts in my mind as to your future usefulness."

But that is to be the end of it. Eisenhower needs Patton's tactical genius. As Assistant Secretary of War John J. McCloy will later remind Ike, Abraham Lincoln was faced with similar concerns about the leadership of Gen. Ulysses S. Grant. "I can't spare this man," Lincoln had responded to those calling for Grant's dismissal. "He fights."

Patton fights.

★ ★ ★

Field Marshal Bernard Law Montgomery is in his command post far from the front lines when he receives news that lead elements of the British army are marching into Messina. Montgomery beams. He believes he has won the race. Brigadier J. C. Currie of the British Fourth Armored Division, who will lead the British forces as they enter the ancient city, has even brought along bagpipes to celebrate their victory.

Currie and his commandos enter Messina. Many of the men are perched on the exterior of their American-made Sherman tanks as the overjoyed people of Messina spill into the streets and throw bouquets of flowers at them. But when the British column rumbles into the town center, Currie is shocked to see American soldiers standing in formation. Their uniforms are filthy from days of fighting, and many are so exhausted they can barely stand. But they have clearly won the race. And then, even as Currie struggles to make sense of this surprising scenario, George S. Patton rumbles into the piazza in his specially modified jeep command car, its three-star pennants on either side of the front hood flapping in the breeze. Patton's arrogant grin is not lost on Currie.

The British general has no choice but to step down from his Sherman tank and extend a hand in greeting. "It was a jolly good race," Currie concedes to Patton. "I congratulate you."

Patton shakes Currie's hand and thanks him. He revels in the victory, and in the look of surprise on the British officer's face. "I think the general was quite sore that we had got there first," Patton writes in his journal that night.

Any doubts about the efficacy of the American fighting men are now banished—thanks to George S. Patton. His picture graces the cover of *Time* magazine. President Franklin Delano Roosevelt hails him as a national hero. To the victor go the spoils, and Patton's glory spreads worldwide.

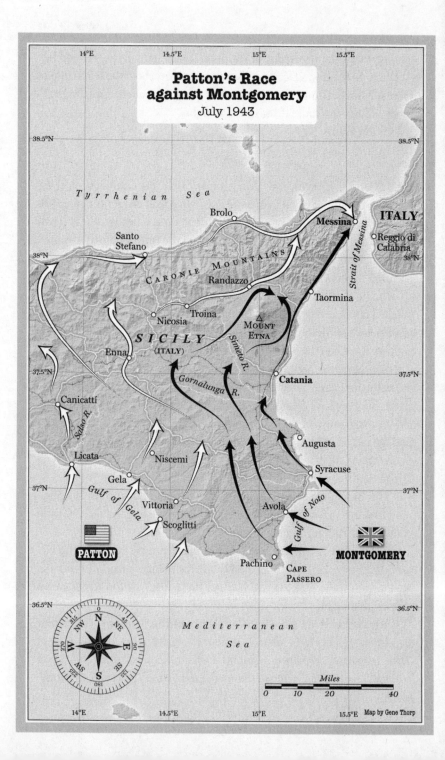

Patton's Race
against Montgomery
July 1943

Tyrrhenian Sea

ITALY

Brolo

Messina

Reggio di Calabria

Santo Stefano

CARONIE MOUNTAINS

Randazzo

Taormina

Nicosia Troina

SICILY
(ITALY)

△ MOUNT ETNA

Strait of Messina

Enna

Simeto R.

Gornalunga R.

Catania

Canicatti

Salso R.

Niscemi

Augusta

Licata

Syracuse

Gela

Vittoria

Avola

Scoglitti

Gulf of Noto

🇺🇸
PATTON

Pachino

CAPE PASSERO

🇬🇧
MONTGOMERY

Mediterranean Sea

N

Miles

0   10   20   40

Map by Gene Thorp

But that glory will be short-lived. Despite Eisenhower's best attempts to cover up the slapping incidents, the story is leaked to the press. For three months, nothing happens. Patton personally apologizes to both soldiers and to the medical staff who witnessed his actions, and for a time the matter seems settled. But Ernest Cuneo, a liaison officer in the Office of Strategic Services, leaks details of the slaps to NBC radio correspondent Drew Pearson, who announces the story to the nation on November 21, 1943. Public outrage leads the American Congress to call for Patton's immediate dismissal, even in the face of his battlefield triumphs.

"I have been a passenger floating on the river of destiny," he writes to Beatrice, adding a hopeful comment: "At the moment, I can't see around the next bend, but I guess it will be alright."

Patton is correct. Ike firmly believes that Patton's methods are deplorable, and he fears that Patton's ego is so monumental that he will sacrifice the lives of other men to gain greater fame.

But Patton fights.

And more than anything else, Eisenhower needs fighters.

★ ★ ★

By October 21, 1944, as Eisenhower passes a quiet afternoon in his villa at the Hotel Trianon, and Hitler plots far to the east in the Wolf's Lair, the fall of Messina is a distant memory. Since then, Dwight Eisenhower, a man whose keen sense of self-preservation has led him from civilian obscurity to wartime fame, did something extremely unusual: he defied the U.S. Congress and protected George Patton.

Patton has repaid Eisenhower's largesse by enraging Russia, defying orders, instructing soldiers of the Third Army to steal gasoline and other supplies from other U.S. armies, and openly sulking when he is not allowed to do as he pleases. "I am not usually inclined to grumble or to think the cards are stacked against me," Patton wrote to Beatrice during the Metz offensive, "but sometimes I wish that someone would get committed to do something for me."

Still, Patton fights. And Patton wins. Army Air Corps general Jimmy Doolittle compared the relationship to that between a fighting dog and its master: "When Eisenhower releases Patton," Doolittle notes, "it's like releasing an English pit bull—once you let him go, it's hard to make him stop."

General George Patton confers with a lieutenant colonel near Sicily

What Eisenhower doesn't know is that Adolf Hitler is furtively sending soldiers, tanks, and artillery toward a weakness in the American lines near the Ardennes Forest of Belgium. And that Operation Watch on the Rhine will utilize radio silence and deception in ways that will veil the attack from the Allied forces until it is far too late for them to effectively block it.

Eisenhower lives in the moment, trying to balance the many needs and demands of his lonely job. He has absolutely no idea how he will end the war by New Year's Eve, but taking Aachen in Germany is certainly a good start.

The time once again to unleash his prize pit bull is about to arrive.

4

BOLSHOI THEATER
MOSCOW, RUSSIA
OCTOBER 14, 1944
7:00 P.M.

The houselights are up in Moscow's legendary Bolshoi Theater as Olga Lepeshinskaya waits in the wings. The twenty-eight-year-old prima ballerina adjusts her costume and stretches her long, willowy legs as she prepares to take the stage. The acoustics in this legendary auditorium are among the best in the world, allowing Lepeshinskaya to hear with utter clarity the sounds of the last-minute tunings of violins and clarinets arising from the orchestra pit, and also vivid snippets of conversation from the 2,185 Russians noisily filing into their seats. She can hear their words of eagerness about enjoying this sold-out Saturday night performance, and the relief in their voices that after many hard-fought years the tide of war is turning in their favor.

Ever since Adolf Hitler ordered his armies to attack more than three years ago, the people of the Soviet Union—or Russia, as it is still commonly known—have seen more than ten million of their men and boys in uniform die. Amazingly, an equal number of civilians have also perished, done in by military bombardment, the random shooting of innocent women and children, and starvation. The German invaders cut off food supplies and appropriated harvests for themselves. Moving quickly and ruthlessly, the German war machine advanced a thousand miles from its own borders to the outskirts of Moscow before being repelled. At one point, German tanks and infantry stood just twenty-two miles from where these Muscovites sit right now.

But during the past six months, fate has turned against the German army. A summer offensive by Soviet forces pushed the Wehrmacht back. The long siege of Leningrad has come to an end, and just a few days ago that city was lit in the evening after three long years of blackouts. Truly, this is a night for all Russians to celebrate.

In keeping with the wartime austerity, the once-stately Bolshoi no longer sports gold leaf decorations. These have been painted over with a stark white paint, and the seats upholstered in plush crimson have been replaced by hard-backed chairs that not only fit more bodies into the ninety-year-old theater, but also make it possible to stage political rallies here in addition to the world's finest ballets—thus, the countless hammer-and-sickle emblems lining the walls.

Olga Lepeshinskaya smiles as she peeks her head around the curtain to clandestinely observe the house. Tonight she will dance *Giselle*, in one of the most famous romantic roles in ballet. Just having a stage is a luxury, for as part of her wartime service Lepeshinskaya has performed in woods, meadows, and bombed-out churches to entertain the Soviet troops as part of the Bolshoi's First Brigade frontline theater. Everything about the Bolshoi—the cavernous hall, the polished wood of the stage, and the many boxes lining the walls—feels like an extravagance after dancing in the dirt and rubble of the battlefield.

Suddenly a roar sweeps through the crowd. The audience turns and looks upward to the balcony that houses what was called the Imperial Box back before the days of Communist rule. A short, very overweight man bobs down toward his seat at the front of the box. The whole world knows the sight of Winston Churchill, prime minister of Great Britain. Why he happens to be in Moscow, attending the ballet, is a mystery to the crowd. But his presence here reinforces the solidarity between the Allied forces of the United States, Great Britain, and the Soviet Union. Together they will surely defeat Hitler and Germany.

The ovation is thunderous, and Churchill obliges the audience with a great wave of his hand before taking his seat.

As the house lights go down, Olga Lepeshinskaya gazes up at the box where Churchill sits. Her eyes study its other occupants, searching

Winston Churchill watching a military operation through a window

in vain for her lover. She sees American ambassador to the Soviet Union W. Averell Harriman; his young daughter, Kathleen; and Soviet diplomat Vyacheslav Molotov—but not the man she longs to see.

Then: commotion. However, it is dark, and the blinding footlights obscure Olga's view. What could be happening?

Twenty minutes later, as Lepeshinskaya's flawless dancing once again proves that no one—perhaps with the possible exception of her nemesis, Galina Ulanova—deserves the title of prima ballerina more than she, a quick look up at Churchill's box explains the source of the commotion.

For there, sitting next to Churchill, is the unmistakable profile of Olga Lepeshinskaya's lover. He has not been to the ballet once since the war began. Iosif Vissarionovich's face is pockmarked, his left arm shorter than the right, and he is the tiniest man in the box.* Olga Lepeshinskaya

---

*His left arm was seriously mangled when he was twelve, in an accident involving a horse-drawn carriage.

does not call him Iosif, not even when they are alone. Instead, she knows him by his adopted name, the one that translates to "man of steel."

Then, strangely, just before the end of the first act, Olga Lepeshinskaya is puzzled to see him move to the back of the box, where he cannot be seen.

When the first act of the ballet is complete, the houselights come back up, and the whole audience once again rises to its feet to give Churchill an ovation.

But the British leader refuses to bask in the acclaim alone. He beckons to the back of the box, encouraging another man to step forward.

So it is that Olga Lepeshinskaya's lover appears and stands at Churchill's right. The Soviet audience applauds thunderously, dazzled to see in the flesh the man whom they alternately love and fear.

All hail Marshal Joseph Stalin.

★ ★ ★

In his lifetime, Stalin will murder millions of people. Some will be shot, others will be denied food and ultimately die of starvation, millions will be

Joseph Stalin in 1945

sent to die in the deep winter snows of Siberia, and many will be tortured to death. Already, during one infamous murder spree in April and May of 1940, some twenty-two thousand Polish nationals were shot dead. What began as an attempt to execute every member of the Polish officer corps soon expanded to include police officers, landowners, intelligence agents, lawyers, and priests. The shootings were conducted for nights on end, often beginning at dusk and continuing until dawn. Some were mass killings carried out in the Katyn Forest, while others were individual executions inside the Kalinin and Kharkiv prisons. Mikhailovich Blokhin, chief executioner at Kalinin, personally shot seven thousand men in the back of the head as they knelt before him. Those killings took place inside a cell whose walls were lined with sandbags to deaden the sound. As soon as a victim fell dead, he was dragged from the room and thrown onto a truck for delivery to the burial site, while another handcuffed prisoner was marched before Blokhin and told to kneel. Noting that Russian pistols had so much recoil that his hand hurt after just a dozen killings, Blokhin opted for the smoother feel of the German Walther PPK.

The killings continued for two long months.

In order to prevent global outrage in case word of the atrocity spread, Stalin ordered his troops to make it seem as if German soldiers had carried out the executions.

His cruelty is so perverse that even those who serve him are in constant fear for their lives. Stalin has a standing order that none of his bodyguards are to enter his bedroom. Ever. Once, just to test them, he lay on his bed and screamed out in agony. Thinking the Soviet leader was in mortal danger, the guards rushed into the room to save his life. Stalin's scream was fake. He was testing his guards.

Each man was then executed for failure to follow orders.

★ ★ ★

Stalin will ultimately order between fifty million and sixty million deaths, far more than his hated rival Adolf Hitler.

The entire population of Great Britain is forty-seven million people. Stalin, in effect, will eventually slaughter the equivalent of every man, woman, and child in Winston Churchill's beloved homeland. He will do so without compassion or guilt, all the while living a life of luxury and debauchery in stark contrast to the rigors of the Communist lifestyle his government imposes.

Yet Winston Churchill has not come to Moscow to repudiate Stalin. He has come to befriend him.

For even though Stalin and his American counterpart, President Franklin D. Roosevelt, often treat Churchill as a drunken fool, the British leader is a most astute man. He is well aware that Roosevelt and Stalin are making plans to exclude Britain from the redrawing of maps once the war is over. Churchill has flown to Moscow to negotiate directly with Stalin. Tonight he has shown his solidarity with the Soviet leader by requesting that the performance include not just *Giselle*, but also a special demonstration of songs and dances by the Red Army choir.

Since the evening of October 9, when Churchill first met with Stalin at the Kremlin, a rather precarious diplomatic dance has been taking place between the two men. The Russians have pushed the German army hundreds of miles back, and it is clear that the Soviet Union will become the reigning superpower in Eastern Europe.

Rather than retreating once the war ends, Stalin has indicated that he will occupy countries such as Poland and Hungary. Churchill has no plans to stop him. Britain's global empire has been almost completely lost during the war—he seeks to regain some of the lost territory by dividing control of Europe between the Soviet Union and England.

Already, Soviet forces have captured all of eastern Poland. Rather than sympathize with the Polish people, who are vowing to fight for their homeland, Churchill upbraids them for being arrogant, and for wanting to "wreck" Europe. "I don't know if the British government will continue to recognize you," Churchill has informed the Polish government, which is now operating in exile. Meanwhile, even though Poland is not his to give away, American president Franklin Roosevelt has already secretly promised this sphere of influence to the Soviets.

Even the fearful Polish people themselves cannot foresee the horrors of the day in the not-so-distant future when every aspect of their lives will be overseen by a secret police loyal to their Soviet masters. They will live in constant fear of being hauled off to Mokotów Prison, in Warsaw,

Eastern Europe
October 1944

10°E   15°E   20°E   25°E   30°E   35°E

60°N

Leningrad

Tallinn ✪

ESTONIA

SWEDEN

Baltic Army Groups

Baltic Sea

Riga ✪   **LATVIA**

Dvina R.

55°N

LITH.

GER.

Minsk ○

White Russian Army Groups

GERMANY

Vistula R.

FRONT LINE, JUNE 1944

Warsaw   Brest

Berlin ✪

HITLER

POLAND

U. S. S. R.

Oder R.

Prague ✪

50°N

Kiev ○

Krakow ○

FRONT LINE, OCT. 1944

CZECHOSLOVAKIA

Ukrainian Army Groups

Vienna ✪

Budapest ✪

AUSTRIA

HUNGARY

R O M A N I A

45°N

Belgrade ✪

Bucharest ✪

YUGOSLAVIA

Danube R.

Adriatic Sea

Black Sea

Sofia ○

BULGARIA

N
NW NE
W E
SW SE
S

ITALY

GREECE

TURKEY

40°N

Miles

0   100   200   400

15°E   20°E   25°E

Map by Gene Thorp

where some of them will be tortured in a most horrific manner: skulls crushed, fingernails ripped off, torsos beaten with everything from brass rods to rubber truncheons. All because Churchill and Roosevelt gave their nation away to Joseph Stalin in the name of world peace.

But the rest of Eastern Europe is still up for grabs. Churchill has brought with him a handwritten piece of paper that he jokingly calls his "naughty document." On it, he's scratched out the names of Eastern European countries and the percentage Great Britain will control. Russia will get 90 percent of Romania, and Britain 10 percent. Britain will get 90 percent of Greece, and the Soviets will get 10 percent.

So it goes for each nation in Eastern Europe: Yugoslavia, Bulgaria, Hungary, and so on.

The negotiations continue for days. Stalin and Churchill go back and forth diplomatically, but the truth is that Stalin has no plans to honor this agreement.

Churchill inspired and encouraged the British people during the harrowing early days of the war, when Britain was under daily German attack, but this political mission reflects the darker side of his character. An island nation is in constant need of resources to ensure stability and prosperity. British politician Horace Walpole, speaking two hundred years earlier, spoke emphatically about England's need to control other countries so that they might provide the wealth Britain's limited size could not. Without these resources, Walpole wrote, "we shall be reduced to a miserable little island, and from a mighty empire sink to as insignificant a country as Denmark or Sardinia. Then France will dictate to us more imperiously than we ever did to Ireland."

Churchill understands this harsh political reality. And though he won't admit it to Stalin, both men know that England has already seen its global power seriously diminished. Without the Americans, the Germans most likely would have defeated the British long ago. Even now, as Churchill attempts to seduce a madman, American soldiers flood the streets of London. They are paid a higher salary than their British counterparts, and spend it freely. British soldiers seethe at the sight of American GIs with English girls on their arms, but there is nothing the Tommies, as they are called, can do about it.

Horace Walpole's prediction has come to pass. Instead of France, as it was in Walpole's time, it is Stalin and the Soviet Union who are now dictating terms to Churchill and Great Britain.

★ ★ ★

Olga Lepeshinskaya beams as Joseph Stalin and Winston Churchill join in the ovation. She has danced *Giselle* beautifully. The two world leaders now clap their hands enthusiastically to show their approval as the ballet comes to an end.

Her days of dancing on the front lines are most assuredly over. The German threat against Moscow is no more, and those Soviet soldiers fighting their way west into Czechoslovakia and Hungary push the buffer between the Soviet people and imminent peril farther and farther into the distance. But Olga does not know that for every mile the Soviet soldiers conquer, their insatiable desire to rape and plunder goes unchecked. In *Giselle*, such rapists are hunted down by spirits from beyond the grave for their barbarous acts. Yet in the real world, their acts not only go unpunished, but they are seen as acts of heroism by the barbaric Soviet leadership.

A large bouquet of roses, grown in the warmth of a greenhouse for just this purpose, is carried onstage and presented to Olga Lepeshinskaya. The audience is still on its feet. She curtsies as she accepts the bloodred flowers. But when she looks up at the box where her beloved sat just moments ago, he and Winston Churchill are gone.

In six days of negotiations, the two men have redrawn the map of Europe. But Churchill has been wasting his time. For the Russians have no plans to honor their promises. When the war finally ends, they plan to grab as much land as possible, ensuring that millions of people will soon live their lives under the murderous thumb of Marshal Joseph Stalin.

Time to celebrate.

5

The man with five months to live surveys the joyous crowd, as he revels in the ongoing applause.

Unbeknownst to him, Franklin Delano Roosevelt is waiting to deliver the last campaign speech of his long and storied political career. Red, white, and blue bunting covers the stadium. The surface of the old ballpark is dark. Roosevelt stands tall atop the speaker's platform in center field, stretched up to his full six-foot-two height, awash in the cheers of forty thousand Bostonians and bathed in brightness by giant spotlights shining down from atop the roof.

FDR has been president of the United States for nearly twelve long years—and is just days away from being elected to a record fourth term. He wears a gray fedora and thick gray overcoat on this brutally cold autumn night. His legs are withered and weak from the polio that has long ravaged his body. Even with steel braces encircling his hips, thighs, and knees, FDR must grip the lectern to balance himself.

"This is not my first visit to Boston," Roosevelt reminds the crowd, gently trying to calm their boisterousness. The president's subtle request for quiet is spoken into the microphone in that genteel upper-crust voice that these working-class men and women recognize from the radio.

But the good people of Boston refuse to sit down and let him speak. Most have never glimpsed the president in person until this moment.

President Franklin Delano Roosevelt

Indeed, many have only heard his voice and seen his picture in the *Boston Globe*.

"Free admission," reads the ticket that got them all into the ballpark on this cold Saturday night. "Bring your friends."

And they did.

The voices of those cheering are made up of men too old to fight, veterans home on leave, rosy-cheeked young children, and "Gold Star" mothers—those mournful women who have lost a son in combat.

The night is being broadcast nationwide on the radio. Festivities began with the twenty-eight-year-old Italian American matinee idol Frank Sinatra singing the national anthem. Sinatra's given name is Francis, but he claims that he was inspired to name his newborn son, Frank Jr., after the president. "What a guy," Sinatra marvels after his performance, referring to Roosevelt. "And boy does he pack 'em in."

Despite the adoration of the public, Roosevelt is not a man of the people. He was born into wealth and privilege and has never known hard labor. As a young man, FDR collected stamps and shot birds, which he then stuffed himself and put on display. These are his hobbies to this very day. The president still spends his free time tending to the more than one million stamps in his possession, and his ornithological collection is on display at the family home in Hyde Park. Somewhat ironically, he speaks fluent German, thanks to his early years of schooling in Germany, near the warm springs at Bad Nauheim, where his father temporarily moved the family so that the elder Roosevelt might recuperate from a heart problem. The cure did not take, and FDR's father died when Franklin was just eighteen, leaving the future president a sizable inheritance that would ensure him a life of luxury. His wealth made him stuffy and elitist, even as his foppish behavior led his cousin Alice Roosevelt, daughter of Franklin's macho distant cousin Teddy, to sneer that FDR was a "Good little mother's boy." She took to insulting FDR's manhood even further by giving him the nickname Miss Nancy.*

At age twenty, Franklin married Eleanor Roosevelt, his fifth cousin and the niece of Teddy Roosevelt. While he was at first madly in love with Eleanor, he found his affection soon waned. FDR is a man who craves constant approval, and he chafed at Eleanor's constant criticism. The range of her scorn included their bedroom activities. Although their fruitful marriage has produced six children, Eleanor once stated that sex with FDR was an "ordeal to be endured." Their relationship is now a platonic political arrangement—as it has been since Eleanor caught Franklin having an affair with her social secretary almost thirty years ago.

The American people know none of this. Despite FDR's upper-crust mannerisms, his public policies have done much to benefit the working class, and the folks love him. In Roosevelt, they see the man who led the

---

*Alice Roosevelt was extremely loyal, and her flair for the cutting remark was later put to good use in defense of her cousin Franklin. When it was said that Wendell Willkie, FDR's opponent in the 1940 presidential election, was a grassroots candidate, she agreed, noting that it was "the grass of 10,000 country clubs." And of FDR's 1944 opponent, the nattily attired and immaculately coiffed Thomas Dewey, she remarked, "He looks just like the little man on the wedding cake." Dewey, a man so sensitive about his height that he sometimes sat on a phone book to look taller in his office chair, would be haunted by that remark the rest of his career.

Eleanor Roosevelt at work

nation out of a crippling economic depression. They see a president who brought the nation together in the devastating wake of the Japanese surprise attack on Pearl Harbor. They see a president who has gone to great lengths to assist the German Jews who are now being persecuted in their homeland, even going so far as to recall the American ambassador to Germany, thus enduring the rage of American anti-Semites. And they see the commander in chief who has guided the country so skillfully through three long years of war. The good people of Boston have turned out in force this evening to show their gratitude.

"I shall not review all my previous visits. I should have to go on talking for several days to do that," Roosevelt says into the microphone, the veteran politician making a joke in the hope that a ripple of laughter will get the people to sit down so that he might speak.

It doesn't help. The cheering continues.

Outside Fenway Park, the crowd is even larger. The sidewalks are packed all the way out to Kenmore Square, about a quarter mile away. Some in the throng are able to brag that they were also on hand when the president's cousin, former U.S. president Teddy Roosevelt, spoke at Fenway back in 1914, just as the First World War was breaking out in Europe.

But Teddy came in the summer, during the warmth of baseball season. This is different. Roosevelt has come at a time of freezing temperatures. On his way into Fenway just moments ago, sound wagons blaring patriotic songs preceded him. To counter rumors that he is in poor health, Roosevelt made sure the top was down in the Sunshine Special, as his bulletproof black Lincoln limousine is known. The president looked vigorous and strong, seemingly unbothered by the damp chill of the night air, as he drove into Fenway with famous actor and director Orson Welles sitting next to him in the backseat. "Nice lights," Welles said in awe as the Lincoln turned left—appropriately, as the liberal president will joke with his Secret Service protection.

Welles was the warm-up act at Fenway, and did his job splendidly. With his deep, dramatic voice and Shakespearean delivery, Welles insisted that the nation must elect Roosevelt to a fourth term. The director, who has achieved lasting fame with the movie *Citizen Kane,* had Fenway at a fever pitch long before Roosevelt clambered as gracefully as possible to the lectern to speak.

Now comes a delicate moment for Franklin Roosevelt. He must maintain Welles's momentum while hiding the fact that he is, in the language of the day, a cripple. In 1921, at the age of thirty-nine, he was afflicted with polio, a stunning blow to the privileged man. Since then, he has seen that great doses of funding have gone to cure the disease, but to no end. The president now spends his days in a wheelchair, a fact that can easily be concealed in pictures of him sitting behind his Oval Office desk or at the wheel of a car. But he is not completely paralyzed, and has never lost his roving eye. FDR maintains a bevy of mistresses—among them, his personal secretary; a sixth cousin; and even a former princess from Sweden. But there are no long walks in Franklin Delano Roosevelt's life. No hikes. No midnight rambles on the White House lawn.

The only time his paralysis becomes a serious issue is at moments like this, when tens of thousands of people are watching his every move. He must rise and stand so that not a soul outside his closest circle will ever know of his health problems.

Roosevelt has practiced and plotted and seen to the evening's every last detail. His car was driven through the center field garage and straight up a ramp onto the speaker's platform. When it came time to get out of the car and move to the lectern, he continued the ruse by holding a cane and leaning on the arm of an adviser. Since his legs will not move, Roosevelt must swing his hips from side to side in a much-practiced method of forward movement. He would never dare let this, or any, crowd know that he is paralyzed, for that would convey weakness.

In a time of world war, a man such as Roosevelt must be made of the same sturdy timber as Adolf Hitler, Winston Churchill, and Joseph Stalin.

But there is a far greater truth behind Roosevelt hiding his affliction: America is not ready for a paralyzed president. A nation that is intolerant of racial differences is even more unable to come to terms with physical handicaps.

Truth be told, Roosevelt's physical problems extend far beyond his polio. He suffers from hypertension. He has bronchitis. After a lifetime of smoking cigarettes, his lung function is compromised, and he often assumes a gray pallor. He cannot ride on a train traveling more than thirty-five miles per hour, because the atrophied muscles in his lower body are unable to absorb the vibration.

In a word, Franklin Delano Roosevelt is dying. The greatest cause is something he cannot even see: Roosevelt's arteries are completely clogged and hardened, so much so that when he dies the embalmer will be unable to poke a needle into them.

Yet FDR now stands out in the cold, just like any veteran politician seeking reelection. This is something he must do. The race between him and Republican nominee Thomas Dewey is just too close. So he endures a cold Boston night, just as he endured a four-hour car ride through New York City in the rain two weeks ago. Nothing must stop him from reelection.

"Radio time costs a lot of money," Roosevelt finally barks into the microphone.

There is a moment of stunned silence.

This voice is not that of a frail old man, or of one who is tentative about speaking his mind.

It is the sound of ultimate authority.

Franklin Delano Roosevelt, despite the physical maladies that have made him a shell of his former self, is the most powerful man in the world. His decisions will determine the fate of peoples and nations, and even the shape of the global map, for decades to come. So as Roosevelt talks, the people of his nation listen.

The crowd finally sits down.

* * *

Franklin Roosevelt speaks for thirty-five minutes before being bundled into his Lincoln and driven back to his train, the *Ferdinand Magellan*, by his Secret Service detail. His speech has been a rousing success, touching on a wide array of themes, including race relations, the rise of trade unions, and America's diversity: FDR points out the fact that the U.S. Army is comprised of "the Murphys and the Kellys, the Smiths and the Joneses, the Cohens, the Carusos, the Kowalskis, the Schultzes, the Olsens, the Swobodas, and—right in with all the rest of them—the Cabots and the Lowells."

He's saying that everyone, from all strata of American society, is doing his part.

The massive fighting force that has banded together to battle its way across Europe is not just a combination of the established wealthy and the Irish, Italian, Jewish, Polish, and Scandinavian immigrants, but of blacks as well. To the people of Boston, most of whom come from Irish and Italian stock, and who can remember the words "Irish Need Not Apply" when seeking jobs, those words are a heartfelt reminder that the nation is changing for the better.

Not everyone believes this to be true. Many believed that FDR's strategy of government-funded jobs and the public works projects of the New Deal were socialistic, even though they may have rescued the nation from the Great Depression. Roosevelt's Republican opponent in the presidential election of 1944, New York governor Thomas Dewey, has relentlessly attacked FDR for promoting a form of "communism."

But Franklin Roosevelt is not a Communist any more than Thomas Dewey plays center field for the Yankees. FDR is a natural leader whose foremost objective is to push the nation in a positive direction, first as governor of New York in 1928, and then during the legendary "First 100

Days" as president in 1933, when he realized that drastic experiments in government were required to halt a four-year economic slide that was being called the Great Depression.

The American Dream had evaporated. One fourth of all American workers were out of a job. Banks were failing. Poverty was epidemic. The American people felt that they were on their own. The government to whom they paid taxes and the men they voted into office were either unwilling or unable to fix the problems. Millions of Americans were desperate, families were falling apart, and prosperity looked as if it might never return.

Working closely with Congress, Roosevelt crafted a series of fifteen bills that fixed the banking system and made possible a number of monumental public works projects designed to put Americans on the job. Thus began the long climb back to prosperity. Republicans and Democrats set aside their differences and worked closely to get Roosevelt's ideas passed into law. They enacted the legislation so quickly that comedian Will Rogers joked on the radio that Congress didn't vote on the bills, "they just wave at the bills as they go by."

FDR's social experiments have worked. The American Dream has been revived, and the nation is reaching new heights of prosperity because of the production necessary during World War II. But those new laws also drastically expanded the size and reach of the federal government. This has made some voters angry. More than 150 years since Americans fought for independence and deposed a king, the specter of a powerful authority controlling private lives is alienating many citizens, and Dewey feeds that discontent by comparing large government with the oppression of communism.

Tonight in Fenway, Roosevelt fires back. He speaks out against communism, distancing himself and his administration from what many in the world—even Adolf Hitler—perceive as the world's greatest threat. "We want neither communism nor monarchy," Roosevelt tells the crowd. "We want to live under our Constitution."

But Roosevelt says nothing about which sort of government will rule postwar Europe. One thing is for certain: thanks in part to him, communism will play a very large role.

Winston Churchill isn't the only one making deals with Joseph Stalin.

Franklin Roosevelt has made any number of secret arrangements with the Soviet leader dividing the postwar world between America and the Communist Soviet Union. Giving eastern Poland to the Soviets is just a start.

The high-stakes nature of the global intrigue being played out in Washington, Moscow, London, and Berlin means that FDR can trust very few people. It's quite clear, however, that he needs someone to represent him in this new, turbulent world. Even if FDR were not president of the United States, his physical handicaps do not allow him to parachute behind enemy lines. His world-famous jaunty profile does not allow him to go undercover. And the constraints of his office do not allow him to perform the unethical work of political assassination or other messy intrigues.

But war is war, and lethal things must be done. So Roosevelt has appointed one special individual to do the dirty work. The man's name is William "Wild Bill" Donovan.

At age sixty-one, Donovan is just a year younger than the president. The two have known each other since they were classmates at Columbia Law School. But there the similarities end. Roosevelt is a liberal while Donovan is a staunch conservative Republican. Roosevelt is in failing health; Donovan is so robust and larger-than-life that he seems bullet-proof. And while Roosevelt is happiest basking in the adulation of a large crowd, the swaggering Donovan prefers to work in the shadows. Even before the war began, Roosevelt brought in this quick-thinking former attorney and Medal of Honor* winner to be his global eyes and ears—and Donovan has done a spectacular job.

As Roosevelt gives his speech in Fenway on this cold Saturday night,

---

*Donovan won his Medal of Honor during World War I, as leader of a mostly Irish American regiment from New York known as the Fighting Sixty-Ninth. He was shot and wounded while battling German positions in France on October 14 and 15, 1918. Donovan refused to be evacuated, so that he might continue to lead the charge. In addition to the Medal of Honor, in his lifetime he was also awarded the Distinguished Service Cross, Distinguished Service Medal, and the National Security Medal. No other individual has won all four of America's top decorations. Also of note is that upon his return from World War I, Donovan worked with Teddy Roosevelt to form a new institution for veterans known to this day as the American Legion. *The Fighting 69th*, a film about the exploits of the regiment, starring James Cagney and Pat O'Brien, was released in early 1940. The actor George Brent played Donovan.

Wild Bill is busy sabotaging America's relationship with Winston Churchill and Great Britain—in order that the United States and the Soviet Union can achieve a tighter bond.

Donovan's location seems innocuous enough. He is at home in Washington, DC, safe and secure in his tony Georgetown mansion on Thirtieth Street. Donovan has a sizable fortune, and lives a lavish lifestyle that would make few suspect he is America's top spy.

Yet Donovan's Office of Strategic Services (OSS, as this covert group of top-secret operatives he commands is known) is in constant contact with him. While he might be relaxing at home, Donovan is well aware that troops of the Soviet Red Army are rolling into Yugoslavia on board American tanks, trucks, and jeeps. Donovan soon orders that ten tons of medical supplies be flown into the Balkans at U.S. expense, an extravagance that will assist the Communist takeover. The OSS is also sowing seeds of discord in Greece, the country that Winston Churchill covets more than any other.

Thus begins a sideshow to the war itself: the undercover battle led by William Donovan and the OSS to ensure that Eastern Europe fall into the hands of Soviet Russia. Above all else, FDR does not want a confrontation with the Soviet Union. He thinks of Joseph Stalin as his friend, and a true ally. Better to let Stalin have a part of the world where the United States has few interests. And even when Winston Churchill complains that the Soviet expansion is hurting England, it is explained to him that Donovan is out of control—and unstoppable. "I have always been worried by his predilection for political intrigue," Gen. Walter Bedell "Beetle" Smith, one of Dwight Eisenhower's top staff members, writes to Churchill about Donovan, "and have kept a firm hand on him so he keeps away from me as much as possible."

But Wild Bill Donovan reports only to the president of the United States.

★ ★ ★

Two weeks after that triumphant night in Fenway Park, Franklin Delano Roosevelt relaxes in the White House, safely reelected to a fourth term. No other American president has ever served this long.

Roosevelt sits at his Oval Office desk in his wheelchair, the one specially built to look as much as possible like a normal piece of office furniture. The day is not a busy one, not beginning until almost noon with a private meeting with British admiral James Somerville, a war hero who has just been assigned to Washington as head of Britain's naval delegation. Later on there will be a brief reception with a group of female newspaper correspondents and a small formal dinner for fourteen guests in the cavernous East Room of the White House. The affair will be short, lasting from 7:30 to precisely 9:00 p.m. Roosevelt will rattle around the White House for three more hours after that, but the time will be unstructured, unplanned, and completely his own. November 18, 1944, will mark that rarest of all days for a wartime president: one without crisis.

But today will one day be seen to hold monumental significance, thanks to a memo Roosevelt now grasps in his hand. Typed and organized into a single sheet in the form of a letter, it arrived between appointments. The memo comes straight from the desk of Wild Bill Donovan, who has scrawled his signature at the bottom. Roosevelt personally requested this piece of paper on October 31. Its highly confidential contents will soon get leaked, through no fault of Roosevelt's, and he will be forced to defend Donovan when the newspapers report that the OSS chief is trying to create an "American gestapo."

When that moment comes, Roosevelt will have no choice but to distance himself from Donovan in the same manner as Beetle Smith. Noting to an aide that Donovan loves "power for its own sake," Roosevelt will try to "find a way to harness that guy, because if we don't he'll be doing a lot of things other than what we want him to do."

But Roosevelt has no intention of stopping Donovan, because Wild Bill is doing what FDR wants.

"Pursuant to your note of October 31, 1944," Donovan writes, "I have given consideration to the formation of an intelligence service for the postwar period.

"Though in the mist of war, we are also in a period of transition," he adds. "We have now in the government a trained and specialized personnel needed for the task."

Neither Roosevelt nor Donovan has any further concern about the German army. The war will soon be won; that is a foregone conclusion. And just as Donovan once traveled the globe at Roosevelt's behest in the days before Pearl Harbor, warning that the United States should expand its navy and army in anticipation of the day it would join the war, Roosevelt now asks him to see the future once again. Both men anticipate that another great conflict might follow once Germany is defeated. But rather than suffer another surprise attack, as at Pearl Harbor, Donovan is pressing Roosevelt to allow him to design a new postwar intelligence agency that will anticipate clear and present dangers. In the absence of openly belligerent enemies, this new agency's role will be to spy on America's friends as well as her adversaries.

Roosevelt endorses the new group. His typewritten reply is signed, simply, "FDR."

And so the Central Intelligence Agency is born.

★　★　★

As history will show, both Roosevelt and Donovan are taking their eyes off the ball much too early. Adolf Hitler and the armies of Nazi Germany are far from conquered. As Wild Bill Donovan strategizes about postwar power consolidation, Wehrmacht soldiers, guns, and tanks are quietly grouping near the German border. They do so under strict radio silence, lest the Americans hear their chatter and anticipate the biggest surprise attack since Pearl Harbor.

The Germans face west, toward the American lines, and the thick wilderness in Belgium known as the Ardennes Forest. It is here that U.S. forces are weakest, because it is assumed that an attack through this primeval wood is impossible. To tilt the odds even further in the Germans' favor, it has been ascertained that George Patton and his Third Army are more than one hundred miles southeast, still in dire need of gasoline, guns, and soldiers—and still unable to conquer Metz.

Hitler and his generals are sure that Operation Watch on the Rhine will be a successful counterattack that not even the great George Patton can thwart. The Nazis are poised to turn defeat into victory with this counterattack and the development of a new atomic weapon that Hitler believes is almost ready.

The Führer is still certain of ultimate victory.

Very certain.

6

WAR ROOM
THIRD ARMY HEADQUARTERS
NANCY, FRANCE
DECEMBER 9, 1944
7:00 A.M.

Col. Oscar Koch thinks that Hitler is up to something.

The G-2, as General Patton's top intelligence officer* is known in military parlance, is certain that the German army is far from defeated. In fact, he is the only intelligence officer on the Allied side who believes that the Wehrmacht is poised to launch a withering Christmas counteroffensive.

Only, until now, nobody will listen to him.

The sun has not yet risen on what promises to be yet another bitter cold and wet day in eastern France. Koch stands amid the countless maps lining the walls of his beloved War Room, thirty miles south of the front lines. The forty-six-year-old career soldier stands ramrod straight. He is bald, and wears thick glasses that give him a professorial air.

Just a few feet away, George S. Patton sits in a straight-backed wooden chair as Koch begins the morning intelligence briefing. Patton wears a long overcoat and scarf to ward off the cold, even indoors. He is pensive,

---

*Patton served as G-2 in charge of Hawaiian Islands security from 1935 to 1937. During that time he wrote a paper entitled "Surprise" in which he predicted the growing power of the Japanese military and its potential to attack the Hawaiian Islands through the use of aircraft carriers, submarines, and fighter-bombers. This made Patton the first American officer to accurately predict the Japanese surprise attack on Pearl Harbor four years later.

and eager to be once again on the attack. In just ten days, Patton is launching his Operation Tink, a bold new offensive that will take the Third Army into the heart of Nazi Germany for the first time. Metz has finally fallen after two long months of battle. Patton systematically worked his way toward Metz, bypassing the network of forts as needed, while at the same time depriving their inhabitants of food and water. Fort Driant surrendered on December 8, 1944. The invasion of Germany now awaits. Patton plans to cross the Rhine and press hard toward Frankfurt, then on to Berlin.

Unlike many generals, who plan an attack without first consulting their G-2, Patton relies heavily on Koch.

And with good reason. A humble veteran soldier who worked his way up through the ranks, Koch is perhaps the most driven man on Patton's staff. He is consumed with the task of collecting information on every aspect of the battlefield. Koch arranges for reconnaissance planes to fly over enemy positions, and then has a team of draftsman construct precise terrain maps of the towns, rivers, railway lines, fence lines, creeks, farm buildings, bridges, and other obstacles that might slow down the Third Army's advance.

Koch also arranges for German-speaking American soldiers to exchange their military uniforms for peasant clothing at night and travel behind enemy lines, mingling in bars and restaurants to collect information about Wehrmacht troop movements.

And Koch and his team carefully scrutinize data radioed back from the front lines by American patrols.

Every bit of that information comes together in the War Room's centerpiece, an enormous series of maps detailing the entire Western Front. British, American, Canadian, French, and German positions are all carefully marked.

The maps' transparent acetate coverings are marked in grease pencil, with special notations for armored, infantry, and artillery. Each unit is denoted by a special symbol. Once an army is on the move, its progress is closely tracked. A rag made wet with alcohol wipes the acetate clean, and a unit's new location is once again marked in grease pencil. In this way, Col. Oscar Koch knows with almost pinpoint accuracy the location

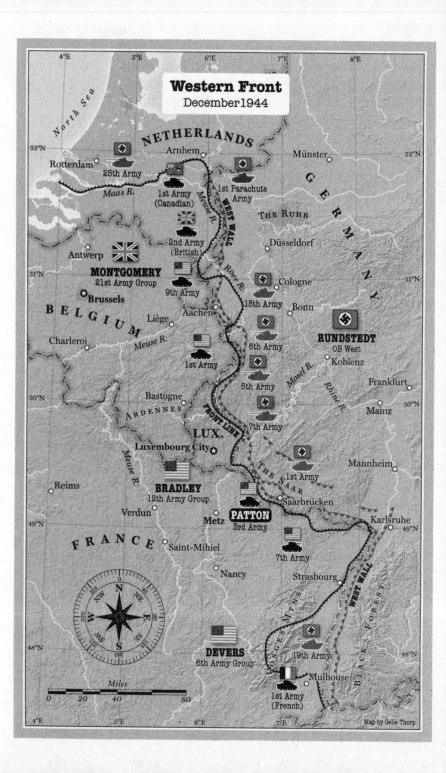

Western Front
December 1944

North Sea

52°N

Rotterdam
25th Army
Maas R.

NETHERLANDS

Arnhem

1st Army
(Canadian)

Meuse R.

1st Parachute
Army

WEST WALL

Münster

GERMANY

52°N

Antwerp

2nd Army
(British)

MONTGOMERY
21st Army Group

9th Army

THE RUHR

Düsseldorf

Roer R.

51°N

BELGIUM

Brussels

Liège

Aachen

Charleroi

Meuse R.

1st Army

15th Army

Cologne

Bonn

6th Army

RUNDSTEDT
OB West

Koblenz

Mosel R.

Frankfurt

Rhine R.

51°N

50°N

Bastogne

ARDENNES

FRONT LINE

LUX.

Luxembourg City

5th Army

7th Army

Mainz

Mannheim

1st Army

THE SAAR

50°N

Reims

Meuse R.

BRADLEY
12th Army Group

Verdun

Metz

Saint-Mihiel

Nancy

PATTON
3rd Army

Saarbrücken

7th Army

Karlsruhe

Strasbourg

VOSGES MTS.

WEST WALL

BLACK FOREST

49°N

FRANCE

N
NW   NE
W   E
SW   SE
S

Miles
0   20   40   80

DEVERS
6th Army Group

19th Army

1st Army
(French)

Mulhouse

48°N

4°E   5°E   6°E   7°E

Map by Gene Thorp

of every tank, howitzer, airfield, fuel dump, supply depot, railway station, and infantry detachment between Antwerp and Switzerland.

And that, Koch now explains to Patton as the general listens with his usual intensity, is what troubles him. There is something missing.

The Third Army's proposed route across the Rhine and into Germany is defended by a small and vulnerable German force. So, in all likelihood, Patton's Operation Tink will begin as a rousing success—though Koch never goes out on a limb to predict a victory. War is too uncertain. But, Koch goes on to point out, a real problem lies farther north, on what will be the Third Army's left flank during Operation Tink.

In particular, Koch is wary of an enormous German troop buildup. Despite the fact that the roads are empty during daylight hours, Koch has discovered that thirteen enemy infantry divisions have been relocated under cover of darkness to an area near the Ardennes Forest. This means there are an additional two hundred thousand Wehrmacht soldiers at the very location where the U.S. lines are thinnest. German forces in the Ardennes currently outnumber Americans by more than two to one.

In addition, advance scouts from the U.S. First Army report that they hear the rumble of truck engines and the heavy clank of tank treads coming through the forest from the German lines. Koch has confirmed that five Panzer divisions containing some five hundred tanks recently moved toward the Ardennes. German railway cars loaded with men and ammunition are proceeding toward the Ardennes with increasing frequency. Just three days ago, the Allies intercepted a coded message showing that a major German fighting force had requested fighter plane protection as it moved troops and supplies toward the Ardennes.

Perhaps spookiest of all: the Germans have shrouded this major movement in complete radio silence.

Koch doesn't have to remind Patton that radio silence usually precedes an attack.

Patton quietly absorbs what Koch has to say, sometimes taking notes or interrupting with a specific question. He thinks that Koch is "the best damned intelligence officer in any United States command," but almost every single other Allied intelligence analyst believes the Germans are too beaten down to launch a major offensive.

Should it take place, a German attack would be launched against positions currently occupied by the U.S. First Army, but Col. Benjamin "Monk" Dickson, the First's G-2, is not concerned. He will later claim that he foresaw the German attack, but at this moment he behaves as if he doesn't believe that the Germans pose a threat. Dickson, too, has been told of the hundreds of Panzers, the railway cars packed with elite SS divisions, and the recent appearance of Messerschmitt fighter planes in the sky after months of Allied air superiority. Dickson considers the German movements to be a regular rotation of troops in and out of the area.

This lack of concern is mirrored throughout the highest levels of the Allied command. British field marshal Bernard Montgomery writes to a fellow British general that Hitler "is fighting a defensive campaign on all fronts. He cannot stage a major offensive operation." Monty is so certain there will not be a surprise attack that he is making plans to return home to London for Christmas.

Col. Oscar Koch is the only man who believes that the Germans are ready to attack.

"Although the Allied offensive is destroying weekly a number of German divisions," Koch notes, "the enemy has been able to maintain a coherent front without drawing on the full of his infantry and armored reserves, thereby giving him the capability to mount a spoiling offensive in an effort to unhinge the Allied assault on Festung Deutschland."

Koch ends his briefing. Patton's excitement about Operation Tink is temporarily set aside as he absorbs the heavy weight of this new information. Koch is a cautious man and reluctant to speculate, preferring to speak in hard facts. His certainty about a major new German attack means a great deal.

Patton remains seated for quite some time, silently pondering the situation. Despite aggressive Third Army patrols into Germany's Saar region in the past few weeks, there has been almost no enemy resistance. This is very unusual. The Germans normally fight viciously for every inch of ground. Patton knows that ever since the time of Julius Caesar, when Germanic tribes battled the Romans, the Germans were fond of going on the offensive and employing unique tactics to gain the element of surprise. Patton finds himself reminded of the story of "the dog that did not bark," in which a cunning predator conceals himself before suddenly lunging out to fight his victim. Patton wonders if Hitler is playing such a deadly game.

But Patton is conflicted. The lack of clear-cut intelligence is easily explained. The German army is now based in its own country, rather than in a hostile nation such as France. The local citizens are patriots who will not spy on their own soldiers, as the French Resistance movement has done so successfully. And because German telephone lines are still largely intact, achieving radio silence is as simple as ordering all military officers to use the telephone instead of the radio. Seen from this perspective, the behavior of the German army is completely logical. The warnings of Col. Oscar Koch might be an exercise in paranoia.

Patton still has every intention of launching Operation Tink on December 19. It will be glorious, starting with the biggest aerial bombardment the Americans have ever poured down on the German army. He finally has the bridging material necessary for his tanks and men to continue their winter offensive for as long as their guns and their gasoline will take them. With any luck, the war might be over by New Year's Eve after all.

But what if Koch is right? What if there is danger on the Third Army's northern flank?

Finally, Patton stands to leave. He orders that in addition to fine-tuning the last-minute details of Operation Tink, planning is to begin immediately on emergency measures to rescue Gen. Courtney Hodges and his First Army should the Germans attack to the north in the Ardennes Forest. If that happens, "Our offensive will be called off," he tells his staff. "And we'll have to go up there and save their hides."

Patton's private sentiments indicate serious concern. "First Army is making a terrible mistake," he worried in his diary two weeks ago. "It is highly probable the Germans are building up east of them."

★　★　★

As General Patton leaves the War Room, Colonel Koch goes back to the endless business of acquiring information. It is a skill that he will one day put to good use while working for the CIA. For now, he is most pleased that General Patton wants the Third Army to be "in a position to meet whatever happens."

But Patton needs to do more than just make backup plans. He calls Gen. Dwight Eisenhower and passes on Koch's assessment. Ike, in turn, passes this on to his own G-2, Gen. Kenneth Strong, who relays Patton's concerns to the First Army.

Where the warning is promptly ignored.

7

GERMAN FRONT LINES
DECEMBER 16, 1944
5:29 A.M.

Sunrise is still two hours away. The morning sky is completely black, without even moon or starlight. German artillery crews stand at their guns, making happy small talk and stomping their feet to keep warm. Their cheeks sting from the record December cold. They have been awake for hours, waiting for this moment. Someday they will tell their grandchildren about the great instant when Unternehmen Wacht am Rhein (Operation Watch on the Rhine) commenced, and how they were among the lucky gunners who fired the first rounds into the American lines, turning the tide of war in favor of the Fatherland, once and for all. They will regale their descendants about the brilliant deception that allowed a quarter million men, more than seven hundred tanks, and thousands of huge artillery pieces to remain camouflaged in the Ardennes Forest for weeks. And these young soldiers will talk about the glory of the surprise attack that split the American and British armies, and then the relentless push to reclaim the strategically vital port city of Antwerp. Next, Adolf Hitler successfully sued for peace with the west, thereby preserving the Third Reich and preventing an Allied invasion of the German homeland. With the Americans and British neutralized, Hitler activated step two of Operation Watch on the Rhine and launched his legendary second attack against Stalin and Russia that defeated the Communists.

That is the story they hope to tell.

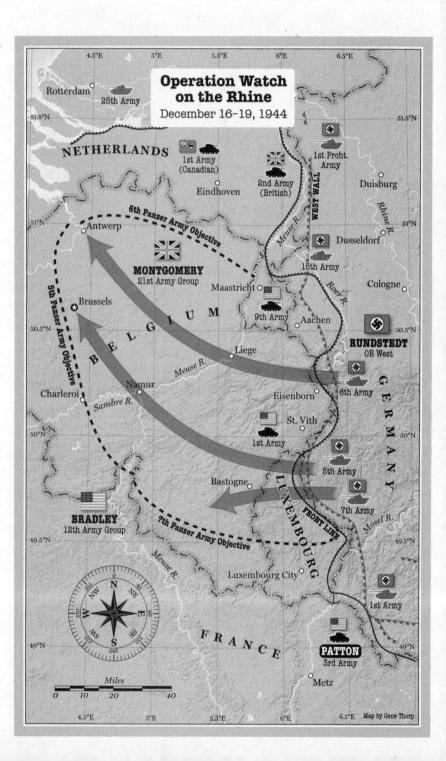

Operation Watch on the Rhine
December 16–19, 1944

NETHERLANDS

Rotterdam

25th Army

1st Army
(Canadian)

Eindhoven

2nd Army
(British)

WEST WALL

1st Prcht.
Army

Duisburg

Rhine R.

Antwerp

6th Panzer Army Objective

MONTGOMERY
21st Army Group

Maastricht

Dusseldorf

15th Army

Cologne

Meuse R.

Brussels

BELGIUM

9th Army

Aachen

RUNDSTEDT
OB West

5th Panzer Army Objective

Liege

Meuse R.

Charleroi

Namur

Sambre R.

Eisenborn

6th Army

GERMANY

St. Vith

1st Army

5th Army

Bastogne

7th Army

BRADLEY
12th Army Group

7th Panzer Army Objective

LUXEMBOURG

FRONT LINE

Mosel R.

1st Army

Meuse R.

Luxembourg City

Miles

0   10   20   40

FRANCE

PATTON
3rd Army

Metz

Map by Gene Thorp

But all that is in the future. Right now these young Germans are eager, awaiting the command to rain down hellfire on their enemies.

At 5:30 a.m. that order is delivered. Up and down the eighty-mile German front lines, some sixteen hundred pieces of field artillery open fire. The silent forest explodes, and muzzle blasts light the sky as the furnaces of hell are thrown open. "Screaming Meemie" rockets screech into the darkness, a deadly sound that American soldiers everywhere find unnerving. And big 88 mm guns fire their fifteen-inch-long shells at targets almost ten miles away, hitting U.S. positions before they even know they're being fired upon. Every German soldier within a hundred yards is rendered temporarily deaf from the noise. Hand gestures replace the spoken word.

SS Obersturmbannführer Otto Skorzeny has never once fired an artillery piece, but he has waited for this moment just as eagerly as those men manning the big guns. His life has been a whirlwind of activity since his meeting with the Führer less than two months ago. For his special role in Operation Greif, as the offensive is known, he has scoured the ranks of the German military for men who speak English. He has outfitted these men in American uniforms, and acquired American tanks, trucks, and jeeps to help them travel effortlessly behind U.S. lines. Their ultimate goal is to make their way through this rugged, snow-covered terrain as quickly as possible to capture three vital bridges over the Meuse River. But their more immediate task is to sow seeds of confusion throughout the American lines. They will spread rumors and misinformation, tear down road signs, and do everything in their power to mislead the Americans as the German army pours into the Ardennes Forest.

The problem facing Skorzeny is that the Americans know all about Operation Greif. Shortly after his Wolf's Lair meeting with Hitler, some idiot in the Wehrmacht high command circulated a notice up and down the Western Front: "Secret Commando Operations," the directive stated in bold letters at the top of the page. "The Führer has ordered the formation of a special unit of approximately two battalion strength for commando operations." It went on to ask all English-speaking soldiers, sailors, and pilots who wished to volunteer to report to Skorzeny's training center in Friedenthal.

An irate Skorzeny went directly to Hitler to have the notice withdrawn, but the damage had already been done. As Skorzeny knew it would, the paper fell into Allied hands. It was the sort of intelligence coup that G-2s such as Oscar Koch live for. And while Skorzeny insisted that Operation Greif be canceled for this blunder, the Führer personally requested that it proceed. Skorzeny reluctantly complied. In the weeks of training that followed, his men were sequestered in a special camp, set apart from other German soldiers. To brush up on their English, they conversed with captured U.S. soldiers and pilots in prisoner-of-war camps. They learned to chew gum like Americans, how to swear, and casually banter using American slang. One German soldier who made the mistake of writing home about his whereabouts was immediately shot.

The sound of the 75 mm guns thundering up and down the lines signals that the time has come for Operation Greif to begin. It is a moment that fills Skorzeny with equal parts euphoria and dread.

The legendary commando is known for his ruthlessness, which is just one reason the Allies have named him the most dangerous man in the German army. But he is also extremely loyal, and fond of his men. As Operation Greif commences, he fusses over them, quietly worrying about their fate. Every mission has peril, but this one is especially dangerous, as all the men in Skorzeny's elite commando unit know.

If captured by the Americans, they will not be treated as prisoners of war, as regular German soldiers would be.

By disguising themselves as Americans, Skorzeny's men of Panzergruppe 150 are deliberately violating the Geneva Convention. If captured in German uniforms, they could expect to spend the rest of the war in U.S. captivity, but at least they would live.

But Skorzeny's soldiers will be wearing U.S. uniforms, and therefore will be classified as spies. The punishment for being captured while not wearing an enemy uniform is death by firing squad.

Skorzeny gives the order to move out.

★ ★ ★

Confusion reigns. The narrow, muddy roads leading from Germany into the Ardennes are now clogged with German tanks, trucks, horse-drawn carts, and halftracks as thirty German divisions flood toward the American lines. The front extends north to south through three countries, meaning that Wehrmacht forces are now on the attack in Germany, Belgium, and Luxembourg. Their movement was supposed to be lightning quick. But with the roads too narrow to handle all the German vehicles, the biggest surprise attack of the war has become an enormous traffic jam.

Still, Hitler's gamble is achieving some success. The American army has been caught off guard. Even as German infantry creep through the forest in their winter-white uniforms, the highest levels of Allied leadership still believe that Germany is incapable of launching a major offensive. Some dismiss this as a "spoiling attack"—a diversion that weakens the American lines by forcing them to shift men and supplies from some other location. Convinced that an attack through such wooded and mountainous terrain is impossible, Dwight Eisenhower considers the Ardennes to be a place of rest and sanctuary for weary American troops. "Of the many pathways that lead to France, the least penetrable is through the Ardennes," notes Gen. Omar Bradley, the commander in charge of the American front lines. "For there the roads are much too scarce, the hills too wooded, and the valleys too limited for maneuver."

Bradley is George Patton's immediate superior, in command of the U.S. Twelfth Army group, which stands poised to invade Germany. Only Dwight Eisenhower has more power among American forces in Europe.

Yet before Patton's troubles with his temper on the island of Sicily one year ago, Bradley was his subordinate. Patton now reports to Bradley. Even worse, Eisenhower has chosen Omar Bradley for several important assignments that before might have come Patton's way. In particular, it was Bradley who was chosen to lead U.S. ground forces in the D-day invasion back in June. Meanwhile, Patton and the Third Army languished in England, not allowed to join the greatest ground force in history until two long months later.

Ike's message to others was clear: Omar Bradley is predictable, easily controlled, and safe. Patton, as audacious and tactically brilliant as he might be, is too unpredictable to be given command of all American ground forces.

Yet Eisenhower's pick quickly proved costly. Bradley's decision to halt Patton's troops instead of allowing them to attack prevented the encirclement of fifty thousand Wehrmacht soldiers and SS troops in mid-August. The Germans took heavy losses, but many more quickly escaped through what was called the Falaise Pocket. If Patton had had his way, his tanks

General Omar Bradley (center) with General George Patton (left)
and General Bernard Law Montgomery (right)

would have slipped the noose around those trapped German troops, taking thousands of their best soldiers prisoner and seriously damaging the Wehrmacht's ability to wage war. "We're about to destroy an entire hostile army," Bradley noted of the opportunity. "We'll go all the way from here to the German border."

But in the end Bradley grew timid. He ordered Patton's tanks to halt at the town of Argentan, leaving a gap between the American and Canadian units that would have encircled the Germans—a gap through which the Germans soon escaped.

Patton knew Bradley was wrong but had no choice but to obey orders. On August 16, Patton wrote in his diary that Bradley's blunder was "of historical importance." Those same German units that Patton nearly captured lived to fight another day. Many of those men are arrayed against the Allied forces on the German border at this very minute. Now, even as Bradley reassures himself that the German offensive in Ardennes is nothing more than a spoiling attack, many of those same Wehrmacht and SS fighters—among them a clever young SS tank commander named Joachim Peiper—are heading toward the American lines.

Nevertheless, Bradley, who graduated alongside Eisenhower in West Point's class of 1915,* and who commands the million men of the Twelfth Army Group, does not see the threat. In fact, he has allowed his troops to relax.

Meantime, Patton and his intelligence officers are anxious, well understanding that there is danger in the Ardennes. But again Patton can do nothing. And it is his own fault.

★ ★ ★

Even as the furor over his Sicily slapping incidents was dying down, George Patton made a second great public relations blunder, on April 25, 1944. It happened in Knutsford, England, while he was speaking to a group comprised largely of British women. The occasion was the low-key opening of a "Welcome Club" for American soldiers, which would allow troops a place to unwind and meet their British hosts in a comfortable setting. Though Patton at first declined to attend, his headquarters was nearby, and he finally consented to drive over and say a few words. Yet his trepidation about the event was so great that he ordered his driver to arrive fifteen minutes late, hoping that the conference would already be over.

But the women of Knutsford were waiting for him.

Patton's remarks were supposed to be brief, just a few paragraphs. After citing George Bernard Shaw's famous quote that "the British and Americans are two people separated by a common language," Patton reassured the ladies that the Americans and British would rule a postwar

---

*Many refer to the West Point class of 1915 as "the class the stars fell on." Fifty-nine of its graduates achieved the rank of general. Among them were Eisenhower and Bradley, who both attained five-star rank, the highest rank in the U.S. Army. At this point in history, only nine men had been selected for this honor, which also carries the title of general of the army. Ulysses S. Grant, William Tecumseh Sherman, and Philip Sheridan all held this title, but in the Civil War era, when there was no rank higher than four stars. General John Pershing held the same title just after World War I. Those who wore five stars are army generals Dwight Eisenhower, Omar Bradley, Henry "Hap" Arnold, Douglas MacArthur, and George Marshall. The navy equivalent of five stars has been awarded to admirals Chester Nimitz, William Leahy, Ernest King, and William F. Halsey.

world. The women were thrilled, not understanding that Patton had slighted the Russians.

At the time, Patton was supposed to be keeping a low profile so that the Germans would be unclear of his whereabouts before the D-day invasion. So there was just a handful of reporters present that warm spring day in Knutsford, and the few photographers on hand swore not to publish their pictures of Patton. Yet the general's comments somehow got leaked. His well-intentioned words made headlines around the world.

Stalin and the Russians were infuriated.

Patton had done it again. "This last incident was so trivial in nature," a distraught Patton wrote in his journal, "but so terrible in its effect."

As with the slapping incidents, there were public demands that Patton be fired. Controversy, it seemed, followed him everywhere.

Eisenhower elevated the agony by waiting almost a week to discuss the controversy and Patton's future. The meeting would take place at Ike's headquarters. The results were not likely to land in Patton's favor. Friendly relations with the Soviets were of vital importance to President Franklin Roosevelt. "Wild Bill" Donovan of the OSS was working hard to maintain that friendship, as was Eisenhower's boss back in Washington, Gen. George Marshall. A weary Eisenhower, exhausted from planning the D-day invasion, was furious at what he considered to be Patton's immaturity. Those errant remarks in Knutsford, as simple as they might have been, had the potential to unravel a peaceful postwar world.

Patton drove five hours to be at the meeting with Eisenhower. The date was May 1, 1944. There was a very good chance he would be sent home to America, and even reduced in rank to colonel. Patton described the moments before entering Eisenhower's office as a time of awaiting "possible execution."

"It is sad and shocking to think that victory and the lives of thousands of men are pawns to the 'fear of They,' and the writings of a group of unprincipled reporters, and weak-kneed congressmen," Patton wrote in his journal. "But so it is."

Unbeknownst to Patton, it was Winston Churchill's spies who had leaked his comments, so it was appropriate that the cunning prime minister himself weigh in on Patton's side, stating that the general was "just speaking the truth." The politically astute Eisenhower could read between the lines in Churchill's comments.* So while the meeting with Patton began badly, Eisenhower had to admit that he sorely needed the general's skills as a battlefield commander. As Patton himself once predicted, referring to the partnership between two legendary Confederate generals in the Civil War, "Ike, you will be the Lee of the next war, and I will be your Jackson."

Eisenhower knows his military history. He knows that Stonewall Jackson was brilliant and unpredictable. And he is also well aware that Robert E. Lee's army was never the same after a Confederate sentry accidentally shot and mortally wounded General Jackson.

So George S. Patton was spared—but damaged. From May 1, 1944, forward, Patton's chances of leading all U.S. forces in Europe were nonexistent. He was too much of a political liability. His hopes of assuming a major postwar command in a world divided between the United States and the Soviet Union had all but vanished. The military career that George S. Patton loved so much would last only as long as the world needed his fighting skills.

"When I came out," he wrote after the meeting, "I don't think anyone could tell that I had just been killed. I feel like death, but I am not out yet. If they will let me fight, I will."

★ ★ ★

As the German offensive in the Ardennes gathers speed, George Patton keeps track of events from his headquarters sixty miles south, in Nancy. He is frustrated because his immediate boss is Gen. Omar Bradley, whom Patton considers his inferior and as completely lacking in the prescience and strategic forethought necessary to win a war.

The Ardennes proves it. Totally off guard, Bradley has allowed a group of professional American baseball players to tour the area the Germans are

---

*There is still a great deal of conjecture about who leaked the story, but due to the severe restrictions on what the press could and could not publish, the story would never have made it into print without the blessing of British and American authorities at the highest level. Churchill's ongoing efforts to insert Britain in the postwar argument at the expense of the Soviet Union would have allowed him to seize Patton's comments as an opportunity to heighten U.S.-Soviet tensions.

now attacking.* The alluring film actress Marlene Dietrich is also on hand. She has just finished performing in the Belgian crossroads town of Bastogne. Tonight she is scheduled to put on a show for the men of the Ninety-Ninth Division in the Belgian hamlet of Honsfeld.

That concert has been abruptly canceled.

★　★　★

The Ninety-Ninth Infantry Division of the American First Army is digging in, trying desperately to stop the elite Twelfth SS Panzer Division from capturing a spot on the map known as Elsenborn Ridge, a vast, treeless hill, beautiful in the summer when wild grasses cover its summit. But there is no beauty right now. Just frozen mud, corpses, and shell craters. Except for those moments when fog covers the hilltop or the powerful winds are driving rain and snow into their eyes—which is often—the men of the Ninety-Ninth have optimal fields of fire from their lazy semicircle of foxholes. Any German attack will require the enemy to cover a half mile of open ground, all while running uphill.

But one hundred yards down the slope, a thick forest offers the Germans complete concealment. The woods are dark and gloomy. A dense fog makes the Germans even less visible. The Ninety-Ninth are easy targets for the German artillery guns hidden in the forest below—including the high-velocity 88 mm guns, which fire a round that travels a half mile per second.

Many men in the Ninety-Ninth are new to combat and came to the Ardennes to ease into the frontline action. They lack winter-camouflaged uniforms, ammunition, and warm clothes, and yet they stand ready to hold the line at all costs.

---

*The group consisted of right fielder and player-manager Mel Ott of the New York Giants; pitcher Bucky Walters of the Cincinnati Reds; Dutch Leonard, a retired former pitcher who'd once played for the Detroit Tigers and Boston Red Sox; and Frankie Frisch, the retired second baseman who enjoyed an eighteen-year career as a player with the New York Giants and then St. Louis Cardinals, and later managed the Cardinals. The greatest of these was Ott. Just five foot nine, he hit 511 career home runs, was the first player in history to have eight consecutive 100-RBI seasons, had a lifetime batting average of .304, and retired only 124 hits shy of 3,000. The lifetime Giant would tragically die in a car crash at the age of forty-nine.

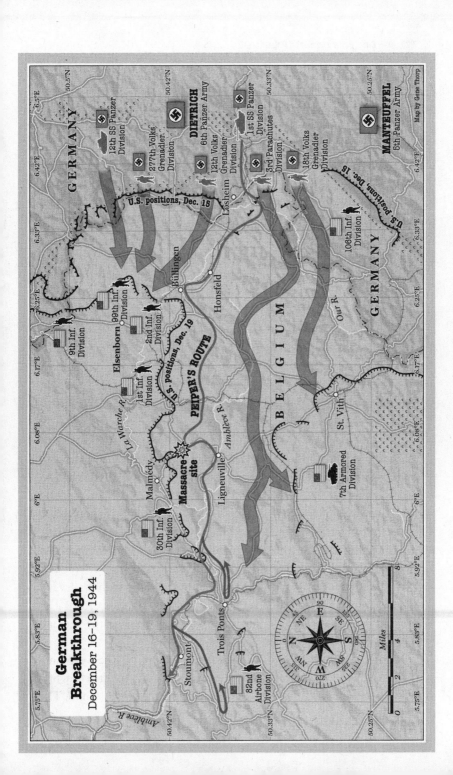

German Breakthrough
December 16–19, 1944

GERMANY

12th SS Panzer Division

277th Volks Grenadier Division

DIETRICH
6th Panzer Army

12th Volks Grenadier Division

1st SS Panzer Division

3rd Parachutes

18th Volks Grenadier Division

MANTEUFFEL
5th Panzer Army

U.S. positions, Dec. 15

U.S. positions, Dec. 18

106th Inf. Division

9th Inf. Division

Elsenborn

99th Inf. Division

2nd Inf. Division

Büllingen

Honsfeld

Losheim

1st Inf. Division

U.S. positions, Dec. 19

La Warche R.

PEIPER'S ROUTE

Malmedy

Massacre site

Ligneuville

Ambleve R.

30th Inf. Division

BELGIUM

St. Vith

Our R.

GERMANY

7th Armored Division

Trois Ponts

Stoumont

Ambleve R.

82nd Airborne Division

N NE E SE S SW W NW

Miles
0   2   4   8

Map by Gene Thorp

Because if they don't, Hitler's crazy gamble in the Ardennes just might succeed.

Like the equally strategic nearby location known as the Losheim Gap, the Elsenborn Ridge represents a vital corridor that the German army must possess in order for Operation Watch on the Rhine to be successful. The Losheim Gap is a narrow valley through which the Third Reich successfully invaded France in 1940, and is known to be the pathway for funneling tanks through the rugged Ardennes. The ridge is critical because a network of key roads lies on the other side. Capture the ridge, gain access to the roads, and the Twelfth Panzer Division suddenly stands a very good chance of making it all the way to Antwerp.

The Ninety-Ninth must hold the line.

Just yesterday they were thinking about Mel Ott, Marlene Dietrich, and Christmas. Many were even living in a warm barrack that had once belonged to the Germans, where they slept in beds and ate hot meals each morning and night.

Not today.

The Ninety-Ninth is made up of mostly green recruits who arrived in Europe just weeks ago. The unit was activated in October 1942, but many of those original members who trained together at Camp Van Dorn in Mississippi and Camp Maxey in Texas are either dead or in a hospital somewhere. Some units within the division are at half strength, meaning that cooks and clerks are now serving temporary duty as riflemen. The ground is almost frozen, but it is still possible to dig a deep foxhole, leaving the Ninety-Ninth less exposed and vulnerable. Their boots are not waterproof or insulated, so when they finally scrape away enough earth to make the home in the ground that will protect them from shrapnel and snipers, trench foot and frostbite add to their misery.

The German artillery and tanks fire from the safety of the valley forest, pounding the Ninety-Ninth as they huddle in their foxholes. The ground shakes so badly from the explosions that the few nearby trees fall over without being touched.

Snipers, meanwhile, kill anyone who exposes his head aboveground. And even when the Germans aren't firing, the sounds of their laughter and snippets of conversation carry up the hill to the Ninety-Ninth. The

Americans grow depressed and anxious as they hear the clank of tank treads from the forest, reminding them that the force now gathered below is, indeed, an enormous army.

It is only a matter of time before that army races up the Elsenborn Ridge to wipe out the Ninety-Ninth. The German forces outnumber the Americans by a ratio of five to one.

Those in the Ninety-Ninth who live to tell the story will long remember the scream of the high-velocity 88 mm shells, a sound that gets higher and more pronounced just before impact. They will remember reciting the Lord's Prayer over and over as those assault guns pound their position. They will remember "the filth, the hunger, the cold, and the life of living like an animal."

They abide by a new list of unwritten rules: They cannot sleep for any length of time because the German attacks have no set routine. They cannot leave their foxholes during daylight because German gunners zero in on any sign of movement.

Over the next four days, the Ninety-Ninth will see 133 more of its men die. Six hundred will fall back to the battalion aid stations to be treated for frozen feet. As many as 1,844 will go "missing," meaning that their loved ones will never enjoy the closure that comes with having a body to bury. "This was our Valley Forge," one soldier will remember.

Through it all, the leadership skills of the Ninety-Ninth's officer corps will be sorely tested. Some will show themselves to be true leaders of men. Others will not. One senior officer will drive away in terror. Another will favor total surrender to fighting. After all, the Ninety-Ninth is facing elements of the Waffen SS, Hitler's most elite and brutal fighting force. Surely it is better to raise the white flag of surrender and live to see home and family when the war ends than to face almost certain death or go "missing" at the hands of the SS.

It is Heinrich Himmler, the psychopathic leader of the SS, who preaches a philosophy that if an enemy is made to feel enough terror, there is no need for battle. He will simply quit.

But the Ninety-Ninth will soon learn that surrender does not always prevent violent death.

★　★　★

As the second day of Operation Watch on the Rhine begins, the First SS Panzer Division is on the move. They are the lead element in the much-larger Sixth Panzer Army, tasked with racing through the countryside to capture three vital bridges over the Meuse River.

The First comprises the best of the best, a fighting force so highly regarded by Hitler that he has allowed them to sew his name onto their uniform sleeves. In the buildup to Operation Watch on the Rhine, a lack of manpower was solved by shifting men from the Luftwaffe and German navy into the infantry. This is not the case with the First. They are all hardened fighters who have seen more than their share of combat in this war. And their armament bears testimony to their elite nature. It's nothing but the finest for the First SS Panzer: sixty tanks, three flak tanks, seventy-five halftracks, fourteen 20 mm guns, twenty-seven 75 mm assault guns, and numerous 105 mm and 150 mm self-propelled howitzers.

"The morale was high throughout the entire period I was with them despite the extremely trying conditions," an American officer will later write of his time as a prisoner of the First SS Panzer. "The discipline was very good. The physical condition of all personnel was good . . . The equipment was good and complete with the exception of some reconditioned half-tracks among the motorized equipment. All men wore practically new boots and had adequate clothing. Some of them wore parts of American uniforms, mainly the knit cap, gloves, sweaters, overshoes, and one or two overcoats. The relationship between officers and men . . . was closer and more friendly than I would have expected."

In command of this magnificent fighting force is the dashing poster boy for the SS, twenty-nine-year-old Joachim Peiper. "He was approximately 5 feet 8 inches in height, 140 lbs. in weight, long dark hair combed straight back, straight well-shaped features with remarkable facial resemblance to the actor Ray Milland," the American POW major will later write.

Peiper is a graduate of the SS military college at Bad Tölz, the German equivalent of the U.S. Military Academy at West Point, or Britain's Royal Military Academy at Sandhurst. The requirements for admission are rigorous, and include a background check to ensure Aryan racial purity* and personal behavior that the SS considers to be proper. The curriculum includes ample time in the classroom combined with hours of long-distance running to ensure maximum physical fitness. Combat exercises include using live rounds of ammunition to inure the future warriors to the feel of combat. The end result is an officer in the tradition of the legendary Greek Hoplites, who formed the backbone of the Spartan heavy infantry.

Amazingly, an advanced education is not necessary for admission to the SS-Junkerschule at Bad Tölz. The most important qualification is total loyalty to Adolf Hitler. Which is why a man such as Joachim Peiper, who dropped out of school to join the army, not only was accepted to the school but became a star alumnus.

Upon graduation, Peiper was selected to serve as a top assistant for SS leader Heinrich Himmler, a calculating and brutal man whom Peiper came to idolize. He even allowed the Reichsführer-SS to arrange his marriage.

Himmler was loyal to Adolf Hitler's *Nationalsozialismus* (National Socialism, later shortened to Nazi) long before the Führer achieved absolute power over the German people in 1933. As such, he enjoys Hitler's confidence,

---

*Top-level members of the SS had to prove their racial purity by providing records of their family lineage dating back to 1750. This practice of achieving racial superiority was based on something known as "scientific racism," which stated that some races were more advanced than others. Beginning on April 7, 1933, German law required that obtaining a certificate known as the *Ariernachweis* was mandatory for any individual wishing to hold public office in Germany or to gain membership in the Nazi Party. This "Aryan Certificate" was attained by showing a complete record of family lineage (through birth and marriage certificates) that proved racial purity. It was believed that the Caucasian race was divided into three sectors: Semitic (descendants of Noah's son Shem, most often associated with Jewish ethnicity); Hamitic (descendants of Noah's son Ham, often associated with North African and Middle Eastern ethnicity); and Aryan, construed by the Nazis to be of Nordic and Germanic ethnicity. The defining characteristics were blue eyes, blond hair, a statuesque physique, and Caucasian skin pigment. The Aryan bloodline was thought to be purer because it had not intermingled with that of other ethnicities. The extermination of Jews, Gypsies, homosexuals, and mentally and physically handicapped individuals was a way of cleansing Europe of people with non-German impurities. Scientific racism was discredited after World War II. It's worth noting that members of the SS were all German at the beginning of the war. By its end, combat deaths had seen its ranks so depleted that soldiers of foreign birth, such as Czechs, Poles, and Norwegians, were conscripted into the Aryan brigades.

Joachim Peiper

Heinrich Himmler inspecting a German POW camp in the Soviet Union

and is given the harsh task of carrying out the extermination and suppression of those races, ethnicities, and enemies whom Hitler deems a threat to the Reich, including Jews, Gypsies, homosexuals, and Nazi political opponents. Under Himmler's tutelage, Peiper developed the philosophies of intolerance that now guide his military tactics. He stood at Himmler's side to witness the shooting of Polish intellectuals in the early days of the war, and was an eyewitness to the first gassing of Jewish civilians, including women and children. When Himmler rewarded Peiper with an assignment to lead a half-track battalion on the Russian front, the fanatical young officer developed a reputation for battlefield cunning. His men and tanks moved quickly, thrusting and feinting in a manner reminiscent of George S. Patton's lightning-fast maneuvers. In one daring nighttime raid, his men rescued a German infantry division surrounded by Soviets who, on the verge of decimating the German unit, the 320th Infantry, had ceased their attack in order to rest and recoup. After waiting until well past midnight to make sure the Russian tank crews were sound asleep, Peiper's First Panzer smashed through their lines, guns blazing. Not only were the able-bodied members of the 320th saved, but so were more than fifteen hundred wounded Wehrmacht fighters.

It was Adolf Hitler himself who presented his dashing Aryan tank commander with the prestigious Knight's Cross of the Iron Cross, making Peiper the youngest officer in the German army ever to be so honored.

During their time on the Russian front, Peiper's men took few prisoners, believing that the *Untermenschen*, or "subhumans," as the Germans called the Russians, did not deserve to live. They also developed a nickname for themselves, based on their passion for using fire in battle: the Blowtorch Brigade. On two occasions Peiper's tanks completely surrounded Russian villages. His assault troops then set fire to every building, burning to death every man, woman, and child inside them. This is how Peiper punishes the subhuman.

Since the suicide of Field Marshal Rommel, there are few other German tank commanders who can compare to Peiper. He and his men now bring their ruthless talents to Operation Watch on the Rhine, where the need for speed on the battlefield is vital. The Germans must destroy the Allied army before replacement troops arrive, giving the Americans a numerical advantage in soldiers and weapons.

In his final act before Operation Watch on the Rhine launches, Peiper issues orders stating, "There will be no stopping for anything. No booty will be taken, and no enemy vehicles are to be examined. It is not the job of the spearhead to worry about prisoners of war."

That job would be left to the slower columns of infantry trailing in their wake.

But the spearhead gets off to a slow start.

Thanks to the Ninety-Ninth's defiant stand at the Elsenborn Ridge, Peiper's intended route toward the Meuse is blocked. Furious at the sight of his Mark IV and Mark V Panther tanks stuck behind the horse-drawn artillery carriages of a support unit known as the Twelfth Volksgrenadier Division, Peiper personally begins directing traffic in order to take charge of the mess. Fourteen hours after the initial artillery barrage that launched Operation Watch on the Rhine, Peiper finally manages to get his tanks on the move. It is after dark. The dirt roads have been turned to thick, sloppy mud after the winter rains, and have not yet frozen for the night. To his chagrin, many German infantry commanders are ordering a halt, so that their men might find a warm house in which to enjoy a few hours' sleep.

But Peiper and the men of the First do not sleep. All night long, the five-man* crews of the twenty-five-ton German Panzers and forty-four-ton Panthers push through the forest, hoping that their tanks do not sink into the mud. Minefields force them to slow even further, and there are brief firefights as they breach the American lines. By morning the breakout is complete. There is no more American opposition. December 17 is a new day for Joachim Peiper and the men of the First Panzer Division. Knowing that overcast skies will keep American fighter-bombers grounded, Peiper races toward the Meuse.

Just before dawn, he and his men pass through the tiny village of Honsfeld, where they spot American jeeps parked outside a row of local houses. As Peiper presses on to the town of Büllingen, where he knows there to be a fuel dump, he leaves the SS infantry behind. They quickly search the houses and emerge with a group of American soldiers, who were literally caught napping. The seventeen men are marched outside wearing nothing but thin army-issue boxer shorts. The Americans stand barefoot in the darkness, cursing their fate even as they marvel at the enormity of the German caravan passing before them. Tanks, halftracks, and trucks curve

---

*Commander, gunner, loader, driver, machine gunner/radio operator.

into the distance as far as the eye can see. Clearly this is no mere spoiling attack.

Suddenly, SS troopers open fire on the unarmed captured Americans. Sixteen are shot dead where they stand. The remaining soldier pleads for his life, but the SS takes no pity, murdering him by throwing him in front of a tank.

Peiper successfully locates the American fuel dump in Büllingen, where two hundred U.S. soldiers are taken prisoner and forced to refuel the German tanks. Meanwhile, twelve members of the Second Infantry Division's signal company have a bittersweet moment of luck. They manage to avoid detection by the SS, and spend the morning hiding in a cellar. When it becomes obvious that Tuffy, their beloved company dog, might bark and give them away, they reluctantly strangle the animal.

The twelve men later manage to sneak back to American lines. The Americans who have been taken prisoner in Büllingen, meanwhile, are not murdered once they finish gassing up Peiper's Panzers. These men of the Second Infantry Division are marched back to German lines, where they are locked in POW cages.

They are the lucky ones.

★ ★ ★

As George Patton remains in his headquarters in Nancy, unaware of the extent of the German offensive, Joachim Peiper and his men race toward the town of Huy, sixty miles away, where the first key bridge crosses the Meuse. Impatient and frustrated, Peiper urges his crews to press forward with all due haste. He does not need to remind them that American bombers have been leveling German cities, killing innocent civilians—perhaps even some of their own family members. Operation Watch on the Rhine is a chance to achieve vengeance as well as victory.

Dressed in their trademark gray tunics, with the SS lightning-bolt logo on their collars and the death's-head insignia on their caps, Peiper's SS troopers have served with him on the cruel battlefields of Russia, in the hills of northern Italy, and during the American invasion of Normandy. The men of the Leibstandarte think of Peiper as a father figure, even though the blue-eyed officer is younger than many of them. Peiper's men are considered a cut above their fellow members of the Waffen SS, as the military branch of the SS is known. The regular army soldiers in the

SS death head insignia

Wehrmacht would never dream of comparing their battlefield skills or prestige with those of the First SS Panzer Division Leibstandarte SS Adolf Hitler.*

---

*The differences between the Wehrmacht and the SS can be summed up in the translations of their names. *Wehrmacht* means "defense force" in German, while SS roughly translates as "protection squadron"—as in the protection of Adolf Hitler and the Nazi Party ideology. The Wehrmacht comprised all the German armed forces, including the SS (army, navy, air force, and SS; or, in the original German, *Heer, Kriegsmarine, Luft-waffe,* and *Schutzstaffel*). The two groups wore separate uniforms, with the Wehrmacht clad in gray wool, while the SS wore camouflage or earth-gray uniforms. In addition to being a branch of the military, SS troopers swore to be loyal to Adolf Hitler unto death, and could be ordered to do anything in the name of the Führer. This led them to commit scores of unconscionable acts of terror and brutality, acts that included murdering prisoners of war, Jews, and other innocent civilians. The *totenkopf* ("skull") emblem worn on the SS uniform signified that "you shall always be willing to put yourself at stake for the life of the whole community," in the words of SS leader Heinrich Himmler. Beginning in 1934, the SS was put in charge of the concentration camps that would systematically murder millions of Jews, homosexuals, Gypsies, handicapped individuals, and political prisoners. The barbaric behavior of the SS stands in sharp contrast to that of Wehrmacht soldiers such as Field Marshal Erwin Rommel, whose troops were forbidden from mistreating civilians. Rommel and other German commanders ignored SS admonitions to murder Jews and enemy prisoners. Nevertheless, many German fighting men participated in civilian atrocities, especially against the people of Poland, France, and the U.S.S.R. "I have come to know there is a real difference between the regular soldier and officer, and Hitler and his criminal group," Dwight Eisenhower said. "The German soldier as such has not lost his honor. The fact that certain individuals committed in war dishonorable and despicable acts reflects on the individuals concerned, and not on the great majority of German soldiers and officers." Ironically, Eisenhower would later censure George S. Patton for publicly making very similar remarks.

The First surprises a convoy of thirty-three American trucks between Modershied and Liegneuville just after noon. The Americans of Battery B, of the 285th Field Artillery Observation Battalion, have just driven through Malmedy. This timeless village is nestled in the valley formed by a ring of low, thickly forested hills. It is a quaint crossroads, with narrow lanes spoking out to the north, southwest, and east. It is the sort of place where cows clog the country roads and where everyone knows one another.

★ ★ ★

The first and last trucks in the American column are quickly destroyed by Peiper's Panther tanks. This makes it impossible for the Americans to flee on the one-lane roads, so they leap from their vehicles and dash in all directions. Some hide as best they can, while others sprint for the cover of a nearby tree line.

Twenty-year-old corporal Ted Paluch, who is thousands of miles away from the safety and comfort of his family home in Philadelphia, crouches in a roadside ditch. He clutches his M-1 carbine, which proves no match for the Panzer that lowers its main gun. Paluch has no choice but to surrender, as do more than one hundred other men from Battery B.

Joachim Peiper watches the herding of prisoners dispassionately from the seat of his halftrack, then orders his driver and the rest of the tank column to continue their rush to the Meuse. He chooses a route to the southwest, not knowing that a single thrust north to Elsenborn Ridge would link him up with the Twelfth Panzer Division, allowing them to destroy the Ninety-Ninth Division and open up those vital roads to Antwerp.

Meanwhile, Paluch and the men of Battery B are marched away from the road, into a small field that offers them no place to hide should they attempt to run. The Americans were on their way to the town of St. Vith. They had stopped in Malmedy for lunch, and enjoyed almost two hours of peace and calm. Now they are led into a field with their hands high. They can clearly see the skull-and-crossbones insignia on their captors' tunics, denoting that they are not normal German soldiers but the feared SS. The one hundred Americans are frisked and, in defiance of Peiper's orders, stripped of everything of value: socks, watches, gloves, cigarettes. As this is happening, German halftracks and tanks rumble past just fifty yards away, as part of the long procession following Peiper to the Meuse.

The Americans are tense and confused. The Germans seem to be polite, if a bit brusque.

The first pistol shot comes without warning.

An American POW falls dead.

As if they have been waiting for this signal, machine guns from the single-file column of tanks and halftracks open fire, stopping only to reload as they slaughter the Americans. Terrifying bursts of German automatic weapons fire echo across the wintry countryside. Each weapon is capable of firing at least 850 rounds per minute, meaning 14 bullets per second from every single MG-34 machine gun zoom toward the American targets. Every tank carries more than 5,000 rounds, but the men of the First Panzer are too professional to waste ammo on prisoners. Instead, the gunners fire off a quick burst for fun as they pass through the crossroads. They leave helpless U.S. prisoners in their wake, jerking in spastic dances as bullets riddle their young bodies. Many more have already fallen limp into the snow, where some will remain until the spring thaw reveals their corpses.

The initial round of shooting continues for two full minutes. When it finally stops, SS men walk the field, pistols in hand. "Hey Joe," they call out, using their best American accents in the hope that a fallen soldier will respond. "Hey, Jim."

The deception succeeds. Every man who makes a sound is immediately shot in the head.

The SS troopers ask if any of the Americans need medical assistance, then shoot those who reply.

Any man who moans is shot in the head. Any man whose breath can be seen on this cold Sunday afternoon is shot in the head. Any man who flinches or cries out when he is kicked is shot in the head.

Cpl. Ted Paluch lies very still on the cold pasture, playing dead. He hears the Luger pistol shots as his buddies are executed one by one, and the German laughter that accompanies every new murder. Nearby, Cpl. Charles Appman lies beneath a fellow soldier, and feels the body quiver as that man is shot in the head. Appman wonders if he is next, and whether he will feel any pain as the bullet enters his skull. Seeing a bright white light, he will later recall that he feels the presence of God.

In all, eighty-four Americans are murdered in cold blood in what will come to be known as the Malmedy Massacre.

But the killing of POWs is not limited to Malmedy. Even as Ted Paluch and Charles Appman play dead throughout the afternoon, Peiper's men are slaughtering more American POWs as the SS tanks continue their race to the Meuse. In the next three days, Hitler's elite bodyguards will murder more than 350 American soldiers and 100 Belgian civilians.

★ ★ ★

Corporals Paluch and Appman remain motionless for hours. Their hands and faces are numb when they hear the last tank rumble past. Finally, the coast may be clear. Desperate, Paluch and Appman climb to their feet and sprint across the field and over a barbwire fence to safety, destined to marry, raise children, have careers, and live well into their eighties. Once they and the other survivors reach the American lines and report their atrocities, the horror story of the Malmedy Massacre races up the Allied chain of command.

The speed of the news is unparalleled. A patrol from the 291st Engineer Combat Battalion comes upon the first survivor at 2:30 that afternoon, even as Ted Paluch and Charles Appman are still playing dead. Four hours later the First Army's top generals know what happened. And four hours after that, every soldier up and down the American lines knows that the SS is murdering American POWs in cold blood.

The Americans seethe. The rules of war make it a crime to kill a man who has surrendered. Many American commanders tell their men that there will be no SS troopers taken prisoner. If the Germans are not going to comply with the rules of war, then neither are the Americans.

8

———◆———

George S. Patton is cold.

Patton hunkers down in the passenger seat of his open-air jeep, puffing quietly on a cigar. The lamb's wool collar of his parka is cinched against his throat, and his helmet is pressed down tight on his head. He says very little as his driver navigates the streets of this ancient French town. The general ignores the arctic cold air that has been blasting him throughout the ninety-minute drive from his headquarters in Nancy. It is not Patton's way to let the elements affect him.

Patton's driver, Sgt. John Mims* of Abbeville, Alabama, slows at the entrance to the old stone barrack serving as Twelfth Army headquarters. The sentry snaps to attention and salutes. In return, Patton touches the gloved fingertips of his right hand to his steel helmet. The jeep passes onto a muddy parade ground, and a quick glance at the assembled cars shows that Dwight Eisenhower and his staff have not yet arrived from Versailles. Nor is Omar Bradley's official vehicle in view. Courtney Hodges, the general in command of the First Army, is also not in attendance—though this does not surprise Patton. Hodges failed to anticipate the German attack through the Ardennes, and then spent two days denying that it was happening. He even passed the time procuring a new hunting rifle and then

———

*Mims served as Patton's driver from September 1940 until May 1945.

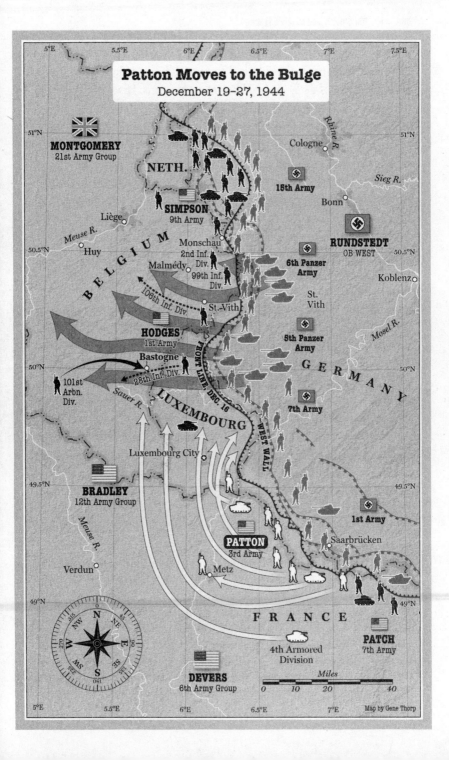

Patton Moves to the Bulge
December 19-27, 1944

MONTGOMERY
21st Army Group

NETH.

SIMPSON
9th Army

15th Army

Cologne

Rhine R.

Sieg R.

Bonn

RUNDSTEDT
OB WEST

Liège

Meuse R.

Huy

B E L G I U M

Monschau
2nd Inf.
Div.

Malmédy

99th Inf.
Div.

106th Inf. Div.

St.-Vith

6th Panzer
Army

St.
Vith

Koblenz

HODGES
1st Army

Bastogne

5th Panzer
Army

Mosel R.

101st Arbn.
Div.

28th Inf. Div.

Sauer R.

LUXEMBOURG

G E R M A N Y

7th Army

FRONT LINE, DEC. 16

WEST WALL

Luxembourg City

BRADLEY
12th Army Group

Meuse R.

Verdun

Metz

1st Army

Saarbrücken

PATTON
3rd Army

F R A N C E

N
NW NE
W E
SW SE
S

DEVERS
6th Army Group

4th Armored
Division

Miles
0   10   20   40

PATCH
7th Army

Map by Gene Thorp

actually held a raucous staff Christmas party. Now that the extent of the carnage is known, Hodges has locked himself in his office, where he sits hunched over his desk, his head buried in his arms. His staff explains to all who ask that he has the flu.

General Bradley is surprised and distraught. As recently as last night, he was still telling an aide that the German offensive did not concern him.

Bradley now looks like a fool. The German army has been decimating American forces for the last twelve hours. The situation has led Eisenhower to call an emergency meeting of the top Allied commanders. Patton's Operation Tink is no more. As the irascible general predicted almost two weeks ago, Courtney Hodges and his First Army need to be rescued. And it is Patton's Third Army that will have to do it.

★   ★   ★

"The present situation is to be regarded as one of opportunity for us and not of disaster," Dwight Eisenhower tells the crowd of generals and senior officers seated at the long conference table. Ike will officially be promoted to five-star general tomorrow. But rather than looking elated, he is pale and tired. A glance around the dank second-floor room shows that British field marshal Bernard Law Montgomery is not in attendance.* A situation map covers one wall. The air smells of Patton's cigar, other officers' cigarettes, wet wool, and wood smoke from the fire burning in a potbelly stove. The low flame fails to warm the room, meaning that almost no one has removed his thick overcoat.

Eisenhower continues, forcing a smile: "There will be only cheerful faces at the conference table."

"Hell," Patton interrupts, "let's have the guts to let the sons of bitches go all the way to Paris. Then we'll really cut them up and chew 'em up."

Patton's brash remark fails to get much more than a grim chuckle.

---

*Though several British officers were in attendance—and laughed out loud at Patton's plan—Montgomery chose to skip the meeting. This act of grandstanding at such a crucial moment did not get him punished for insubordination. Quite the opposite. The next day, Eisenhower reassigned large chunks of Bradley's forces to Montgomery's command. This led many in the British press to claim that the U.S. forces were helpless without the field marshal's tactical expertise. Understandably, this infuriated many American soldiers.

But it sets a tone. As it was on the desperate battlefields of North Africa, Sicily, and France, Patton's aggressiveness is once again vital to Allied success.

"George, that's fine," Eisenhower responds, once again reclaiming the room. "But the enemy must never be allowed to cross the Meuse."

This is the line in the sand. Joachim Peiper and his SS Panzers are desperate to reach the Meuse River and secure its bridges in order to advance the German attack.

Eisenhower's G-2 intelligence chief, the British major general Kenneth Strong, briefs the room on the current location of the American and German forces. Since late September, the German army has successfully prevented the U.S. and British forces from making any significant advances into the Fatherland. The war has become a stalemate. The Allies were foolishly assuming the Germans could never reverse the tide. That was a mistake.

If the seventeen divisions of German soldiers now marching through the Ardennes can somehow make it across the Meuse, the war could change radically—and not in the Allies' favor.

"George," Eisenhower states. "I want you to command this move— under Brad's supervision, of course." Here Eisenhower nods at Omar Bradley. Bad weather delayed Bradley on the long drive down from Luxembourg City, but he made it just in time. He is tense because he clearly was fooled by the enemy, and could be seen as to blame for the German advance. This is something no general can allow to happen in wartime.

Ike continues: "A counterattack with at least three divisions. When can you start?"

Patton is ready. He has not only come to the meeting equipped with three different battle plans, but he met earlier this morning with his staff and arranged a series of code words. Launching the Third Army's attack is as simple as Patton calling his headquarters and saying the code for whichever of the battle plans is to be set into motion.

"As soon as you're through with me," Patton replies.

"When can you attack?" Eisenhower presses.

"The morning of December twenty-first," Patton responds, referring to two days from now, "with three divisions," he adds, still clutching his lighted cigar.

The room lapses into embarrassed silence. These career military officers know to be diplomatic when a man makes a fool of himself. And Patton has clearly crossed that line. Three divisions is not a small, nimble fighting force. It is a slow-moving colossus, spread out over miles of front lines. The idea that one hundred thousand men and supplies can somehow be uprooted and moved one hundred miles in forty-eight hours is ludicrous. If the men make it, but the guns and gasoline don't, all will be lost. Attempting such a task in the dead of winter, on narrow and icy roads, borders on the impossible. Once again, Patton's big mouth appears to be his undoing.

Eisenhower has seen this play out one too many times. "Don't be fatuous, George."

Patton looks to his deputy chief of staff, Lt. Col. Paul Harkins. Harkins says nothing, but nods, confirming that Patton is standing on solid ground.

"We can do that," says Patton, staring straight into Eisenhower's eyes.

Charles Codman, Patton's aide-de-camp, will later write of "a stir, a shuffling of feet, as those present straightened up in their chairs. In some faces, skepticism. But through the room, the current of excitement leaped like a flame."

Patton seizes the moment. Stepping to the map, he points out German weaknesses. This goes on for an hour. Omar Bradley says very little, realizing that this operation belongs to Patton and Patton alone.

Finally, as the meeting breaks up, Eisenhower jokes with his old friend. "Funny thing, George, every time I get a new star, I get attacked."

"Yes," Patton shoots back. "And every time you get attacked, I bail you out."

★ ★ ★

This time, Patton might be too late.

Brig. Gen. Anthony McAuliffe is already racing to the front lines. He is part of Dwight Eisenhower's desperate effort to stem the German advance by throwing reserve troops into the fray. A career army officer, McAuliffe is a less-than-imposing physical specimen. He stands five feet, seven inches, and his slicked-back hair makes him look even shorter. McAuliffe is trying to reach the city of Werbomont, Belgium, before the

Germans can capture it. But the journey is frustrating. Rather than speeding down icy roads, McAuliffe's jeep is facing an onslaught of traffic.

Allied tanks, trucks, halftracks, and soldiers are all headed in the wrong direction—right into McAuliffe's face.

They are not lost; they are defeated. They have done all they can to stop the German offensive, and their units have been decimated. They fought against hopeless odds to buy time for the 101st to get to Bastogne. Now they retreat from the front in droves. Their grimy, frostbitten faces are lined with grief after seeing their buddies blown to bits. The retreating men clog the narrow farm roads, utterly broken by the German advance. Never before has an American army been so devastated.

It does no good for McAuliffe's driver to honk the horn or order a path cleared for the general. Most of the soldiers barely respond to anything. Some mumble lines of gibberish. Others are crying. Among these groups is the 110th Infantry, which has just lost 2,750 of their 3,200 men in battle. "They shambled along in shock and fear," one eyewitness would later recall. "I have never seen such absolute terror in men."

But McAuliffe can do nothing to halt the retreat. These men are not his concern. He has been ordered to the town of Werbomont, where he will lead the veteran 101st Airborne Division into battle. These hardened warriors now trail miles behind him aboard a ten-mile-long column of open-air cattle trucks.

The forty-six-year-old McAuliffe isn't supposed to be in charge, but it seems that every man above him has taken Christmas leave—or, in the case of the division's former chief of staff, shot himself. So McAuliffe rides hard for Werbomont. Rapid response is vital to stopping the Nazi penetration. In military terms, the blast hole that has been created in the Allied lines is known as a salient.

American newspapers are simply calling it "the Bulge."

McAuliffe is a kind, plainspoken man. He is that rare West Point graduate and general army officer who doesn't sprinkle his conversation with swearing. And he is pragmatic. These shattered soldiers are clear evidence that the Krauts, as American soldiers call their Wehrmacht opponents, are hardly defeated. They have already slaughtered thousands of Americans in just four days.

The Krauts will be striving mightily to slaughter the 101st, as well.

★ ★ ★

It wasn't supposed to be like this. The 101st had been pulled back to rest after months of hard fighting. They were quartered in Reims, one hundred miles behind the lines, where they were awarded leave in nearby Paris and allowed to catch up on their sleep. There was no hurry to supply them with winter underwear, galoshes to keep their boots dry, or even extra ammunition. The 101st didn't need it. They were not expecting to see action until after the winter.

But that was then. Now they are on the move. They are supposed to be enjoying some well-earned rest after being dropped behind the Normandy beaches back in June, and then again at Operation Market Garden in late September. But Dwight Eisenhower desperately needs them on the front lines. Some were resting in their barracks when their orders arrived. Others were actually pulled, drunk or hungover, out of Paris's brasseries by military police. They travel in a special caravan made up of almost four hundred vehicles. Many drive with headlights blazing. This is normally forbidden in a combat zone, but now allows them to travel at a quicker speed. The downside is that if German planes are flying overhead, any member of the 101st would be butchered from the air, their silhouettes standing out in the snowy fields beside the roads, completely visible to the Nazi pilots.

But the calculated gamble is paying off. The skies are leaden with clouds and fog. The Luftwaffe is not flying tonight.*

Freezing, the American soldiers are lined up "nut to butt" for hour after hour in the swaying trucks. When the mass of retreating men slow their caravan, members of the 101st call down to them, asking for supplies. Ammunition is hurled up to them. Helmets. K-rations. Even rifles.

---

*The German air force once dominated the skies over Europe. But the Battle of Britain cost the Luftwaffe almost 1,900 fighters and bombers, as well as 3,500 air crew killed and another 967 captured. The Luftwaffe never recovered. The buildup of Allied forces in Europe before and after D-day was complemented by an increasing reliance on airpower to assist ground forces in close combat support and to pummel enemy installations and cities. Though the Luftwaffe was still mounting coordinated strikes in late 1944, the Allies had almost complete air superiority.

But not heavy winter coats. Not wool socks. And certainly not long underwear. Those in retreat will not part with them.

"What's going on up there?" a chorus of men yell. "How many Krauts are there? How close are they? Do they have tanks?"

To which one of the retreating men simply replies, "You'll all be killed!"

Undaunted, the 101st moves ahead. Any man can break. But the advancing Americans know they don't have that luxury. Just like the Roman legions who once fought off the Germanic hordes on this same stretch of land, they hold the fate of Europe in their hands.

Despite the last-minute call to arms, General McAuliffe and the 101st are more than ready to fight. When a captain in the command of one column of defeated men inexplicably blocks the road and refuses to move his trucks so that the 101st can pass, the paratroopers reach for their fighting knives.

An airborne officer promptly defuses the situation by unholstering his pistol and promising to put a bullet through the captain's head.

Thankfully, the captain sees "the wisdom in prompt obedience," in the words of a unit chaplain.

"No one would have missed him," chimes in a paratrooper.

And so the 101st rolls on.

But Brig. Gen. Tony McAuliffe, West Point Class of 1918, never makes it to Werbomont. Nor does the 101st Airborne.

Instead, they are diverted to a tiny hamlet that is no more than a speck on the Ardennes map. The Germans call the village a "road octopus" because seven different highways sprout in seven different directions from its center. The key to success in Operation Watch on the Rhine means controlling the local roads, which allow heavy tanks to travel more quickly. Thus, the Germans covet this town.

The road octopus is more commonly known as Bastogne.

Until a few days ago, McAuliffe had never heard of it. But now, for better or worse, he is here. As his jeep roars into the town center, he finds a miserable scenario. There is little natural charm or beauty to Bastogne under the best of circumstances. But now it is a scene of utter devastation. There is no power, and the *centre ville* is choked with refugees and dray carts piled high with the possessions of the fleeing. Ongoing German shelling has reduced most of Bastogne to rubble.

Yet McAuliffe must defend this horrible little burg at all costs. He sets up his command post in the basement of a hotel across the street from the train station and impatiently awaits the arrival of his troops. A quick glance at the situation map boards erected along the compound walls show how desperately the Germans want to capture Bastogne: they have committed three divisions and parts of four more. McAuliffe's eleven thousand para-troopers and Combat Command B of the Tenth Armored Division num-bering three thousand tanks and soldiers are on the verge of being surrounded by a force numbering fifty-five thousand Wehrmacht fighters and Panzers.* Once the Germans close the noose, there will be no way for the Americans to escape. Their only hope to survive is for Gen. George Patton and his Third Army to break through and rescue them.

"Now, Tony, you're going to be surrounded here before too long," says Maj. Gen. Troy Middleton, briefing McAuliffe before hightailing it out of Bastogne. Middleton is commander of the U.S. Army's VIII Corps, and McAuliffe's immediate superior. He is pulling his headquarters back to the safety of a town named Neuchâteau. McAuliffe can't help but notice that VIII Corps is so eager to pull out that they are leaving behind their ample liquor stores.

"But don't worry," Middleton emphasizes. "Help is on the way from Patton."

With that, Middleton hurries to his staff car and quickly drives out of town, knowing the Germans are just two miles away. He has performed admirably since December 16, but the arrival of the 101st means that it

---

*The Mark IV Panzer formed the backbone of the German army's tank corps, with more than seventeen thousand seeing service during the war. But when the invasion of Russia revealed that the Soviet T-34 had thicker armor and more powerful armament, the Panther tank was designed and built. Its 75mm gun and sloped armor (to deflect shells) proved highly effective on the Russian front and was considered the best Ger-man tank of the war. The Tiger, designed in 1942, was originally supposed to be named the Panzer VI, but Adolf Hitler ordered that a new name be used. Both the Tiger I and the Tiger II were formidable heavy tanks, easily the equal of any other armored weapon on the battlefield. But the Panzer II, in particular, was rushed into service, and suffered from mechanical issues that limited its effectiveness.

Soldiers of the 101st Airborne Division marching in Bastogne, Belgium

no longer serves any purpose for him and his headquarters staff to remain in Bastogne and potentially become captured.

McAuliffe now assumes the full weight of command. He is distinctly aware that many might see the situation as the 101st's version of Custer's Last Stand.

But McAuliffe does not believe this will be the case.

Or as a medic in Bastogne's field hospital sums up the situation, "They've got us surrounded. The poor bastards."

★ ★ ★

Meanwhile, fifty miles northeast of Bastogne, as the sun rises over the Elsenborn Ridge, the Germans attack.

Firing from a forest, they zero in on the frozen American force dug in on the ridge, almost two thousand feet above sea level. Members of the Ninety-Ninth Infantry Division hear the thunderclap of a single 88mm shell being fired. Its flight is short and intense, screaming louder and louder as it finds an American foxhole. Dirt, snow, blood, and body parts erupt into the sky. Instant death. The men of the Ninety-Ninth press their frostbitten bodies deeper into their fighting holes. For the better part of a week, the Ninety-Ninth have held the Elsenborn Ridge, knowing that sooner or later the Germans would attempt the frontal assault. Now it has begun.

That lone shell is the first of hundreds. The Germans barrage the Americans for over an hour. There is no pattern to where the shells fall. Some American soldiers become nauseated when the shells explode close by. Their ears ring. Some wet themselves without knowing it, and quietly revel in the brief sensation of warmth on this subzero day.

And then silence.

But only for a short time.

At 9:00 a.m. the German army's Third Panzergrenadier Division emerges from the tree line near the Schwalm Creek Valley. The hardened Nazi soldiers sprint toward the American foxholes.

They should know better.

It is impossible to run through fresh snow. The Germans sink up to their knees. They quickly lose their breath. Instead of running, they wade through the snow, making great postholes with each step.

This is when the machine gunners of the Ninety-Ninth take aim. It is now their turn to inflict death.

And they do.

For the first time all morning, the Americans poke their heads up above the rims of their foxholes and fire back. Machine gunners on the front of the slope make use of their unobstructed fields of fire, each man slowly pivoting his gun barrel from left to right, and then back again, fingers firmly squeezing triggers. The hillside is pocked with craters where German shells have fallen short, but otherwise there is no place for the Krauts to hide on this vast expanse of white.

The American-made automatic weapons fire at a slower clip than the German models. But the Browning water-cooled .30-caliber machine gun more than gets the job done, firing off seven two-inch-long bullets every second. It is especially lethal in a setting such as Elsenborn Ridge, which has the wide-open feel of a shooting range. In fact, finding targets to kill is not a problem for the machine gunners of the Ninety-Ninth. The real trick in aiming downhill is not firing too high, lest the bullets whiz above the enemy's head.

So as the foot soldiers of the Third Panzergrenadier Division lumber up the long and empty half mile between their lines and those of the dug-in Ninety-Ninth, they are, in reality, sealing their own doom.

Some Germans wear winter white. Others are clad in Nazi battle gray. But the color red soon carpets the snow as American bullets mercilessly mow them down.

The soldiers of the Ninety-Ninth cannot remember a moment in their lives when they have felt so wretched. Their units are broken from the relentless bombardment. They are beyond exhausted. Many are battling pneumonia and dysentery. Some are not even riflemen, but rear echelon cooks and clerks who have never learned simple infantry tactics.

But that does not stop them from fighting. And with every German who falls dead in the snow, they feel just that much more hopeful that they will live to see another sunrise.

The clatter of rifle shots and automatic weapons from the Ninety-Ninth continues, and thick swarms of Germans crumple atop one another. Soon the Germans have no choice but to retreat.

Two hours later, they attack again.

Once again, they fail.

Finally, as night falls, the German soldiers of the Third Panzergrenadier attempt one more assault of Elsenborn Ridge.*

But the Ninety-Ninth Division repels them a third time. As the Americans hunker down in their foxholes for their fifth straight subzero and sleepless night, they hear the moans of the dying German troops who now litter the snowy slopes below the ridge fill the air. They are crying out for relief. But none will be forthcoming.

The Ninety-Ninth has held the line for five consecutive days. Even as Americans almost everywhere else are retreating en masse, they are

---

*Precise German casualties are not known. All told, the Americans lost five thousand, either dead or missing, and the incidence of death was disproportionately high among the fifty-six thousand attacking Germans, who also lost more than one hundred tanks and armored vehicles.

holding. But for how long? They continue to take enormous casualties, and are still outnumbered five to one. A fifteen-mile-long caravan of Panzer tanks and halftracks is backed up in the valley below, waiting with growing impatience for the Ninety-Ninth to be killed to the last man so that they might obtain those vital roads through the Ardennes.

Should the Ninety-Ninth fail to hold their lines, the Germans will be able to quickly redirect their attack toward the Meuse and toward Bastogne. If this should happen, George Patton's hopes of relieving Bastogne will not come to pass.

So the question remains: How much longer can the Ninety-Ninth hang on?

*　*　*

"Ike and Bull are getting jittery about my attacking too soon," Patton writes in his diary, referring to Eisenhower's G-3, Maj. Gen. Harold Bull. His army is racing to Bastogne, encountering stiff German resistance along the way. "I have all I can get. If I wait, I will lose surprise.

"The First Army could, in my opinion, attack on the 22nd if they wanted (or if they were pushed), but they seem to have no ambition in that line.

"I had all my staffs, except for VIII Corps, in for a conference. As usual on the verge of an attack, they were full of doubt. I seemed always to be the ray of sunshine, and by God, I always am. We can and will win, God helping."

*　*　*

The Germans also inch toward the city, unaware that they are racing Patton and the Third Army for control of this vital crossroads. Now, five miles from the center of Bastogne, the Nazis are trying to overrun a town called Noville.

Blocking the way is a tall and determined young major named William Desobry and his ridiculously small band of soldiers and tanks known as Team Desobry.

They make their headquarters in the village schoolhouse. The village church is across the street. When the battle is over, the SS will enter the same church and shoot the village priest for offering comfort to the

Americans. For good measure, they will also shoot six other residents of this otherwise sleepy town.

But that is all to come.

Desobry is twenty-six and has been in the army just four years. Though he chose to attend Georgetown University instead of West Point, his quick thinking and sound judgment have already seen him promoted over men a dozen years his senior. With that kind of talent come great expectations. The scarecrow-thin Desobry has been ordered to place his small team of defenders between the German advance and the heart of Bastogne. For while a quick map study shows Desobry that Noville is utterly indefensible, the town is also tactically vital—of the three roads leading out of Noville, one aims straight into downtown Bastogne. The road is paved and wide, the closest thing the Ardennes has to a superhighway leading directly to Bastogne.

"If this situation gets to the point where I think it necessary to withdraw," Desobry nervously asked his commanding officer when first given the order to defend Noville, "can I do that on my own, or do I need permission from you, sir?"

Desobry's superior, and commander of CCB of the Tenth Armored Division, is Col. William Roberts. The two are so close that Desobry considers Roberts to be his second father. He listens intently to the colonel's response, determined to follow it to the letter, for fear of letting the older man down.

Roberts is kind—yet direct. "You will probably get nervous tomorrow morning and want to withdraw, so you had better wait for any withdrawal order from me."

That order has not yet arrived.

Armed with just fifteen Sherman tanks and four M-18 Hellcat tank destroyers, Desobry holds Noville long enough for an element of the 101st Airborne to reinforce his small command. The battalion of paratroopers works with Team Desobry to thwart several German attempts to capture Noville. Panzers and Sherman tanks soon burn alongside the road. Wounded soldiers are trapped inside many of these. The heat from the flames is too intense for rescue, and so they roast to death in their steel coffins.

The town is burning as well. At times the smoke from burning buildings mixes with the thick fog to give Noville an otherworldly appearance.

Men fire their guns into the morass, unsure of where they're aiming or what they've hit. German shells from the ridgelines outside town fall on the Americans at the rate of two dozen every ten minutes. The schoolhouse is destroyed, and Major Desobry is forced to find a new command post. Not even night stops the German shelling.

As the evening descends, Desobry hunkers down with his airborne counterpart to discuss strategy. He has no problem ceding command of the situation to Lt. Col. James LaPrade, a Texan who graduated from West Point in 1939. LaPrade is the rare man who not only is Desobry's superior officer and near equal in height, at just under six-four, but who has a career arc even more accelerated than Desobry's. At the young age of thirty, LaPrade is just two promotions away from making general.

But unbeknownst to the two officers, one of Desobry's men has just made a fatal mistake. With dusk not yet complete, an American maintenance officer parked his vehicle directly in front of the command post, rather than a few hundred yards down the road. A German tank crew on a distant ridgeline spotted the vehicle through binoculars. Now they waste no time zeroing in on this choice target. Within seconds of estimating distance and trajectory, their big 88 mm gun belches its trademark green fire, and a shell races toward Desobry and LaPrade.

The two men sit in the quiet of the command post. A clerk writes in his journal. The careless maintenance officer enters the cramped room, with its wall-to-wall collection of maps, chairs, and telephones, to report that he is back from towing broken tanks into Bastogne. An armoire has been pulled across one window as protection from snipers.

The 88 mm lets out its trademark scream before impact—an impact that absolutely no one in the command post is expecting.

The armoire explodes into a thousand splinters. The roof collapses, as do the stone walls. Desobry is buried under a pile of rubble, his body shot through with pine wood. His left eye is nearly ripped from its socket, and his head is slashed and punctured by metal, wood, stone, and glass.

But he is alive.

Lt. Col. James LaPrade lies beside Desobry, all but unrecognizable. Tony McAuliffe thinks he's the best battalion commander in the 101st. His wife's name is Marcy. His brother, Robert, a marine, won the Navy

Cross and had a ship named after him for his heroism on Guadalcanal, where he was killed in action.

"LaPrade," reads the name on the dead commander's dog tags.

If not for that, his shattered body could belong to anyone, on either side of the war. Not even his wife would be able to recognize the man she loves.

A medic quickly attends to Desobry, and helps lift his stretcher into an ambulance. The driver guns the engine and races for the tents of the field hospital, on the outskirts of Bastogne. But a German patrol intercepts the ambulance. For some reason, they take pity on Desobry, perhaps thinking he will die soon anyway, and do not shoot him.

For Major Desobry, the war is over. He is taken to a German prisoner camp in the Fatherland.

But he has done his job in Noville. By delaying the Germans' advance and resisting the urge to withdraw, he has given the 101st Airborne the precious time they need to form a tight perimeter around Bastogne.

★ ★ ★

Gen. Tony McAuliffe receives the bad news. The Americans have taken two hundred and seventy-five casualties in Noville. Team Desobry lost eleven of its fifteen Sherman tanks. Under cover of fog and darkness, the 101st Airborne and Tenth Armored, along with what is left of Team Desobry, fall back into Bastogne's inner defenses, soon to make their last stand.

McAuliffe is exhausted. He barely slept last night because the German air force bombed Bastogne, with one bomb almost destroying his command post in the basement of the Hôtel de Commerce. He moves his headquarters to the basement of a Belgian army barracks. Just before noon he steals away to a small, quiet room, zips himself into his sleeping bag, and naps. His staff knows to wake him if anything of importance occurs.

Meanwhile, in the meadows and forests ringing Bastogne, the men of the 101st have managed to turn the problem of being surrounded into a tactically positive situation. They keep their perimeter tight, facing

General Anthony McAuliffe (right) conferring with General George Patton (left)

outward, waiting for the German attack. Despite the light snow that now falls on their positions, they even feel secure enough to climb out of their foxholes for a few minutes to shave and use the slit latrine.*

With a break in the action, rumors and innuendo spread up and down the line, and the men are now hearing that George S. Patton is sending an armored division to bail them out. Maybe two. They can't be sure of this—any more than they could believe the rumor that C-47s were going to airdrop precious supplies of food and bullets into Bastogne last night. That never came to pass. What confuses the men of the 101st is that the weather seems to be too rough for American planes to fly a

---

*A slit latrine was a long, narrow trench just wide enough for a man to straddle while relieving himself. Dirt was thrown over the hole afterward to eliminate odor.

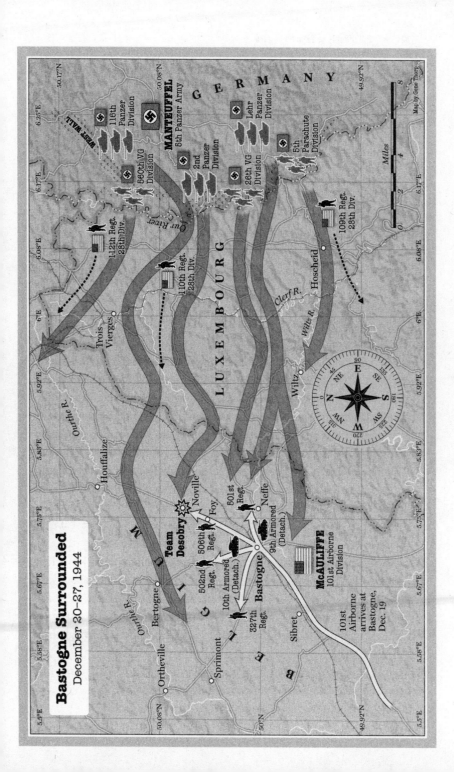

Bastogne Surrounded
December 20–27, 1944

GERMANY

116th Panzer Division

MANTEUFFEL
5th Panzer Army

560th VG Division

2nd Panzer Division

Lehr Panzer Division

26th VG Division

5th Parachute Division

112th Regt. 28th Div.

110th Regt. 28th Div.

109th Regt. 28th Div.

Our River

SKYLINE DRIVE

Trois Vierges

Ourthe R.

Houffalize

Ourthe R.

Bertogne

Clerf R.

Wiltz R.

Wiltz R.

Hoscheid

Wiltz

L U X E M B O U R G

Ortheville

Sprimont

Noville

Foy

Team Desobry

506th Regt.

502nd Regt.

10th Armored (Detach.)

501st Regt.

Neffe

9th Armored (Detach.)

Bastogne

327th Regt.

McAULIFFE
101st Airborne Division

Sibret

101st Airborne arrives at Bastogne, Dec. 19

Miles
0   2   4   8

Map by Gene Thorp

vital aid mission, and yet the Luftwaffe has no problem dropping bombs on Bastogne.*

A depressing (and true) rumor also spreads that the Germans over-ran Bastogne's field hospital last night. The wounded were taken prisoner, as were the doctors and surgical staff. All the medical supplies, including surgical instruments and doses of the antibiotic penicillin, were captured. This will become a life-or-death issue when the fighting resumes, because that penicillin is vital to the survival of the severely wounded.

At noon on December 22, 1944, the situation on the American front lines is tense—but quiet enough for some of the men of the 327th Glider Infantry Regiment to actually stand outside their foxholes on the Kessler family farm south of Bastogne, making small talk.

A most odd sight then presents itself. Marching toward them from the direction of Arlon, carrying a white flag as large as a bedsheet, are four German soldiers. They walk into the American lines fearlessly, even strolling past a bazooka team on the outer perimeter without hesitation. The men of F Company shoulder their M-1 carbines, but the Germans keep coming. "This doesn't make sense," says one American, wondering why the Germans appear to be surrendering.

Three American soldiers walk cautiously up the road to greet the Germans. They soon stand face-to-face with two officers and two enlisted men. The officers wear polished black boots and long, warm overcoats. One of them, the short and stocky captain, carries a briefcase.

The Americans never take their fingers off the triggers of their M-1 rifles, unsure if this is a trick.

It is not.

In fact, it is a gesture on the part of the German general Heinrich Lüttwitz, commander of the forces surrounding Bastogne, that is both gallant and arrogant. He thinks it absurd to needlessly slaughter so many brave American soldiers. Instead, Lüttwitz is offering Tony McAuliffe and the 101st a chance to save their own lives by surrendering. War being

---

*A desperate Hitler had ordered the Germans to fly in all circumstances, while the Americans would not take that risk, which infuriated Patton.

war, however, should the Americans refuse to throw down their weapons, Lüttwitz will order that Bastogne be leveled, and every American soldier annihilated. There will be no prisoners.

"We are *parlementaires*," says the short, stocky German junior officer. His name is Hellmuth Henke, and his English is perfect. "We would like to speak to your officers."

The major wearing the uniform of a Panzer commander says something in German to Henke, who quickly corrects himself: "We want to talk to the American commander of the surrounded city of Bastogne."

Henke motions to his briefcase, in which he carries a note for McAuliffe.

The Germans have brought their own blindfolds, suspecting that the Americans will not let them see their defensive locations. Eyes covered, they are soon marched on a roundabout tour of the American front lines. Nobody, it seems, knows quite what to do with them.

Finally, Maj. Alvin Jones gets the radio message that "Four Krauts have just come up the Arlon road under a white flag to our Company F, and they're calling themselves *parlementaires*. What do we do with them?"

Jones has no idea; nor does anyone know exactly what it means to be a *parlementaire*.* But he retrieves the note, leaving the Germans sitting impatiently in the large foxhole that serves as F Company's forward command post, awaiting a response.

Soon enough, word of the note is passed up the chain of command. Within an hour, Tony McAuliffe is being awakened to the news that a German surrender demand is making its way to his headquarters.

"Nuts," he mutters, still half asleep.

Jones soon arrives with the note. There are two, actually: one typed in German and the other in English.

"They want to surrender?" McAuliffe asks, taking the note from Lt. Col. Ned Moore, his chief of staff.

"No," Moore corrects him. "They want *us* to surrender."

---

*An archaic French term meaning a diplomatic go-between who is free from punishment or persecution while performing his duties.

McAuliffe laughs and begins to read.

The letter is dated December 22, 1944:

To the U.S.A. Commander of the encircled town of Bastogne,

The fortune of war is changing. This time the U.S.A. forces in and near Bastogne have been encircled by strong German armored units. More German armored units have crossed the river Ourthe near Ortheuville, have taken Marche and reached St. Hubert by passing through Hompre-Sibret-Tillet. Libramont is in German hands. There is only one possibility to save the encircled U.S.A. troops from total annihilation: that is the honorable surrender of the encircled town. In order to think it over a term of two hours will be granted beginning with the presentation of this note.

If this proposal should be rejected, one German artillery corps and six heavy A.A. battalions are ready to annihilate the U.S.A. troops in and near Bastogne. The order for firing will be given immediately after this two hours' term.

All the serious civilian losses caused by this artillery fire would not correspond with the well known American humanity.

The German Commander.

McAuliffe looks at his staff. "Well, I don't know what to tell them."

"That first remark of yours would be hard to beat," replies Lt. Col. Harry Kinnard, in his Texas twang.

"What do you mean?" McAuliffe responds.

"Sir, you said 'nuts.'"

McAuliffe mulls it over. He knows his history, and suspects the moment will be memorialized. One French general refused to surrender at the Battle of Waterloo with the far more crass response of "Merde."*

And so the response is quickly typed: "To the German Commander, 'Nuts!' The American Commander."

When the letter is presented to the German emissaries, they don't understand. "What is this, 'nuts'?" asks Henke. The Germans have grown cold and arrogant while awaiting a response. They fully expected to return to their lines as heroes for effecting the surrender.

---

*Shit.

Col. Paul Harper, regimental commander of the 327th, has been tasked with delivering McAuliffe's response. He orders the men into his jeep and drives them back to the no-man's-land between the 101st Airborne and the Wehrmacht lines. "It means you can go to hell," he tells the Germans as he drops them off.

"And I'll tell you something else," he adds. "If you continue to attack we will kill every goddamn German that tries to break into this city."

Henke translates to the others. The Germans snap to attention and salute. "We will kill many Americans," Henke responds. "This is war."

"On your way, bud," snorts Harper.

9

---·◆·---

George S. Patton takes off his helmet as he enters the century-old Catholic chapel. Though Episcopalian, he is in need of a place to worship. The sound of his footsteps echoes off the stone floor as he walks reverently to the foot of the altar. The scent of melting wax from the many votive candles fills the small chamber. Patton kneels, unfolding the prayer he has written for this occasion, and bows his head.

"Sir, this is Patton talking," he says, speaking candidly to the Almighty. "The past fourteen days have been straight hell. Rain, snow, more rain, more snow—and I am beginning to wonder what's going on in Your headquarters. Whose side are You on anyway?"

Patton and the Third Army are now thirty-three miles south of Bastogne. Every available man under his command has joined this race to rescue the city. The Bulge in the American lines is sixty miles deep and thirty miles wide, with Bastogne an American-held island in the center. And while Patton's men have so far been successful in maintaining their steady advance, there is still widespread doubt that he can succeed. Outnumbered and outgunned by the Germans, Patton faces the daunting challenge of attacking on icy roads in thick snow, with little air cover. Small wonder that British commander Field Marshal Bernard Law Montgomery—whom Patton has taken to calling a "tired little fart"—and other British authorities are quietly mocking Patton's advance. He has

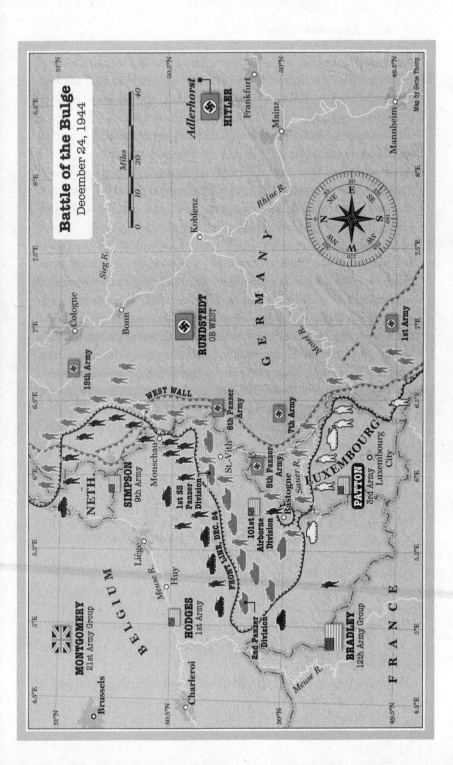

Battle of the Bulge
December 24, 1944

Miles
0 10 20 40

Map by Gene Thorp

even heard that many of them are suggesting he hold his lines and not attack, as Monty is doing, for fear that the wily German field marshal Gerd von Rundstedt may be preparing to launch yet another surprise attack that could do irreparable damage to the Allies. "Hold von Rundstedt?" Patton grumbled in reply. "I'll take von Rundstedt and shove him up Montgomery's ass."

Despite those hard words, the truth is that the Third Army may be in trouble. Patton has vowed to Tony McAuliffe and the 101st Airborne that he will be in Bastogne on Christmas Day. However, thanks to the weather, it is very likely he will not be able to keep this promise.

So the general prays.

"For three years my chaplains have been telling me that this is a religious war. This, they tell me, is the Crusades all over again, except that we're riding tanks instead of chargers. They insist that we are here to annihilate the Germans and the godless Hitler so that religious freedom may return to Europe. Up until now I have gone along with them, for You have given us Your unreserved cooperation. Clear skies and a calm sea in Africa made the landings highly successful and helped us to eliminate Rommel. Sicily was comparatively easy and You supplied excellent weather for the armored dash across France, the greatest military victory that You have thus far allowed me. You have often given me excellent guidance in difficult command situations and You have led German units into traps that made their elimination fairly simple.

"But now You've changed horses midstream. You seem to have given von Rundstedt every break in the book, and frankly, he's beating the hell out of us. My army is neither trained nor equipped for winter warfare. And as You know, this weather is more suitable for Eskimos than for southern cavalrymen.

"But now, Sir, I can't help but feel that I have offended You in some way. That suddenly You have lost all sympathy for our cause. That You are throwing in with von Rundstedt and his paper-hanging god [Hitler]. You know without me telling You that our situation is desperate. Sure, I can tell my staff that everything is going according to plan, but there's no use telling You that my 101st Airborne is holding out against tremendous odds in Bastogne, and that this continual storm is making it impossible to supply them even from the air. I've sent Hugh Gaffey, one of my ablest generals, with his 4th Armored Division, north toward that all-important road center to relieve the encircled garrison and he's finding Your weather more difficult than he is the Krauts."

* * *

This isn't the first time Patton has resorted to divine intervention. Every man in the Third Army now carries a three-by-five card that has a Christmas greeting from Patton on one side and a special prayer for good weather on the other. The general firmly believes that faith is vital when it comes to doing the impossible. Patton sees no theological conflict in asking God to allow him to kill the enemy. He has even given the cruel order that all SS soldiers are to be shot rather than taken prisoner.

* * *

"I don't like to complain unreasonably," Patton continues his prayer, "but my soldiers from Meuse to Echternach are suffering tortures of the damned. Today I visited several hospitals, all full of frostbite cases, and the wounded are dying in the fields because they cannot be brought back for medical care."

Head bowed, Patton prays while Sgt. Robert Mims waits outside with his open-air jeep. When the general is ready, they will set out for yet another day on the road. When Patton finally leaves the chapel and the castle-like headquarters at the Fondation Pescatore, he and Mims will prowl the roads of the Ardennes Forest. Without planes to offer overhead reconnaissance, Patton must see the battle lines for himself.

But these travels also serve another purpose. Patton seeks out his troops wherever he can, encouraging them as they march in long columns of tanks and men up the snowy farm roads. More than 133,000 tanks and trucks travel around the clock toward Bastogne. The infantry wear long greatcoats, many still spattered with the mud of Metz. The tank commanders ride with their chests and shoulders poked out of the top hatch, faces swaddled in thick wool scarves. Heavy snow blankets the roads, forests, and farmlands and also covers their vehicles, muting the rumble of engines and giving the Third Army's advance a ghostly feel. But it can also be deadly:

unable to distinguish which snow-covered tanks are American Shermans and which are German Panzers, some U.S. P-47 Thunderbolt pilots have made the cruel mistake of bombing their own.

Patton's jeep has also been strafed, though by German fighter planes. He is a relentless presence in his open-air vehicle, red-faced and blue-lipped as Sergeant Mims fearlessly weaves the vehicle through the long column of tanks and trucks. "I spent five or six hours almost every day in an open car," he will later write in his journal about his zeal to be in the thick of the action. "I never had a cold, and my face, though sometimes slightly blistered, did not hurt me much—nor did I wear heavy clothes. I did, however, have a blanket around my legs, which was exceedingly valuable in keeping me from freezing."

Just yesterday, a column of the Fourth Armored Division that was advancing on Bastogne were shocked to see Patton get out of his jeep and help them push a vehicle out of a snowdrift. The men of the Third Army are bolstered by Patton's constant presence. They speak of him warmly, with nicknames such as the Old Man and Georgie. His willingness to put himself in harm's way and endure the freezing conditions has many American soldiers now believing the general would never ask them to do something he wouldn't do himself.

Back in America, the Battle of the Bulge has shocked the public. The siege of Bastogne is becoming a symbol of bravery and holding out against impossible odds. All across the country, people are taking time during this Christmas season to do just what Patton is doing right now: get on their knees to pray. They ask God to deliver the "Battered Bastards of Bastogne," as the newspapers are calling the men of the 101st.

Yet Patton's prayer is unique. He is asking not only for deliverance, but for power. Few men are ever given the chance to change the course of history so completely. If the men inside Bastogne are to be rescued, it will be because of the daring of George S. Patton—as he himself well knows.

But to succeed he will need a little help from above.

★ ★ ★

The last words of Patton's prayer are for the ages.

"Damn it, Sir, I can't fight a shadow. Without Your cooperation from a weather standpoint, I am deprived of accurate disposition of the German armies and how in the hell can I be intelligent in my attack? All of this probably sounds unreasonable to You, but I have lost all patience with Your chaplains who insist that this is a typical Ardennes winter, and that I must have faith.

"Faith and patience be damned! You have just got to make up Your mind whose side You are on. You must come to my assistance, so that I may dispatch the entire German Army as a birthday present to your Prince of Peace.

"Sir, I have never been an unreasonable man; I am not going to ask You to do the impossible. I do not even insist upon a miracle, for all I request is four days of clear weather.

"Give me four days so that my planes can fly, so that my fighter bombers can bomb and strafe, so that my reconnaissance may pick out targets for my magnificent artillery. Give me four days of sunshine to dry this blasted mud, so that my tanks roll, so that ammunition and rations may be taken to my hungry, ill-equipped infantry. I need these four days to send von Rundstedt and his godless army to their Valhalla. I am sick of this unnecessary butchering of American youth, and in exchange for four days of fighting weather, I will deliver You enough Krauts to keep Your bookkeepers months behind in their work.

"Amen."

10

ADLERHORST
ZIEGENBERG, GERMANY
DECEMBER 24, 1944
1:00 P.M.

The man with one hundred and twenty-seven days to live can barely see.

The sun shines brightly on Adolf Hitler's pale, exhausted face as he stares up at more than one thousand Allied bombers that have come to destroy the Fatherland on Christmas Eve. The Führer stands one hundred and sixty-five miles east of where Patton knelt to pray. Hitler is ensconced in a drab bunker complex known as the Adlerhorst, and the drone of the bombers has pulled him out of the dining room of Haus 1. As his lunch grows cold, Hitler surveys the danger above him.

"Mein Führer," gasps Christa Schroeder, the striking thirty-six-year-old brunette who has long served as his personal secretary. "We have lost the war, haven't we?"

Hitler assures her that this is not the case. So even as the B-17 Flying Fortresses and B-24 Liberator bombers continue their deadly journey into the German heartland, Hitler saunters back inside to eat, passing a well-decorated Christmas tree that will soon be lit by candlelight.

The Führer's physical condition continues to deteriorate. His unstable gait is that of a senile old man. Lunch is his usual fare of vegetables

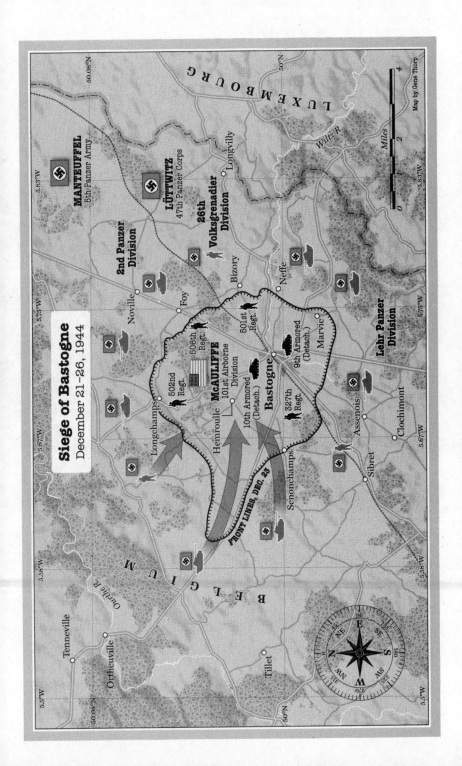

Siege of Bastogne
December 21-26, 1944

MANTEUFFEL
5th Panzer Army

LÜTTWITZ
47th Panzer Corps

26th
Volksgrenadier
Division

2nd Panzer
Division

Lehr Panzer
Division

McAULIFFE
101st Airborne
Division

500th Regt.
501st Regt.
502nd Regt.
327th Regt.
9th Armored (Detach.)
10th Armored (Detach.)

FRONT LINES, DEC. 26

LUXEMBOURG

BELGIUM

Longvilly
Bizory
Neffe
Noville
Foy
Marvie
Hemroulle
Bastogne
Assenois
Clochimont
Sibret
Senonchamps
Longchamps
Tenneville
Orthueville
Tillet

Wiltz R.
Ourthe R.

Map by Gene Thorp

Miles
0 1 2 4

N
NE
E
SE
S
SW
W
NW

and fruit—asparagus and peppers are personal favorites—served with salad and rice. A dozen female food tasters have already sampled the fare to ensure that Hitler is not being poisoned. Now, he once again sits down to eat alongside his mistress, the voluptuous Eva Braun. Hitler inhales his food, even though he is barely strong enough to hold the fork in his right hand, which has grown so weak that he no longer signs most official documents, leaving his staff to forge his signature.

Hitler's left hand is even worse. He cannot stop its palsied shakes, and so it now rests in his lap. The Führer eats maniacally, even leaning his head over the plate to shovel the vegetables in faster. He runs his right index finger along his short black mustache and absentmindedly chews his nails between bites. The Führer's table manners, in the words of one witness, "are little short of shocking."

Yet Hitler is a man who has caused the death of millions, and he is now in a very unpredictable mood. This would not be a good day to correct his etiquette.

The Führer has been holed up in the Adlerhorst since before Operation Watch on the Rhine began, and now directs the battle from this secret fortress. The elaborate collection of seven houses is actually a cleverly concealed military command post. Nestled in the crags of the Taunus Mountains, the Adlerhorst was built in the shadow of the medieval castle Kransberg, which shields the Eagle's eyrie from prying eyes. Each building appears to be an innocent German cottage, with wood exteriors and interior furnishings of deer antlers and paintings depicting hunting scenes.

But the walls are actually reinforced concrete, three feet thick. Antiaircraft guns are hidden in the surrounding forest, where Hitler takes his daily morning stroll with Blondi, his German shepherd. It is to Adlerhorst that Hitler brought his top generals on December 11 to lay out his counterattack strategy, and it is from the concealment of the underground situation room in Haus 2 that an elated Hitler celebrated the operation's opening success on December 16. He was so overjoyed that he couldn't sleep—a condition no doubt exacerbated by the injections of glucose, iron, and vitamin B he receives from Dr. Morell, his corpulent personal physician.*

In the eight days since the Ardennes battle began, Hitler has had much to cheer. His favorite commando, the scar-faced Otto Skorzeny, and the men of Operation Greif successfully roamed behind American lines, spreading lies and innuendos that caused widespread panic. A few of Skorzeny's commandos were caught and swiftly shot by firing squads for the war crime of disguising themselves in enemy uniforms. But by then the damage had already been done.

GIs everywhere became jittery as news that German soldiers were wearing American uniforms and speaking English spread up and down the Allied chain of command. U.S. soldiers became distrustful of any and all strangers. Cases of mistaken identity led Americans to shoot other Americans. Vehicles passing through military checkpoints were halted, and the occupants asked to prove their nationality by answering questions about American culture that only a real GI would know.

Those who did not realize the difference between the American and National Leagues, or the name of actress Betty Grable's last motion picture, were often taken into custody. An American brigadier general who thought the Chicago Cubs were in the American League was placed under arrest and held at gunpoint for five hours. British field marshal Bernard Law Montgomery refused to answer questions, then ordered his

---

*Hitler is fifty-five years old. There is speculation that his shaking left hand and wobbly walk are caused by Parkinson's disease. There is also a theory that he suffered from an advanced stage of syphilis. He referred to it as "the Jewish disease" in his treatise *Mein Kampf*. He reportedly had sex with a Jewish prostitute in Vienna in 1908, and perhaps contracted the disease at that time. What is known for certain is that Hitler's fondness for sugar causes him myriad dental problems, and may explain why he never smiles in public. He is also addicted to cocaine and methamphetamines, suffers from irritable bowel syndrome, has an irregular heartbeat, and has long had a problem with skin lesions on his legs, believed to have been caused by what is known as "neurosyphilis," a late-phase version of the disease that brings on madness. Early in the war, Wild Bill Donovan and the OSS published a report stating that Hitler enjoyed having women urinate and defecate on him, though this appears to be disinformation intended to malign the Führer. However, what is most surely a fact is that by Christmas 1944 Hitler had become impotent.

driver to speed through a checkpoint, at which time the American guards shot out his tires.

When British film actor turned soldier David Niven was unable to recall who had won the 1943 World Series, he answered, "Haven't the foggiest idea. But I did costar with Ginger Rogers in *Bachelor Mother*."

The sentry let him pass.

So great was the Skorzeny-induced hysteria that Dwight Eisenhower was placed under around-the-clock protection after one captured German commando confessed that Skorzeny planned to assassinate Eisenhower.

In the end, the actual damage done by Operation Greif was intense but did not change the course of battle. Even the flamboyant Skorzeny admitted his subterfuge could not turn the tide of the Bulge.

★   ★   ★

Hitler stares at the battle maps spread atop the long rectangular conference table in his underground command post. He stops now and then to nibble on the molasses-filled Lebkuchen* that temporarily appeases his insatiable sweet tooth. What he desperately longs to hear is some good news from the front. Instead, he hears that Bastogne has not yet fallen. And that the Second Panzer Division is just three miles from the Meuse River but has run out of fuel and can go no farther. Rather than waging war, the Second Panzer now hides in the forest, desperately covering their stalled vehicles with tree branches and heaps of snow to camouflage them from the P-47 Thunderbolts that prowl the Ardennes skies.†

But perhaps the most crushing blow is the fate of Hitler's great tank commander Joachim Peiper and the men of the elite First Panzer Division.

"The Butcher of Malmedy," as Peiper will forever be known, is trapped in the small village of La Gleize. For three days Peiper has been using what little ammunition he has left to fend off American artillery and tank attacks.

---

*A baked treat much like a gingerbread cookie.

†Among the many Allied fighter-bombers patrolling the skies over Europe, the single-engine P-47 stood out for its size (ten tons fully loaded, with two one-thousand-pound bombs) and ability to provide close support for ground troops, thanks to the four .50-caliber machine guns in each wing. Patton considered coordinated attacks by the P-47, Sherman tanks, and infantry a vital part of his tactics.

He spends his nights in the cellar of his headquarters, talking with an American major whom his unit has taken prisoner. The two men get along extremely well. "He and I talked together from 2300 hours until 0500 hours," Maj. Hal McCown will later report, "our subject being mainly his defense of Nazism and why Germany was fighting. I have met few men who impressed me in as short a space of time as did this German officer."*

Obersturmbannführer† Peiper and the First are just two bridges away from crossing the Meuse and spearheading a fatal thrust through the Allied lines toward Antwerp. But that goal, as Peiper reluctantly admits to Major McCown, is now unrealistic.

The SS division is cut off. The Americans have blown key bridges in front of them, making it impossible for Peiper to press the attack. The Germans cannot go forward, but cannot retreat, either. Going back would mean their annihilation. This division is just about out of gasoline, medicine, and ammunition. They eat little except hard biscuits and drink sips of plundered cognac and schnapps. Morale is plummeting, with one of Peiper's soldiers caught committing the mortal sin of removing the SS emblems from his uniform, fearing that he might soon become an American POW and be executed. Instead, he was immediately placed against a stone wall and shot by his own countrymen.

Luftwaffe attempts to resupply Peiper from the air have been disastrous. The parachute drop was off course. The gasoline and ammunition (code-named Otto and Hermann) quickly became American property after they missed their marks. The situation is so bad that Peiper has even taken the extreme step of allowing his most severely wounded SS fighters to be taken prisoner. They have shown great loyalty to him. Ensuring that they receive proper medical care is Peiper's way of returning that devotion.

Colonel Peiper does not want his men to die. Thus he hatches a daring plan that may give hope to a hopeless situation.

---

*Peiper is multilingual, so no translator is needed. After the war, he was captured by the Americans and served almost twelve years in prison for war crimes. He moved his family to France, where he made his living as a writer. In 1976, French Communists assaulted Peiper's home, setting it on fire. As Peiper tried to flee the house, he was shot to death.

†A rank available only to members of the SS. The name translates to "senior storm leader," and the rank is equivalent to a lieutenant colonel in the Wehrmacht.

Just after 5:00 p.m. on December 23, Joachim Peiper radios German headquarters and asks permission to destroy his twenty-eight remaining Panzers and escape on foot.

The request is denied. The Führer refuses any defensive action.

Later that night, Peiper once again pleads for the lives of his eight hundred remaining men, arguing that the only way to save them is to flee through the woods.

Again, permission is denied.

A furious Peiper unholsters his pistol and fires several shots into the radio. Its explosion mirrors the depths of his frustration.

Peiper knows the end is coming. There is no way the First can hold out. If they stand and fight, they will all die. But if they surrender, Peiper will likely be put on trial for allowing the murder of American prisoners of war and innocent civilians. If the United States chooses to hand Peiper over to the Russians, there won't even be a trial. Peiper can be sure that his death will be slow and cruel.

Peiper makes up his mind: the First Panzer must escape, even if it means disobeying a direct order.

The word is passed.

By three o'clock on the morning of Christmas Eve, Peiper and every other tanker in the First gather to do something they have not done on a battlefield for a very long time: walk. Tank commanders throughout the division struggle to maintain their stoicism as they leave behind the fighting machines that have given them the godlike power of life and death for one thrilling and sleepless week. A dozen miles and two river crossings lay between Kampfgruppe Peiper and the German lines. The plan is to travel through the woods by night and remain hidden during the day to avoid being spotted by those dreaded American Thunderbolt pilots.

The men of the First form into a long single-file column and begin their march in complete silence. A skeleton crew remains behind to blow up the now useless Panzers and halftracks. Prisoner of war Maj. Hal McCown reluctantly remains at Peiper's side, walking at the front, amazed at the SS discipline. "The noise made by the entire 800-man group was so little that I believe we could have passed within 200 yards of an outpost without detection," he will later write.

The spearhead of Operation Watch is no longer moving forward.

Thirty miles east of George Patton's Third Army, the First SS Panzer Division is now in full retreat, the burning hulls of their tanks lighting up the wintry Christmas Eve sky.

★ ★ ★

Der Heilige Abend, or "the Holy Evening," as Christmas Eve is known throughout Germany, ends late for Adolf Hitler. It is four o'clock on Christmas morning as he slowly ascends the stairs from his War Room and readies himself for bed. Rising at noon, the man who seeks to remove any sort of religious tone from Christmas* receives the news that Peiper and his division have escaped entrapment. This morning, even as Hitler lay sleeping, 770 of the 800 men who began the journey from La Gleize swam the icy Salm River and reached the German lines safely.†

After dressing in his usual formal manner, Hitler meets with his staff to celebrate the holiday, drinking a rare glass of wine and making jovial small talk. Then he descends once again into his War Room. He seeks the latest reports from Bastogne, certain that he can renew his stalled attack if only he captures the road octopus. There is a gleam in Hitler's eye as he scrutinizes the maps, despite his declining physical condition. It is a gleam that his generals know all too well, for it is the look the Führer shows when he is divining some ingenious way to outwit his enemies.

Just yesterday, the German submarine U-486 sank the troopship SS *Leopoldville* off the coast of France, sending eight hundred American

---

*Hitler was raised Catholic. His parents, Alois and Klara, were devout. The Führer's father died in 1903, at the age of sixty-five, and his mother from breast cancer four years later, at forty-seven. Of Hitler's five siblings, only his youngest sister, Paula, lived to adulthood. She was taken into U.S. custody at the end of the war, but was released when it became clear that she had not been a party to her brother's actions. She relocated from Austria to Germany after the war, where she lived in seclusion. Paula Hitler died in 1960 at the age of sixty-four. Like her brother, she had no children. Her death ended the Hitler bloodline.

†Maj. Hal McCown was not among them. He managed to run off and escape during a brief skirmish with forces of the American Eighty-Second Airborne Division. It is worth noting that the Eighty-Second was originally supposed to be the force defending Bastogne, but they were routed to other positions at the last minute, leaving it to the 101st to defend the town.

servicemen to the bottom of the Atlantic. And Hitler's special V-1 rocket-propelled bombs rained down death on the British city of Oldham, killing twenty-seven innocent civilians as they gathered to celebrate Christmas Eve.

No matter what the Allies might think, Adolf Hitler is far from beaten.

11

———◆———

J oseph Stalin is plotting to take over the world.

He does not celebrate Christmas. This religious holiday has no place in the godless Communist Soviet Union. So instead of sitting before a Christmas tree to unwrap presents with his eighteen-year-old daughter, Svetlana, the Soviet dictator now works at his desk in the Kremlin. Because the Communist philosophy frowns on opulence, Stalin's second-floor office is dark and cramped. The room smells of smoke from his Dunhill pipe. He hates noise, so as Stalin hunches over a small desk and dictates to a young secretary, his voice is the only sound breaking the complete quiet of the room.

"I have received your letter regarding sending to Moscow a competent officer from General Eisenhower," Stalin writes to U.S. president Franklin Delano Roosevelt. Outside the window, snow falls on Red Square. The temperature is well below freezing, and the Moscow River will soon be covered in a thick sheet of ice. Should he choose to do so, Stalin could escape to his seaside dacha on the Black Sea, in the town of Sochi, where there is no ice and where the sun shines warm and bright in the dead of winter. He can wade in his saltwater swimming pool, which the architects have kept to a discreet five-foot depth, knowing that the five-foot-four Stalin does not swim.

But the coming holiday, not to mention the ongoing war, would make Stalin's absence from Moscow conspicuous. Instead, the dictator remains in the Kremlin as a show of solidarity with the Soviet people. He works by day and spends evenings smoking his pipe and playing chess. Sometimes he watches Charlie Chaplin films and Russian comedies—but always in private.

Because what the ultrasecretive mass murderer does not want the world to know is that he loves to laugh. It is a secret he shares with his mistress Valentina Istomina—but then, it would be almost impossible to hide this from her, as the buxom "Valechka" is also Stalin's longtime housekeeper.*

"Naturally, I agree with your proposal as well as I agree to meet the officer from General Eisenhower and to arrange an exchange of information from him."

Signed: "J. Stalin."

A little-known fact is that Russian is actually Stalin's second language. He learned it late in life, and still speaks it with the coarse Georgian accent of his youth.† English is his third language, and Stalin understands it far better than he lets on. This has been an advantage in global negotiations with his British and American allies. He eavesdrops on their conversations and adjusts his bargaining position accordingly. Stalin dictates this letter without punctuation and using improper grammar, perpetuating the myth that he is not fluent in FDR's mother tongue.

He uses the same ruse with Winston Churchill, who wrote to wish Stalin a happy fifty-sixth birthday. "Thank you for congratulations," Stalin now pens. "And good wishes for my birthday. I have always greatly appreciated your friendly sentiments."

That note will be sent to 10 Downing Street in London, even though Churchill is currently enjoying a raucous Christmas celebration aboard the HMS *Ajax* off the coast of Greece.‡

---

*Stalin had a roving eye, and was especially fond of ballet dancers, opera singers, and actresses. He had many trysts, including a dalliance with a female Georgian test pilot and a thirteen-year-old Siberian girl that produced a child out of wedlock. His relationship with Valentina Istomina began when she came to work for him in 1934, when she was nineteen. Their relationship continued until his death in 1953.

†Stalin spoke Georgian as a child. This language of the Black Sea region also has its own alphabet.

‡The celebration featured scores of British officers, and the whisky and champagne flowed freely.

Even as the British officers are celebrating, Stalin-backed Greek Communists are on the move. They are attempting to take control of the entire country, despite the agreement between Churchill and Stalin at their Moscow meeting just two months ago that Greece would be a British sphere of influence. Churchill is learning the hard way that Joseph Stalin is not a man to be trusted.

It is a lesson that young Svetlana Stalin knows all too well.

★ ★ ★

Svetlana once enjoyed Christmas Day a great deal.

Her mother has been dead for thirteen years. Natasha Alliluyeva simply went to bed one night and did not come down for breakfast in the morning. A maid found her alone in her bedroom, dead from a pistol shot. A suicide note was visible on the nightstand.*

Natasha was twenty-three years younger than Stalin, a second wife to replace the one who had died from typhus. Due to the dictator's long-standing proclivity for brutal rape, Natasha incredibly may have been his illegitimate daughter.

"The devil knows whose daughter you are—maybe mine," Stalin once sadistically taunted her.

The suicide was Natasha Alliluyeva's final protest against the Soviet leader's nonstop cruelty and philandering, the bitter end to fourteen years of abuse and neglect.

When her mother died, the five-year-old Svetlana knew nothing about her father's monstrous behavior. All she knew was that her mother was suddenly and mysteriously taken from her in the night. It would be years before she'd come to understand her father's evil disposition, and begin to distance herself from his foul temper and hard drinking.

Yet Joseph Stalin was devoted to Svetlana. "He was a very simple

---

*There is evidence that she may have been murdered. Natasha Alliluyeva was right-handed. The bullet wound appeared in her left temple, which would imply that she used her left hand. In addition, the doctor who did the autopsy reported that there were no powder marks on her skin and that the gunshot took place from at least three feet away. That doctor was later executed.

man, very rude, very cruel," she will remember years later. "There was nothing in him that was complicated. He loved me and wanted me to be with him."

Four years after Natasha's suicide, the Soviet dictator received a most curious party invitation.* The year was 1935. Stalin was invited to a Christmas gala at the British embassy in Moscow. Although he did not believe in Christmas, Stalin saw an opportunity for Svetlana—and maybe even for himself.

Clearly, Stalin could not attend a Christmas party. The Russian people would never have understood. Atheism was the established philosophy in the Soviet Union.

Yet Stalin had celebrated Christmas as a boy, back home in Georgia. Even though his tyrannical alcoholic father often beat him so severely that he urinated blood, young Joseph had a loving mother, and knew the joy and warmth that came with the Christmas season.

Christmas remained important to Stalin as he became a young man. From age fifteen to nineteen, he studied for the priesthood. He had always been rebellious and was only at the seminary because his parents forced him to attend. But still, he remained loyal to the church until the seminary raised its fees and Stalin turned his back on his faith.

That cold night in 1935, Stalin sent Svetlana across the river to the British embassy in his place, perhaps thinking that nothing more might come of it than just a unique holiday experience for his precious daughter.

When she returned, Svetlana gushed about the presents and the wonderful decorations, in particular the stately Christmas tree.

It was the image of the tree that got to Stalin.

Svetlana's description thawed his frozen heart. If the British could experience such a magical celebration, why couldn't the Soviet people? Of course, celebrating Christmas was still out of the question. But the ruthless dictator also realized that he could manipulate such a holiday to his advantage.

So even though the date was fast approaching, Stalin decreed that January 1 would mark a new annual celebration throughout the Soviet

*The Christmas story is perhaps apocryphal, an invention of Soviet propaganda.

empire. The people would not honor the birth of the baby Jesus. The only religion in the Soviet Union was communism, and Stalin himself had demonstrated this, in 1931, by ordering that the Christ the Savior Cathedral, a towering monument to Christianity right in the heart of Moscow, be blown to bits.

No, the Russians would not celebrate the birth of Christ. Never. Instead they would celebrate the great moments of Soviet Russia's twenty-seven-year-old history.

Stalin arranged to have one of his top henchmen, Pavel Postyshev, publish a letter in the state newspaper, *Pravda*. Such a letter changing Soviet state policy would never have been printed without Stalin's direct approval. To do so would have been a crime punishable by death. So Postyshev, who just two years earlier had engineered a man-made famine to ensure the death of hundreds of thousands in Ukraine, clearly spoke for the Soviet dictator. In his letter, Postyshev spoke of a new Soviet holiday. Instead of Santa Claus, a white-bearded figure named Ded Moroz (Grandfather Frost) would travel across the Soviet Union in a sleigh pulled by three horses, delivering presents on New Year's Day. Instead of the Christ child, a youngster named New Year's Boy would be pivotal to the celebration.

And of course there was the tree. No longer would the holiday tree be seen as "religious dope" and a "savage custom," as it had been known throughout the Soviet Union. "It is time to put an end to this wrongful condemnation of the tree," Stalin ordered by proxy, thanks to Postyshev's letter to *Pravda*. "Children's New Year trees should be everywhere—in schools, orphanages, young pioneer clubs, cinemas, and theaters!"

Thus a holiday was born.*

Soviet toy factories began producing red stars to serve as tree toppers, along with New Year's garlands and figurines of Grandfather Frost and New Year's Boy. The Kremlin even opened its doors to Soviet children so that they might celebrate the *Yolka*, "fir tree."

★ ★ ★

---

*Long after Stalin's death and the 1991 collapse of the Soviet Union, the Christmastime celebration in Russia is still commemorated on January 1 with the ceremonial New Year's tree.

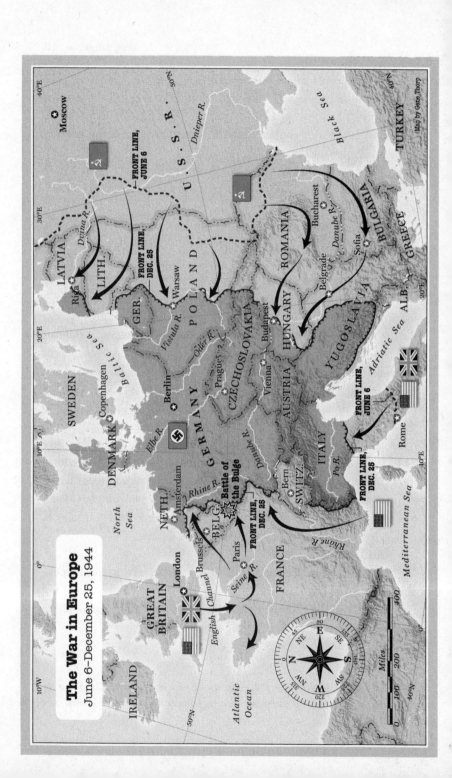

The War in Europe
June 6–December 25, 1944

Map by Gene Thorp

The elaborate staging of a contrived holiday had little effect on Svetlana. Soon, she was completely alienated from her father. The rupture came after she fell in love for the first time in her life, with Alexei Kapler, a Jewish writer and filmmaker twenty-two years her senior—almost exactly the same age gap as that between Joseph Stalin and the suicidal Natasha.

But there will be no marriage between Svetlana and Alexei. Joseph Stalin is determined to be the one and only man in Svetlana's life. On this snowy Christmas Day in 1944, Alexei Kapler now resides five thousand miles away, in the harsh subzero temperatures and round-the-clock darkness of a snow-covered labor camp in Siberia, sent there for "anti-Soviet agitation."

Alexei Kapler would spend ten years in a gulag for the crime of loving Joseph Stalin's daughter.

Merry Christmas, Svetlana.

★ ★ ★

Christmas Day is coming to a close. Stalin finishes his thank-you notes and then turns his attention to reading dispatches from the Battle of the Bulge. He suspects that Adolf Hitler is preoccupied with the Western Front, and perhaps thinks that the Soviet army is using the winter weather to regroup and refortify.

If that is the case, Hitler is wrong. Even at this very minute, the Soviets are hitting the Germans hard in Czechoslovakia and Hungary. And once these nations are wrested from Hitler's grasp, Stalin has every intention of pushing north into the heart of Berlin—planning to get there before the American and British dash, so that he can have all the glory.

If all goes according to Stalin's plan, Eastern Europe will soon be under the control of the Soviet Union. Stalin's troops are not liberating people from the Nazis, they are enslaving them.

With the Americans and British bogged down in eastern France, Joseph Stalin orders his armies to step up their attacks in order to expand his global empire.

The race is on.

12

George S. Patton is tired of breaking his promises. The air in his palatial headquarters, which serves as an old-folks' home in peacetime, is thick with the smell of cigarette smoke and the clack of typewriters. Junior officers and enlisted subordinates make sure to keep their distance from the volatile general as they range in and out of the command post, not wanting to incur the wrath of a clearly exhausted Patton. When a message arrives from Dwight Eisenhower, stating that he "is very anxious that I put every effort on securing Bastogne," Patton nearly explodes.

"What the hell does he think I've been doing for the last week?" Patton will write in his diary, careful, after all his trouble, not to criticize his boss in front of the headquarters staff.

But privately Patton seethes at Eisenhower's poor tactical choices. The Seventeenth Airborne, Eleventh Armored, and Eighty-Seventh Infantry divisions have all been moved one hundred miles back to the French city of Reims as reserves, just in case the German breakthrough goes even deeper into the American lines. "We should attack," he complains to his staff. Patton could sorely use the additional firepower those units would bring to the relief of Bastogne. Instead, they sit in the patient defensive mode that Patton deplores.

"We should attack."

The general broods and studies maps of the front lines. Patton's tank crews are spread out over a thirty-mile-wide front, locked in a stalemate with their German opposites. They are gaining little ground and losing too many men and tanks as they battle for each and every inch of Belgian soil. A German ambush in the hamlet of Chaumont cost Patton eleven Shermans and almost a hundred men. The Fourth Armored also lost scores of tanks in a night attack that advanced their position just a quarter mile.

Even worse is that as soon as the Third Army passes through a town and reclaims it for the Allies, German paratroopers follow right behind. Thanks to intercepted radio messages, they know that the Americans plan to remain constantly on the attack. Thus they move in and take back the towns as soon as the Americans leave.

Dead Americans now lie frozen in the fields outside Bastogne, their faces turned the color of "claret," in Patton's own description, from the blood pooling after death. In his journal, Patton keeps a detailed tally of Allied and German casualties, and knows that Germans are dying in far greater numbers.

But casualties tell only part of the story. The German lines are holding fast. Patton and the Third Army are stuck, and Tony McAuliffe and the 101st Airborne are now enduring yet another day in the violent hellhole of Bastogne. The dirty streets are choked with rubble, and small fires caused by artillery shells are left to burn. The only place a man can feel safe from the constant shelling is hunkered underground in a cellar, where he is at least partially protected from falling debris—thus Tony McAuliffe's decision to relocate his command post to the Belgian barracks. But while there is temporary safety in these bunkers, the tradeoff is the thick, asphyxiating smell of unwashed bodies and clouds of cigarette smoke. And because the soldiers and three thousand civilians that now share Bastogne are reluctant to leave their cellars for any reason, there is also the scent of an aromatic compound known as phenol, or carbolic acid, which is sprinkled on the floors to cover the scent of human excrement and urine.

Elsewhere in Bastogne, American wounded lie atop squalid litters inside an old garage turned into a make-shift field hospital. They cannot help but hear the rasp of the bone saw as army surgeons cut away the destroyed arms and legs of their fellow paratroopers.

The wounded at an aid station on the road leading to the small town of Neufchâteau were helpless to defend themselves when German bombers droned overhead early on Christmas morning. Outside, the nighttime sky was shot through with stars. The weather was beautiful, clear and cold. The wounded could not move. Some were in a drug-induced stupor to halt their pain and others were struggling to sleep. They could hear the sound of Junkers JU-88 long before the bombers were over their targets. After long months on the front lines, they knew how to judge whether a falling bomb was far away or close enough to kill them.

These bombs were very close.

The bomb that struck the field hospital was not a direct hit, but the explosion was so severe that the roof collapsed on top of the wounded men. The building soon caught fire, burning many of the bodies beyond recognition. But most of these were already dead by then, buried under the crushing weight of thousands of toppled bricks.

★   ★   ★

George S. Patton relishes war. He finds it glorious, and thinks there is no finer test of a man's courage. He accepts the fact that horrible death can happen to any man, at any time.

Yet he is not immune to human suffering, and the Battle of the Bulge is taking a hard toll on him. It is within his power to ease the pain and hardship of those embattled men of the 101st Airborne. His failure to do so haunts him.

It has been a week since the meeting with Eisenhower in Verdun. Patton is too keyed up to sleep more than a few hours every night. He is drained and dog-tired. His face is burned bright red from the windblast of too many hours in his open-air jeep. The lines around his blue eyes have become deep fissures. "I saw a tired, aging man," notes a Red Cross volunteer who caught a glimpse of Patton at a Christmas Eve church service. "A sorrowful, solitary man, a lonely man, with veiled eyes behind which there was going on a torment of brooding and depression."

Patton cannot rest. He is failing. "A clear cold Christmas," he wrote in his journal yesterday. "Lovely weather for killing Germans—which seems a bit queer, seeing whose birthday it is . . . I left early this morning to try to visit all the divisions in contact with the enemy. All were very cheerful. I am not, because we are not going fast enough."

There was no Christmas truce, as sometimes occurred during the

First World War. So after arranging for every man in his army to have a turkey dinner—cold sandwiches for the soldiers at the front, a hot meal for those behind the lines—he left early in the morning to visit every one of his combat divisions.

It was a long day, and Patton was not uplifted by what he saw. The only good news came the next morning, when reports that a new sort of artillery fuse was being used effectively against the German strongpoint in the town of Echternach. We "actually killed seven hundred of them," he wrote offhandedly in his journal.

Now he spends the twenty-sixth, Boxing Day,* having heard that some of his tanks are within a half dozen miles of Bastogne. But today, as with yesterday and the day before, victory hardly seems likely. Reports filtering back to his headquarters state that his tank divisions continue to take heavy casualties.

Making matters worse—far worse—is that rather than helping Patton by pushing his own army south toward Bastogne, British field marshal Bernard Law Montgomery refuses to attack. He says his army is not ready. And instead of encouraging Patton's audacious plan to relieve the 101st, Montgomery is deepening their professional rivalry by predicting that Patton and the Third Army will fail.

When Montgomery goes so far as actually to insist to Eisenhower that Patton return to Metz, claiming that Patton's army is too small to take Bastogne, Patton severs all pretense of friendship with his British counterpart. He calls the idea of a retreat to Metz "disgusting."

But Montgomery's behavior only adds to the pressure on Patton, because a simple look at the current battlefield situation map shows that one thing is becoming ever clearer: no one can save the Battered Bastards of Bastogne except for Patton and his Third Army. In fact, no one else is even making the effort.

No one.

---

*So named because this is when British nobility presented their servants with a present known as the "Christmas box." It was understood that they would not receive this present on Christmas Day because they were busy at work, helping their employers with their Yuletide celebration.

★   ★   ★

That same day, the phone in Patton's headquarters rings. Maj. Hugh Gaffey, commanding the Fourth Armored, is on the other end, requesting permission to launch a high-risk attack into Bastogne immediately.

Patton does not hesitate. "I told him to try it," he will write in his journal tonight. With that order, the Fourth Armored Division begins fighting their way toward Tony McAuliffe and the trapped men of the 101st Airborne.

★   ★   ★

Lt. Col. Creighton "Abe" Abrams commands the spearhead Thirty-Seventh Tank Battalion of the Fourth Armored Division. He chews on a long unlit cigar so enormous that his men compare it to the barrel of a gun. Abrams is thirty years old, a lantern-jawed Massachusetts native who graduated from West Point just eight years ago. Some day he will be chief of staff of the army, a four-star general so famous they will name a type of tank after him.

But right now, Abrams is just a bold young tank commander who is making plans to disobey a direct order.

Perched atop a hill just a few miles away from Bastogne, Abrams sits tall in the turret hatch of his Sherman tank, nicknamed Thunderbolt VII. He has already had six Shermans shot out from under him—all named Thunderbolt. In September he was awarded the Distinguished Service Cross for courage under fire. Abrams's men love him, because he is a lax disciplinarian away from the battlefield and knows there is a time and place for fun. But when it comes time to fight, they also know they are expected to do precisely as their commanding officer orders.

A long line of Shermans snakes down the narrow and rutted country road behind Abrams. These tanks also have names: Cobra King, Deuces Wild, Betty, Destruction, and so on.

Abrams has been tasked with capturing the heavily fortified town of Sibret, which lies three miles to the northwest. But his unit is down to just twenty Sherman tanks, and his infantry is short 230 men. Abrams does not like the Sibret scenario, even though that is the plan that his commanding general, George Patton, has just approved.

Lieutenant Colonel Creighton Abrams at his desk in Germany

Scanning the horizon with his high-powered binoculars, Abrams watches hundreds of C-47 cargo planes dropping supplies to the besieged men of Bastogne. Parachutes laden with ammo and food blossom against the leaden sky, but at the same time German antiaircraft fire is shooting down many of the slow-moving, twin-engine supply planes. They spiral to the earth, soon to explode, the pilots consigned to a fiery and instant death.

The sight of this humanitarian airdrop, paired with the knowledge that American soldiers have been suffering and dying inside Bastogne for more than a week, fills Abrams with a sense of urgency. Why attack Sibret? The town is heavily defended, and capturing it will not bring Patton's army closer to Bastogne. Why not bypass Sibret and go directly to McAuliffe's aid?

Abrams ponders that question as he continues to survey the battlefield.

He sees the men of the 101st crouched in their snowy foxholes. He also knows that hundreds of hidden Germans are waiting to destroy any rescuing force.

But Lieutenant Colonel Abrams is convinced he and his men can get through.

So Abrams radios a request for permission to launch an all-out blitz on the tiny hamlets of Clochimont and Assenois. This is the most direct route into Bastogne. If he takes those towns, Abrams can be in Bastogne within hours. But if the impromptu plan fails, his small force will surely be wiped out. The narrow road he plans to use could become a death trap.

The request goes to Major General Gaffey, who passes it along to George Patton.

Patton orders the attack.

★   ★   ★

Abrams soon orders all available American artillery in the area to launch an immediate barrage to soften the German defenses. The thunder of 155 mm guns soon booms across the Belgian countryside, as shell after shell is lobbed on the German positions hidden within Assenois and its forests. In all, more than two thousand rounds will fall on the Wehrmacht fighters today.

"Get those men in Bastogne," Abrams commands his tankers. He waves his arms high in the air, and his tanks churn forward.

There is nothing quick about their movement. The Sherman's top speed is just thirty miles per hour. Nor is there any way to conceal their advance. Thanks to the artillery barrage, the Germans know the Americans are coming. They can now clearly see Abrams and his line of Shermans and halftrack armor steering down the hill into Clochimont.

Abrams closes the hatch and conceals himself inside the three-inch-thick steel of the turret as his and the other Shermans burst through Assenois's ancient town square. German artillery explodes all around. One shell knocks down a telephone pole, blocking the road and bringing the column of five Shermans and a halftrack to a lurching halt.

The pole has to be moved.

Abrams and several other men immediately climb out of their tanks. With sniper fire pinging off steel and glancing off the rutted road, they work as a team to swing the heavy pole out of the way.

Then it's back into their Shermans. Behind them, a column of infantry secures Assenois, and will stay there until the mopping-up action is complete. A second column of foot soldiers travels with Abrams's tanks as

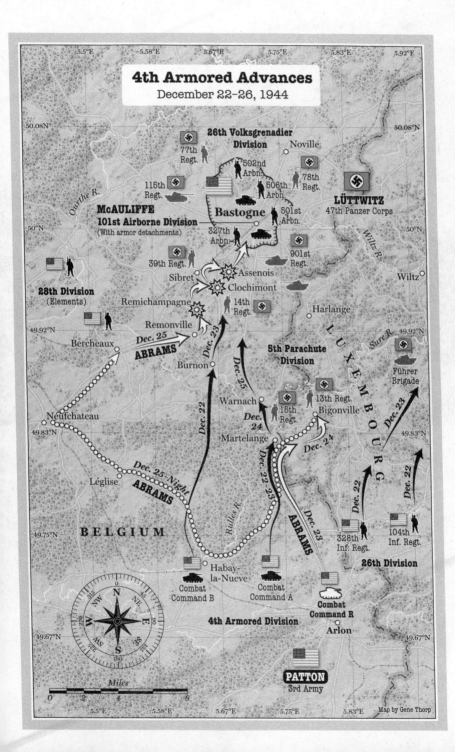

4th Armored Advances
December 22-26, 1944

5.5°E · 5.58°E · 5.67°E · 5.75°E · 5.83°E · 5.92°F

50.08N° · 50.08°N

26th Volksgrenadier Division

77th Regt.

Noville

502nd Arbn.

115th Regt.

506th Arbn.

78th Regt.

LÜTTWITZ
47th Panzer Corps

Bastogne

501st Arbn.

McAULIFFE
101st Airborne Division
(With armor detachments)

50°N · 50°N

327th Arbn.

901st Regt.

Wiltz R.

39th Regt.

Assenois

Sibret

Clochimont

Wiltz

Remichampagne

14th Regt.

Harlange

28th Division
(Elements)

Remonville

L U X E M B O U R G

Sure R.

49.92°N · 49.92°N

Bercheaux

Dec. 25
ABRAMS

Dec. 23

Dec. 25

Burnon

Führer Brigade

5th Parachute Division

Dec. 22

Neufchateau

49.83°N

Warnach

16th Regt.

13th Regt.

Bigonville

Dec. 23

49.83°N

Dec. 24

Martelange

Dec. 24

Léglise

ABRAMS

Dec. 25-Night

Dec. 22-23

Dec. 23

Dec. 22

Dec. 22

ABRAMS

B E L G I U M

Rulles R.

328th Inf. Regt.

104th Inf. Regt.

49.75°N

Habay-la-Nueve

26th Division

Combat Command B

Combat Command A

4th Armored Division

Combat Command R

Arlon

49.67°N · 49.67°N

Miles

0 · 2 · 4 · 8

5.5°E · 5.58°E · 5.67°E · 5.75°E · 5.83°E

PATTON
3rd Army

Map by Gene Thorp

Ourthe R.

American tank destroyers prepare to advance on Bastogne in January 1945

they move toward the concealed German positions in the forest along-side the road through Assenois.

Rather than simply race through the town, Abrams chooses to level it. Every building that might conceal a German becomes a target. The Shermans load and shoot their big 76mm guns as many as seven times per minute. Meanwhile, the infantry ruthlessly hunts down Germans, screaming, "Come out," to induce them to surrender.

"But they wouldn't," one American soldier later remembers. "One poked his head out of a foxhole and I shot him in the neck."

Trouble soon strikes. The jeep carrying the artillery observer is hit before he can give the signal to halt the barrage. The American artillery continues to rain down shells on Assenois, unaware that Abrams and his men are now inside the town. Three hundred and sixty rounds of artillery shells are fired by the American big guns. Geysers of earth erupt throughout the town as each shell forms its own deep crater. Frantic radio calls from Lt. Charles Boggess, who now leads Abrams's spearhead in his tank, Cobra King, go unheard. Americans and Germans both are killed. The American shelling and the nonstop tank barrage are completely decimating Assenois, wiping it off the map as if it never existed. Plumes of fiery smoke and dust turn the daytime sky black. Finally, a spotter plane pilot sees the trouble and orders the artillery to stop.

The Germans lay Teller antitank mines on the road in a last-ditch effort to stop the American breakthrough. None of the Shermans is hit, but an American halftrack explodes when it hits a mine, killing the driver and again bringing the American column to a complete halt. Thinking quickly, Capt. William Dwight, Abrams's operations officer, risks his life by climbing out of his tank and exposing himself to fire as he clears the mines out of the road by hand.

Through the dust and smoke, Pvt. James R. Hendrix, the son of an Arkansas sharecropper, spots two concealed German 88 mm guns. Next to them, hiding in a foxhole, are two Wehrmacht soldiers. Hendrix crouches low and moves toward them through a hedgerow, then presses his body flat in a shell crater as he creeps up on the enemy. Hendrix is just five foot six, and weighs only 125 pounds, but he shows no fear as he prepares to attack the German foxhole alone.

"A feller just figures if it's his time, it's his time, and that's all there is to it," is how he later explains his courage.

Screaming, "Kommen heraus!"—"Come out!" in German—Hendrix runs up to the foxhole with his M-1 aimed squarely at the enemy soldiers.

They don't surrender. Hendrix is forced to shoot one soldier in the head and then smash in the skull of the other with his rifle butt.

"I got their guns and got back in my shell hole and started hollering, 'Kommen heraus,' again, and sure enough, them Germans began coming out from around the different foxholes, and 13 gave up," he will later recall, describing the action that will earn him the Congressional Medal of Honor.

Later that night, in fierce, pitch-black fighting that will see few prisoners taken on either side, Hendrix will add to his legacy by personally knocking out two German machine-gun nests and also braving sniper fire to pull a wounded American from a burning halftrack.*

The battle in the forests surrounding Assenois will continue long into the night, but by afternoon the Americans have carved a small channel through the German lines. The path is less than four hundred yards wide, and Germans are poised on both sides, prepared to counterattack and once again close the road. But for now, American tanks are advancing toward Bastogne.

Boggess fires on a German pillbox on the outskirts of Bastogne. The smoke clears. First Lieutenant Charles Boggess opens the turret of Cobra King and lifts his torso up through the opening. Soldiers in uniform crouch in foxholes across the road to his right, their guns aimed his way. "Come here! Come on out! This is the Fourth Armored," he shouts. He does not yell in German, hoping to find an American reply.

There is no answer. A tense moment passes. With his head and chest completely exposed to rifle fire, Lieutenant Boggess considers his options.

The Sherman 76 mm barrel pivots until it is aimed directly at the foxholes. Pvt. James G. Murphy has already loaded a round, and the gunner, Cpl. Milton Dickerman, awaits the order to fire.

"Come on out!" Boggess nervously shouts again.

A lone soldier walks forward.

"I'm Lieutenant Webster, of the 326th Engineers, 101st Airborne Division," he said. "Glad to see you."

Bastogne has officially been relieved.

Cobra King rolls into the heart of the town, followed by a convoy of Sherman tanks.

Soon, "Abe" Abrams appears.

"Gee, am I mighty glad to see you," says Tony McAuliffe.

Patton's audacious gamble has succeeded. He awards Abrams with the equivalent of a second Distinguished Service Cross and praises him

---

*Hendrix seemed to have been born under a lucky star. A few years later, in September 1949, during parachute maneuvers at Fort Benning, Georgia, he survived a thousand-foot free fall when his primary and reserve parachutes failed to open. He landed on his back, in the soft earth of a freshly plowed field. He suffered minor bruises but no broken bones.

as America's top tank commander—even saying that Abrams is a better tank commander than he.

★ ★ ★

The next morning, December 27, 1944, George Patton once again walks to the front of a small Catholic chapel and drops to his knees in prayer.

"Sir, this is Patton again," he begins with an air of contrition. "And I beg to report complete progress. Sir, it seems to me that You have been much better informed about the situation than I was, because it was that awful weather which I cursed You so much which made it possible for the German army to commit suicide. That, Sir, was a brilliant military move,* and I bow humbly to Your supreme genius."†

★ ★ ★

The German advance stalled on Christmas Eve 1944. Basically, the Germans overran their supply lines. And without ammunition and gasoline, they were unable to wage an offensive campaign. The continued progress of Patton and his Third Army eventually spelled doom for Operation Watch on the Rhine. By January 25, 1945, the Germans had retreated back to the same positions they had held at the start of the offensive six

---

*Another stumbling block was the American Ninety-Ninth Division. They held the northern shoulder of the Bulge assault, inflicting tremendous casualties on the Germans in the Battle of Elsenborn Ridge. Despite the fact that the Wehrmacht offensive had sputtered, the Germans did not give much ground until Patton was able to relieve Bastogne. In fact, on January 1, the Germans launched Operation Baseplate (Unternehmen Bodenplatte), a last-gasp aerial bombardment on Allied airfields by the Luftwaffe. It was a success, resulting in the destruction of 465 American and British aircraft. However, the sorely depleted Luftwaffe also lost nearly 300 planes, which pretty much finished it as a fighting force.

†The citation for Abrams's Bronze Oak Leaf Cluster (awarded in lieu of a second Distinguished Service Cross) concludes by describing the final moments of the Bastogne breakthrough: "Heedless of approaching darkness and strong enemy defenses, he brilliantly led his battalion on to a further objective. Lieutenant Colonel Abrams' intrepid actions, personal bravery and zealous devotion to duty exemplify the highest traditions of the military forces of the United States and reflect great credit upon himself, the 4th Armored Division and the United States Army."

weeks earlier. Thus ended the last great German attack on the Western Front. "The relief of Bastogne is the most brilliant operation we have thus far performed, and is in my opinion the outstanding achievement of this war," Patton writes home to his wife, Beatrice.

"Now the enemy must dance to our tune, not we to his."

13

———•———

WHITE HOUSE
WASHINGTON, DC
JANUARY 20, 1945*
11:55 A.M.

War is never far from the minds of Americans, even on a unique day in the nation's history.

Hope that the Second World War would end by New Year's Day has long been abandoned. Wounded soldiers, many on crutches, are among the seven thousand invited guests tromping through harsh weather to witness Franklin Delano Roosevelt's swearing-in as president of the United States. This will be the first inaugural address during wartime since Abraham Lincoln spoke eighty years ago, in 1865. Also, this is the first inaugural to be held at the White House, in "the president's backyard," as the South Lawn is known. Finally, this is the first and only time an American president will be sworn in for a fourth term.

A light snow dusts the White House on this Saturday morning as spectators show their invitations to the security guards, then pass onto

---

*The Twentieth Amendment officially moved the inaugural date from March 4 to January 20. The reason for this change was that the pace of modern communications meant that news of a president's election no longer took several months to travel around the country; nor did it take months for the president to travel to Washington, DC, to take office. The new amendment was ratified in 1933, and took effect for FDR's second inaugural in 1937. The Twenty-Second Amendment to the Constitution, ratified in 1947, makes it unlawful for a president to be elected to more than two terms.

President Roosevelt speaking at his fourth inauguration ceremony

the wintry lawn. It stopped snowing three hours ago, but the skies are threatening yet another storm. No seats await, so the seven thousand guests remain standing—even those soldiers balancing on crutches. Thirteen of Roosevelt's grandchildren pose for a newsreel cameraman atop the stairs of the South Portico, just a few steps from the podium. FDR's chief of staff, Harry Hopkins, stands ground level at the bottom of the stairs, fastidiously overseeing the proceedings.

In addition to the veterans and dignitaries,* a smattering of black faces can be seen in the crowd, reflecting Roosevelt's hope for a more racially integrated nation. The diverse attendees stand side by side in the elements, awaiting the noon start. Wartime shortages of gasoline and lumber mean that the traditional post-inaugural parade will not happen, and the swearing-in ceremony promises to be brisk.

As the seconds tick down, the crowd presses closer and closer to the White House walls. Only a thin barrier of Secret Service agents and Washington, DC, police protect the curved outcropping known as the South Portico.

---

*Gen. George C. Marshall, Adm. Ernest King, Secretary of War Harold Stimson.

At the stroke of twelve, Rev. Angus Dun steps to the lectern to begin the proceedings. The Right Reverend is bishop of the Protestant Episcopal Diocese of Washington. Dun is a pacifist, which makes him an odd selection to deliver the invocation in a time of all-out war. Even more intriguing, Dun is visibly handicapped. He balances on crutches, having lost one leg to polio. His hands and remaining foot are deformed. Perhaps it can be said that the clergy is the only profession that would embrace a handicapped individual in this day and age, yet the fact remains that Dun has prospered. And unlike President Roosevelt, who would never dare reveal his handicap, Angus Dun* does not hide who he is. Thus it is fitting that just eighty-three days hence, at a time when such fears will be completely meaningless to FDR, Angus Dun will also lead prayers at the president's funeral service.

* * *

Harry S. Truman, the sixty-year-old senator from Missouri, steps to the lectern to be sworn in as vice president. This is a time of austerity in America and around the world, so Truman and Roosevelt have chosen to forgo formal dress, preferring instead to wear dark business suits.

The new vice president places his left hand on a family Bible and raises his right to take the oath of office. He is a small, wiry man with an infectious grin, a man unafraid to cry in public but able to conceal his emotions when a situation turns competitive. Those unlucky enough to sit across the poker table from Harry S. Truman know this all too well. The S does not stand for anything; that single letter is his actual middle name. It was once Truman's dream to attend West Point, but poor eyesight ended that ambition, making necessary the glasses he now wears. Truman, however, fought as an officer in the First World War. He aced the vision exam before his induction into the military by memorizing the eye chart.

---

*The practice of a presidential invocation did not begin until 1937. Chaplain of the Senate ZeBarney Thorne Phillips delivered the prayer then, and again in 1941. He died in 1942, whereupon FDR selected Dun to replace him. With the exception of Billy Graham in 1989, 1993, and 1997, Phillips is the only cleric to perform the invocation more than once. A minor footnote is that Angus Dun's father was cofounder of the credit rating firm Dun and Bradstreet.

President Harry S. Truman in 1945

Truman made the leap from a small-time county commissioner to Missouri senator just ten years ago. And at times the power in Washington still overwhelms him. Now is such a moment. He and FDR barely know each other, and the president clearly has no interest in asking Truman's advice about how to run the country. It is also widely known that Truman did not campaign for this new job. In fact, he was initially reluctant to accept the vice president's spot on the ticket when it was offered at the Democratic Convention last July. Foreseeing his own death, FDR had sought to replace his current vice president, Iowa native Henry Wallace, with someone less liberal and less inclined to align himself too closely with the labor movement. Roosevelt studied the dossiers of several candidates before settling on the pragmatic Truman.

But it was left to a friend and longtime political aide to convince Harry Truman to take the job. "I think, Senator, that you're going to do it," Edward D. McKim told him one night during the Chicago convention.

Truman got angry. "What makes you think I'm going to do it?"

McKim knows Truman well, and has a deep knowledge of how to push his good friend's emotional buttons. "Because there's a little ninety-year-old mother down in Grandview, Missouri, that would like to see her son become president of the United States."

Truman teared up at the image of his mother. He stormed out of the room and refused to speak with McKim.

McKim was unfazed. He was well aware that fear played a part in Truman's reluctance, for there was enormous pressure in accepting the Chicago nomination. "The consensus of opinion at the whole convention was that whoever was nominated for the vice presidency would eventually be president of the United States."

And this does not mean waiting four more years until Roosevelt finishes his term. The president's ill health is now a very poorly kept secret. Even as he swears the oath of office, Truman is quite certain that FDR will soon die—and that he will become the thirty-third president.

That is a notion, in the words of another Truman confidant, "that scares the very devil out of him."

When the ballots were finally cast at the 1944 Democratic Convention, 1,176 delegates were asked to select the party's new vice presidential candidate. Senator Harry Truman garnered 90 percent of the vote. Incumbent vice president Henry Wallace received just 9 percent.

Now, eleven weeks after the Roosevelt-Truman ticket's landslide victory over Thomas Dewey's Republican ticket, the crowd in Washington bears witness as Truman recites the oath. It is an awkward moment, for the man swearing him in is none other than Henry Wallace, the ultraliberal vice president he is now replacing.

Soon it is done. Harry Truman is the vice president of the United States.

Now Franklin Delano Roosevelt is helped to his feet and begins the shuffle of hips and swinging of leg braces that approximates his version of a walk. Supported by the steel bands around his legs and hips that are concealed beneath his dark blue business suit, Roosevelt stands before the chief justice of the Supreme Court, Harlan Stone. His left hand rests on the same Dutch-language Bible as was used in his first three inaugurals. Per FDR's tradition, the Bible is open to 1 Corinthians 13, which teaches that of the three virtues, faith, hope, and love, the greatest trait mankind can display is love.

FDR has six children and is devoted to his thirteen grandchildren, who now watch him from just a few feet away. He also has a wife to whom he has remained married for forty years. In his own way, FDR loves them all.

But Franklin Roosevelt's biggest love is reserved for the American people, whom he has led through twelve daunting years of deprivation and warfare. Roosevelt was first elected president just five weeks before Adolf Hitler became chancellor of Germany, but while Hitler has pursued a course of evil that is destroying his nation, Roosevelt has lifted America up from the lowest point in U.S. history to make it the most powerful nation on earth. He has done the people of America one final great favor by ensuring that his successor will not be an ideological extremist, but a man of the people who will do his best to heal the nation when the war inevitably ends. In this way, FDR does not repeat the mistake of Abraham Lincoln, who selected Andrew Johnson as his second vice president. Johnson's bumbling presidency deepened the rifts and divisions after the Civil War ended and Lincoln was assassinated. As FDR well knows, some of the problems Johnson created exist to this day.*

The crowd pressing in on the South Lawn does not know upon which Bible verse Roosevelt's hand rests. But they can hear his love in the timbre of his voice—so confident and assured, the father figure who will work tirelessly to lead the nation out of danger.

---

*Andrew Johnson was the senator and military governor of Tennessee chosen by Lincoln to serve as vice president during his second term. Johnson showed up severely hungover for his inaugural on March 4, 1865—and then proceeded to take two stiff shots of whisky before delivering a rambling address to the Senate. On the day that Lincoln was assassinated, Johnson was also targeted for murder but was spared when his killer lost his nerve. Upon his ascension to the presidency, Johnson was divisive and inept. Many of the so-called red states and blue states that exist in American politics today can trace their roots back to Johnson's lack of leadership at a time in the country's history when healing instead of settling scores should have been foremost. He was impeached by the House of Representatives but avoided conviction by the Senate by just one vote. He was charged with violating the now-repealed Tenure of Office Act, which was passed the previous year specifically to restrict the powers of his presidency. Johnson managed to fight the charges over the course of the ensuing three-month trial and served out the rest of his term. He actually tried to run for the presidency once again that summer, but his lack of popularity made that impossible. Johnson was so bitter about not getting the chance to serve four more years that he refused to attend the inaugural of his successor, Gen. Ulysses S. Grant.

When they draw him, political cartoonists like to accentuate FDR's strong, uplifted chin. This is how FDR actually appears as he recites the oath of office, a symbol of authority and optimism. And despite the heart disease that is slowly killing him, and the bone-thin legs that can barely support him, the president hardly looks ill. His posture is ramrod straight, his complexion a healthy pink, and his voice strong and clear.

The oath of office complete, FDR now turns to the crowd of seven thousand, and to millions of Americans listening on the radio, and prepares to deliver his final inaugural address.

★ ★ ★

Four thousand miles away, Gen. George S. Patton is not paying attention to the inaugural. Patton, who thinks highly of Roosevelt, and whom the president fondly addresses in person as the "Old Cavalryman" and "Our greatest fighting general—a pure joy," is too busy directing the mop-up to be done on the battlefields of Luxembourg and Belgium, and enduring military politics.

Once again, Dwight Eisenhower is ignoring Patton. Having done the impossible, Patton is once again benched. Rather than having his top general lead the drive into Germany, Eisenhower is putting his strategic weight behind British field marshal Bernard Law Montgomery, who has demanded that he lead the decisive Allied push to the Rhine River. Montgomery cleverly planned for this next wave of combat by withholding most British troops from the Battle of the Bulge. While Patton's Third Army was taking casualties and losing scores of tanks and halftracks, Montgomery was husbanding his resources. Now, fresh and unscathed, the British army and those American units under Montgomery's command are the new tip of the Allied spear. Meanwhile, as the inaugural takes place in Washington, Patton and the Third Army are relegated to rooting out the last pockets of German resistance in the Bulge.

Knowing that being bitter and angry will not help his cause in the slightest, Patton tries to put a positive spin on the situation.

"Saw a lot of dead Germans today, frozen in funny attitudes," he writes to his wife, Beatrice. "I got some good pictures, but did not have my color camera, which was a pity.

"They are definitely on the run, and have suffered more than we hoped."

★ ★ ★

"Wild Bill" Donovan is furious.

He is in Chungking, China, in the last week of a monthlong around-the-world tour that began in Washington, DC, at the same time Bastogne was being liberated. As always, he is driven by personal, not ideological, motivations. It is his deep desire that his Office of Strategic Services (OSS) remain the world's most elite clandestine organization. And as with the Soviet Union and Joseph Stalin, Donovan has no moral or ethical qualms about dealing with the Communists. He is positioning himself and the OSS for a prominent place in the postwar world. Nothing must stand in his way. And since it is clear to Donovan that Communists will be a powerful global presence once Germany and Japan surrender, he is more than happy to deal with them.

The Chinese Communist rebels want twenty million dollars to purchase arms for themselves to battle China's Japanese occupiers. Dono-

"Wild Bill" Donovan during the Nuremberg Trials

van is not concerned that this angers China's existing national government and its leader Chiang Kai-shek, which rightly fears that the Communists will someday attempt to take over the country. Nor is Donovan concerned that twenty million dollars is far more money than the Communists require for such a task.

What concerns Donovan is that his secret slush fund, provided for him by Congress and its War Agencies Appropriations Act of 1944, is just twenty-one million dollars. The terms of the money are that Donovan can spend it any way he likes, without regard to oversight or legality. That money is meant to cover all his far-flung spy operations, from France to Germany to Greece and even into the Vatican. Giving almost all his funds to the Chinese Communists would be ridiculous.

Donovan sends a counteroffer to the Communist Chinese leader Mao Tse-tung,* hoping he will lower their price.

But today the Chinese are not the source of Donovan's fury. His focus is on Europe. Donovan seethes about the capture of OSS operatives near Patton's headquarters. The event happened in September, and began with a flirtation at the bar of Paris's Ritz Hotel between American socialite Gertrude Sanford Legendre and a U.S. naval commander who doubled as one of Donovan's spies. The pair quickly struck up a romantic friendship, then borrowed a rented Peugeot and left for a joyride to the front. Gertrude, an undercover OSS agent, wanted to pay a visit to the headquarters of her friend George S. Patton.

Soon they made the mistake of unwittingly crossing into Germany, where the Nazis promptly captured them. Legendre quickly became the subject of a massive propaganda blast by the Germans, portrayed as the first woman POW on the Western Front.

The story was picked up by the global media. Legendre had the good sense to tell her captors that she was nothing more than a Red Cross employee, but Donovan knows that it is just a matter of time before

---

*The fifty-one-year-old Mao Tse-tung led China's revolutionary Communist regime. After the Japanese surrendered in August 1945, the Chinese Communists overthrew the ruling Nationalist Party government led by Chiang Kai-shek. From 1949 onward, Mao Tse-tung ruled China with a despotic grasp that rivaled that of Hitler and Stalin. Mao died in 1976 at age eighty-two.

Gestapo* interrogators break her. Legendre is privy to an enormous amount of top-secret information that could damage OSS clandestine operations. So while Donovan is concerned about their fates, he is equally outraged that his two spies allowed themselves to be captured in such ridiculous fashion. There will be no forgiveness if they return alive. Wild Bill Donovan is a man who believes in retribution and punishment. Those who run afoul of his agenda will pay a heavy price.

Patton, of course, had nothing to do with their capture. But Donovan is wary of the general, due to Patton's notorious mistrust of the Russians. There is growing sentiment in Washington that Patton's soaring popularity must be brought back down to earth. It was no secret in American G-2 (intelligence) circles or the military press that certain politicians and generals did not want George Patton to garner more laurels, a war correspondent who traveled with the Third Army will write after the war.

So Donovan keeps an eye on Patton as he waits for news about his missing spies, and secretly monitors the many situations around the globe that might somehow affect his postwar power.

Meanwhile, as Donovan is set to fly from Chungking to visit his British counterparts† in Ceylon, the Chinese Communists come back with their counteroffer.

They want more money, not less.

Donovan says he will get back to them.

---

*The Gestapo was Nazi Germany's official secret police. Under the supervision of Heinrich Himmler, this branch of the SS terrorized and murdered anyone who might represent a threat to the Nazi Party. Even law-abiding Germans lived in fear of a visit from the Gestapo, who were often clad in civilian clothing. The Gestapo headquarters, on Prinz-Albrecht-Strasse in Berlin, featured underground cells where prisoners were held and tortured. The remains of those cells can be seen today at the Topography of Terror Museum in Berlin, which is built upon the large city block that was once home to the Gestapo. The buildings comprising Himmler's headquarters have all been demolished. All traces of that awful legacy have been replaced by a stark landscape of gray stones, and no vegetation. The entire city block will never again be developed.

†There is some evidence that Donovan, a well-known Anglophile, was a double agent working for the British. But that has never been proven.

★ ★ ★

The president's voice is strong and clear.

"We Americans of today, together with our allies, are passing through a period of supreme test. It is a test of our courage, of our resolve, of our wisdom, of our essential democracy," Roosevelt tells the nation.

As he looks out on the crowd standing below him on the South Lawn, he does not make eye contact with anyone in that sea of overcoats, scarves, and fedoras. Indeed, he does not make any attempt to recognize them at all. The president's gaze remains fixed on a line of trees in the far distance. His thoughts are focused on the microphone before him, knowing that his pitch-perfect vocal delivery will have far more impact on the millions listening on the radio.

"Our constitution of 1787 was not a perfect instrument; it is not perfect yet. But it provided a firm base upon which all manner of men, of all races and colors and creeds, could build our solid structure of democracy.

"And so today, in this year of war, 1945, we have learned lessons—at a fearful cost—and we shall profit by them.

"We have learned that we cannot live alone, at peace; that our own well-being is dependent on the well-being of other nations far away. We have learned that we must live as men, not as ostriches, nor as dogs in the manger.

"We can gain no lasting peace if we approach it with suspicion and mistrust or with fear. We can gain it only if we proceed with the understanding, the confidence, and the courage which flow from conviction."

After a few final sentences invoking the blessing of the Almighty, Franklin Delano Roosevelt concludes his fourth inaugural address. It is just 558 words long—only George Washington's second inaugural was shorter. Fifteen minutes after the ceremony began, it is over.

The crowd files back out of the White House grounds without commotion or celebration. They have achieved their goal: they have seen history made.

Harry Truman returns to his office in the Senate Building and begins cleaning out his desk.

And Franklin Delano Roosevelt turns his attention to an event even more pivotal than his inauguration: next week's meeting with Winston Churchill and Joseph Stalin to determine the fate of Nazi Germany.

It will take place in a seaside Soviet resort town known as Yalta.

14

AUSCHWITZ-BIRKENAU*
OŚWIĘCIM, POLAND
JANUARY 26, 1945
1:00 A.M.

The earth convulses as Krema V explodes. Tongues of flame turn the coal-black winter sky a bright red. Nazi SS guards watch the inferno intently, but only for as long as it takes to know that the destruction is complete, and there will be no need to place another round of dynamite charges. The grisly evidence is now destroyed.

The guards march to the nearby barracks and order the prisoners out into the snow. The skeletal children with their prison tattoos and shaved heads respond immediately, knowing that the punishment for being too slow is a bullet. The prisoners get in line. The SS guards are normally fond of neat, military-style rows, which allow them to take a head count. But on this night they are in a hurry.

The prisoners are ordered to march. Their destination is unclear, but the road soon takes them past the railroad gate where they first entered this hellhole. They are leaving Birkenau, though they know not why.

---

*While the term *concentration camp* is widely used to describe the many places where the Nazis tortured and killed their enemies, real and imagined, six facilities (Chelmno, Belzec, Sobibor, Treblinka, Majdanek, and Auschwitz-Birkenau) also carried the term *extermination camp*, because most prisoners were murdered immediately upon their arrival. Auschwitz-Birkenau served the dual purpose of forced labor/extermination camp.

The entrance to Auschwitz

Their way is lit by the burning remains of Krema V. That horrible red-brick building where hundreds of thousands of their fellow prisoners entered, but where none walked out. Jews, Gypsies, homosexuals, and the handicapped were led inside, locked in an airtight room, and then gassed when a cyanide-based pesticide known as Zyklon B* was dropped through the ventilation system. Death came slowly as the prisoners, unable to breathe, tried to claw their way out of the room, leaving scratch marks on the walls.

The bodies were then burned inside special ovens, with ashes going up the chimney flu, where they belched forth into the Polish sky and floated to the ground like snow, covering the nearby forests, ponds, and fields. The smell of death dominated the land.

But Krema V is no more. The other four Auschwitz crematoria have also been detonated. Adolf Hitler has ordered that the murders be stopped and that all proof of his atrocities be destroyed. Though taking heavy losses, the Soviet army has blown through the German defenses

---

*Each of the five crematoria at Auschwitz featured a room for gassing victims and ovens for burning the bodies. When the number of bodies became too much for the ovens to handle—as with the deportation of Hungarian Jews from March to November of 1944 following the success of Otto Skorzeny's Operation Mickey Mouse—the bodies were burned outdoors. A large pit behind Krema V served this purpose.

in Czechoslovakia and Hungary, and is rapidly advancing west. To the north, the Russians have captured Warsaw, and are racing through Poland with the intent of occupying Berlin before the Americans and their Allies can get there. The Russians are so close to Auschwitz that the boom of their artillery can be heard in the distance, and the occasional barrel flash of a launching shell limns the horizon. The SS guards who have been ordered to destroy the crematoria are eager to move on, or they will soon become Russian prisoners—a certain death sentence for them.

But even now, when their thoughts are filled with plans to escape, the SS cannot stop themselves from killing. It has become a way of life for them over the past few years, as routine as eating breakfast. They have shot thousands by lining them up against the notorious "Black Wall," as the firing squad barrier next to the medical experiments barracks is known. Now, as the SS men prod the prisoners through the snow, moving them to another section of the concentration camp on a road lined with electrified barbwire fences, those child prisoners unwilling or unable to walk the mile from the Birkenau section of the death camp* to the main section of Auschwitz are immediately shot dead.

Those who bend down to quench their thirst by scooping snow into their mouths are shot dead.

Many of the children now marching through the snow are twins who have been the subject of cruel experiments by a madman named Dr. Josef Mengele.† Those who stop to help their twins are also shot dead.

Ten-year-old Eva Mozes and her twin sister, Miriam, stumble through the snow. As veterans of Mengele's experiments, their bodies are shattered. The "Angel of Death" showed them just one act of kindness by allowing them to keep their hair—but only until a lice infestation forced the shaving

---

*Auschwitz was divided into three sections: the main camp, the extermination camp (Birkenau), and a labor camp four miles away that serviced the IG Farben chemical factory. There were also a number of subcamps in the region.

†Among the experiments were injecting dye into a child's eyes to see if the iris's color could be changed, injecting the bodies with germs and diseases to study the physical reaction, and performing operations without anesthetic. On one occasion, Mengele attempted to create a Siamese twin by sewing the bodies of identical Gypsy children to one another, back to back, and connecting their veins and internal organs. The two girls died a few days later when gangrene set in.

of their heads. The wind cuts through the thin prison rags the girls wear. Eva and Miriam's toes tingle and then go numb in their loose-fitting clogs. They have been in Auschwitz for almost a year. They were the only Jews in their hometown of Portz, Romania, and until 1944 no one seemed to pay much attention to them. But then the Nazis forced them to move out of their home and into a Jewish ghetto to await transport to Auschwitz.

The memory of their arrival is still seared into Eva's brain. After a four-day ride from the Jewish ghetto in Şimleu Silvaniei, they stepped off the cattle cars. Guards* yelled "Schnell, schnell"—"Quickly, quickly!"—as dog handlers allowed their snarling animals to lunge at the new arrivals.

The twins' father, Alexander, and two older sisters, Edit and Aliz, were immediately separated from the rest of the family.

Jaffa, the girls' mother, sought to protect her young daughters. She grasped each one tightly by the hand. But a quick-thinking guard immediately noticed the twins. That's what they'd been trained to do: find twins and dwarves. With a gleam in his eye, that guard took the two girls to the special children's barracks reserved for the patients of Dr. Mengele. Eva and Miriam screamed at the top of their lungs, crying and pleading as Jaffa was torn from them, soon to be gassed and burned. They never saw her again.

At age ten, the girls were completely on their own. Nevertheless, they

---

*Each concentration camp was administered by an SS-Totenkopfverband, or "Death's Head Unit." These units, usually clad in black from head to toe, were divided into two groups, one overseeing daily life in the camps and the other responsible for perimeter security. A commandant oversaw the unit and the camps. Guards had complete discretion regarding punishment and brutality, and many of them had come to their new callings after a prewar life of crime. Wounded SS soldiers on the front were often transferred to concentration camp duty to recover from their injuries. Also, the inverse was often true, with SS guards ordered to leave the camp and serve on the front lines if they showed themselves to be soft or unwilling to commit atrocities. Life as an Auschwitz guard was relatively easy, with steady supplies of liquor, illicit sexual relationships with prisoners, and a social life of which soldiers on the front lines could only dream. For this reason, SS guards were more than willing to follow orders, no matter how brutal or morally questionable they might have been. In the chilling words of SS guard Oskar Gröning, "The main camp of Auschwitz was like a small town, with its gossiping and chatting. There was a grocery, a canteen, a cinema. There was a theatre with regular performances. And there was a sports club of which I was a member. It was all fun and entertainment, just like a small town."

were determined to live. "The first time I went to use the latrine located at the end of the children's barracks, I was greeted by the scattered corpses of several children lying on the ground," Eva will later remember. "It was there that I made a silent pledge—a vow to make sure that Miriam and I didn't end up on that filthy floor."

Auschwitz-Birkenau was built on top of a swamp, so conditions in the cramped barracks are always damp. A railway spur has run through the heart of the camp since spring of 1944, delivering new prisoners several times each day. Once the cattle cars stopped at the unloading ramp, prisoners were ordered to leave their belongings behind and to line up for processing. The elderly and women with children were designated for immediate extermination. Anyone under fourteen was also sent directly to the gas chambers, which made Eva and Miriam very lucky to be alive.

In all, 80 percent of those who survived the horrible journey from their homes to Auschwitz were sent straight to the gas chambers; only those deemed capable of working as slave labor were allowed to live.

There is no good job to have in a concentration camp. Some prisoners are chosen to serve as a kapo, a leader of the other prisoners. Along with that come extra rations, but also the dirty work of collaborating with the Nazis by spying on fellow prisoners, effectively signing the death sentences of those who step out of line.

The worst job of all goes to the prisoners who look fit and strong enough to serve in a Sonderkommando. They will work the ovens, observing the SS Blockführer as he gives the order to fill the gas chambers with Zyklon B, and then, afterward, carrying dead bodies from the gas chambers to the crematoria for burning. Each day they will grow weaker, thanks to the meager Auschwitz meal portions. And once they can no longer work, they themselves will be led into the gas chamber one final time.

The entire Auschwitz complex is ringed by barbwire and overseen by armed SS guards standing in almost three dozen watchtowers. The Birkenau section backs up to a forest, and any inmate who can find a way through the wire to make a run for it is shot on sight.

But this does not prevent escape attempts. Just a few months ago, in October 1944, two hundred and fifty Sonderkommandos smuggled gunpowder into Krema IV and blew it up. They then cut through the fence and escaped into the forest. But the SS quickly surrounded them. Though

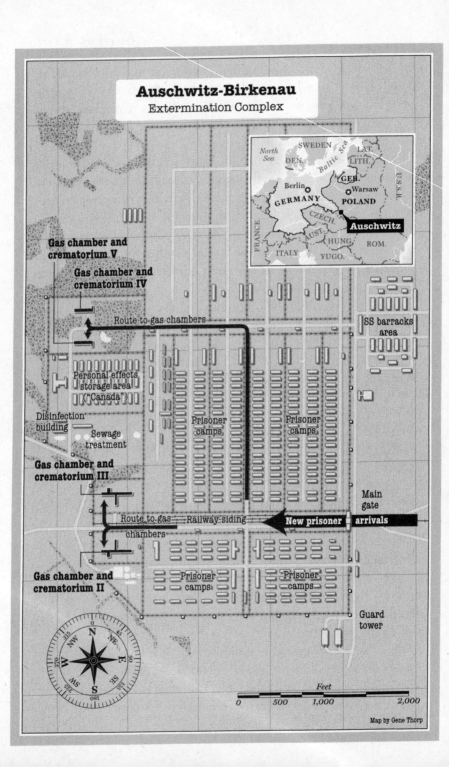

they lost three of their own in the attack, the SS killed all two hundred and fifty Sonderkommandos, then hanged four women suspected of smuggling the gunpowder out of a munitions factory and giving it to the mutineers.*

Upon arrival at Auschwitz, those chosen to live are given a uniform that they will wear night and day: smocks for the women, pants and shirts for the men. Normal footwear is replaced by clogs made of wood or leather, but no socks, causing many prisoners to get blisters, which eventually lead to infection. In many cases that leads to a slow and agonizing death from gangrene.

Hundreds of barracks house the brutalized prisoners. There are skylights but no windows. The floors are bare earth, and inmates sleep on wooden bunks stacked three tiers high. Rats are everywhere. The captives scratch constantly at the lice infesting their clothes and hair. The mattress is lice-infested straw, and blankets are often nothing more than rags.

Food is precious—and hoarded. Breakfast is just a cup of imitation coffee or tea. Lunch is thin soup. And dinner is a piece of black bread and a sliver of sausage. It is common practice to take a bite of bread, and then hide the rest in the lining of clothes until morning. When a prisoner dies in the night, the body is quickly searched for any hoarded bread.

Since March, Eva and Miriam have endured injections that have made their bodies swell and fevers soar. They have even heard Mengele himself laugh that they had just weeks to live. But even when death seemed imminent, Eva and Miriam knew they had to stay alive for each other. "If I had died," Eva later explained. "My twin sister Miriam would have been killed with an injection to the heart and then Mengele would have done the comparative autopsies."

---

*There were 144 successful escapes from Auschwitz, including that of four prisoners who dressed in SS uniforms and drove out through the main gate in Commandant Rudolf Höss's personal automobile. The four were never caught. Höss, on the other hand, was hanged in 1947 for war crimes. A special gallows was constructed in the heart of Auschwitz for the occasion. It stands there to this day.

The monstrous Mengele* fled Auschwitz nine days ago, moving west with his files of research, to keep ahead of the Russians. Eva and Miriam Mozes remained behind, alive. But they are suffering from skin disease caused by lice bites, and their clothes are mere scraps of fabric. So now, with the Soviet army closing in on Auschwitz, they have no idea what will come next. The road on which the twins are marching leads directly to the Black Wall.

The prisoners march through the gates into Auschwitz I, as the main compound is known, passing beneath the sign that mocks them with the words *Arbeit Macht Frei*—"Work Will Set You Free."† This is a lie. Nothing will set them free but death or the liberation of the camps.

Normally a small city of prisoners, Auschwitz is nearly empty. The Nazis are dependent upon slave labor, and have transported sixty thousand Auschwitz prisoners off to other concentration camps.‡

Eva and Miriam stand in the heart of Auschwitz. Corpses are everywhere. Some have been shot, and others simply starved to death. The bodies are contorted and unattended, frozen into the exact shape as when they breathed their last.

The twins have been left behind because the SS guards believe they

---

*Josef Mengele went on to be captured by the Americans soon after the war ended, but was released because he'd faked his identity. Mengele then successfully fled Germany to begin a new life in South America, where he was protected by corrupt local authorities in Argentina and Brazil. Ongoing efforts by Israel and West Germany to have him repatriated for trial failed. In 1979, Mengele suffered a stroke while swimming off the coast of Brazil and drowned. He was buried under a false name, but his body's location was discovered six years later. To this day, the body is stored in the São Paulo Institute for Forensic Medicine. His story was the basis for the novel *The Boys from Brazil*.

†On a normal morning in Auschwitz, a prison orchestra played music near the sign as prisoners marched to work. The rhythm made it easier for them to march in time, which also made it easier for the guards to perform the daily head count.

‡Of those sixty thousand, fifteen thousand died in the death marches just before the arrival of the Soviet army. Some froze due to lack of clothing and shoes, but most were shot when they became unable to continue walking. Their bodies lined the roads leading to the railheads of Loslau and Gleiwitz, where unheated cattle cars awaited them. The trains took them to infamous concentration camps such as Dachau, Bergen-Belsen, and Buchenwald. Many who made the march called it the worst period they spent in Nazi captivity.

will not survive. With the Soviets so close, they have no time for any more killing. Instead, SS men pile into trucks and frantically race away from Auschwitz, leaving the prisoners either to starve to death or to fall into the hands of the Russians.

A thousand prisoners mill about the camp or huddle inside the barracks. Among them is Dr. Adelaide Hautval, a French psychologist who was convicted of being an *asozial*—Nazi parlance for anyone whose behavior disrupts their idea of what constitutes proper social etiquette. Jesuit priests also fall into this category, as do Communists, socialists, and the more than one hundred thousand homosexuals who have died or will die in the death camps.

Hautval's crime was publicly protesting that Jews in Nazi-occupied France were being treated unfairly. For this, she was sent to Auschwitz almost two years ago, where she has stayed alive by working in the hospital, treating those women suffering from the typhus that so often accompanies rat infestation. Many prisoners call her the Saint, but what the twins do not know is that Dr. Hautval refused to follow Mengele's direct order that she perform grotesque surgeries on them.

And so the prisoners wait. Are they really free? Or will some worse fate befall them? Because if they've learned anything from their time in the death camps, it's that just when things can't seem to get more horrific they always do.

Meanwhile, the SS guards have vanished into the night.

★　★　★

A fifty-five-year-old German Jew lies in his wooden bunk in the men's sick barracks at Auschwitz. It is 3:00 p.m. on January 27, 1945. Otto Frank's daughters are not as lucky as Eva and Miriam Mozes, who will survive Auschwitz and go on with their lives. The Frank family moved to the Netherlands when the rise of Nazism increased anti-Jewish sentiment in Germany. On May 25, 1942, the London *Telegraph* ran a story with the headline "Germans Murder 700,000 Jews in Poland." The *Times* of London was soon reporting, "Over One Million Jews Dead since the War Began," whereupon the *Guardian* noted that seven million Jews were now in German custody, and that Eastern Europe was a "vast slaughterhouse of Jews."

Still, neither Franklin Roosevelt nor Winston Churchill nor Joseph

Stalin could effectively confront the atrocities.* This was not a sinister plot, but rather an awareness that the Germans could not be stopped. The Jews could be saved only by the Allies' winning the war. In a radio address to the American people on March 29, 1944, President Franklin Roosevelt made clear not only that he knew about Hitler's determination to kill every Jew in Europe, but also his own plans ultimately to punish all involved.

Frank's family went into hiding soon after those news reports emerged, moving into a secret apartment in Amsterdam. Life there was squalid and claustrophobic, but at least they were free. For two long years the Franks evaded detection by the Nazis. They were less than a month away from Amsterdam's liberation by the Allies when the end came.

On August 4, 1944, a secret informant, whose name has never become known, gave away the family's hiding place to the Gestapo. The Franks were arrested, and within a month Otto; his wife, Edith; and his teenage daughters, Margot and Annelies, arrived at Auschwitz.

---

*Roosevelt's radio address was very specific in informing Americans about the reality of the Holocaust: "In one of the blackest crimes of all history—begun by the Nazis in the day of peace and multiplied by them a hundred times in time of war—the wholesale systematic murder of the Jews of Europe goes on unabated every hour. As a result of the events of the last few days hundreds of thousands of Jews who, while living under persecution, have at least found a haven from death in Hungary and the Balkans, are now threatened with annihilation as Hitler's forces descend more heavily upon these lands. That these innocent people, who have already survived a decade of Hitler's fury, should perish on the very eve of triumph over the barbarism which their persecution symbolizes, would be a major tragedy. It is therefore fitting that we should again proclaim our determination that none who participate in these acts of savagery shall go unpunished. The United Nations have made it clear that they will pursue the guilty and deliver them up in order that justice be done. That warning applies not only to the leaders but also to their functionaries and subordinates in Germany and in the satellite countries. All who knowingly take part in the deportation of Jews to their death in Poland or Norwegians and French to their death in Germany are equally guilty with the executioner. All who share the guilt shall share the punishment."

In the end, while there was great awareness at the highest levels of government on the Allied side of the murder of the Jews, the actual horror of what was taking place was beyond what any rational person could conceive. "The things I saw," Gen. Dwight Eisenhower said after an April 12, 1945, visit to a former concentration camp, "beggar description."

As soon as they disembarked from their cattle cars, families were disrupted. Otto Frank has not seen his wife and daughters since September.

As he lies in his bunk this cold January day five months later, Frank does not know if his family members are alive or dead. He does not know that the women in his life, whom he loves so much, have suffered the indignity of being stripped naked within moments of their arrival at Auschwitz, their heads shaved for delousing, and then made to stand in line to have a number tattooed on their left forearms. That number, they were soon told, was their new identity. They no longer had a name.

During their time in Holland, young Annelies—just "Anne" to her family—kept a detailed journal of what their life in hiding was like. She was five feet, four inches tall, with an easy smile and dimples. Her eyes were gray, with just the slightest trace of green. Anne's wavy hair, before the Germans shaved her skull smooth, was brown and fell to her shoulders.

Incredibly, both girls are still alive as Otto Frank hears ecstatic shouts from outside his barracks. "We're free," the prisoners are shouting. "We're free."

Soviet soldiers are marching into the camp, taking careful and cautious steps, suspicious of a surprise German attack. They wear winter-white camouflage uniforms and appear out of the snowy mist like apparitions. Eva

Anne Frank in 1941

Mozes cannot see them at first, because they blend into the winter landscape so well.

But just as she is not sure of what she sees, so the Soviet soldiers are not sure of what they have stumbled upon: corpses everywhere, living skeletons, and the hollow faces of those who are being liberated but who are so close to death that it does not matter. "When I saw the people, it was skin and bones. They had no shoes, and it was freezing. They couldn't even turn their heads, they stood like dead people," the first Russian officer into the camp will later remember. "I told them, 'The Russian army liberates you!' They couldn't understand. Some few who could touched our arms and said, 'Is it true? Is it real?'"

The Soviet soldiers move from barracks to barracks, shocked at what they see.

"When I opened the barrack, I saw blood, dead people, and in between them, women still alive and naked," Russian officer Anatoly Shapiro will remember. "It stank; you couldn't stay a second. No one took the dead to a grave. It was unbelievable. The soldiers from my battalion asked me, 'Let us go. We can't stay. This is unbelievable.'"

Despite their brutal reputations, the Soviet soldiers are kind to the prisoners, who stare back at them "with gratitude in their eyes." But the Russians have seen so much in this time of war that many are numb to the horrors before them. "I had seen towns being destroyed. I had seen the destruction of villages. I had seen the suffering of our own people. I had seen small children maimed—there was not one village that had not experienced this horror, this tragedy, these sufferings," one Soviet soldier will note wearily.

And yet the Soviets see that Auschwitz is different. "We ran up to them," Eva Mozes and her sister, Miriam, will later recall. "They gave us hugs, cookies, and chocolates. Being so alone, a hug meant more than anybody could imagine, because that replaced the human worth we were starving for. We were not only starved for worth, we were starved for human kindness, and the Soviet Army did provide some of that."

Eva Mozes has kept the promise that she made to herself. Neither her corpse nor that of her sister will ever litter the filthy floor of a barracks lavatory.

* * *

As Otto Frank rises from his sickbed to celebrate his newfound freedom, his thoughts immediately turn to finding his family.

But he will never find them. Instead, in the weeks and months and years to come, he will discover threads of their travels, which will allow him to piece together the horrible ways in which they died.

Otto Frank's beloved wife, Edith, died of starvation, right here at Auschwitz. His daughters were transferred to Bergen-Belsen, in northern Germany. Margot Frank died soon afterward.

Her sister, Anne, had just five weeks to live. She would die bald and covered with insect bites, her emaciated body finally done in by a typhoid outbreak that would kill seventeen thousand inmates at Bergen-Belsen.

She was just fifteen years old.*

* * *

"Judaism," Adolf Hitler tells the German people on the twelfth anniversary of the day he became chancellor, "began systematically to undermine our nation from within."

Hitler's physical health has further deteriorated. His hands shake. His eyes water. He is now taking twice-a-day injections of methamphetamine so he can function. And yet he and Eva Braun carry on the charade that

---

*In one of the most famous stories to come out of the Holocaust, Anne Frank was given a blank diary for her thirteenth birthday, which fell just weeks before her family went into hiding in 1942. She went on to chronicle, in great detail, what it was like to mature from childhood into adolescence in such claustrophobic circumstances. The last entry is August 1, 1944, three days before her arrest. Upon his return to Amsterdam after the war, Otto Frank was amazed to discover that the journal had survived. Anne's insightful comments on the war and her personal relationships were so profound that he sought to have the diary made public. This came to pass in 1950, when it was published in German and French, and then in English in 1952. Though marginally successful at first, *Anne Frank: The Diary of a Young Girl* has since become a classic work on life in Nazi-occupied Germany and the Netherlands, and has spawned a film and stage play. In 1999, *Time* magazine included Anne Frank in its TIME 100: The Most Important People of the Century list.

the war can still be won. But Hitler's location inside the bombed-out ruins of Berlin tells the true story. It has been two weeks since his personal train slunk into the once-proud capital of Germany in the dead of night. The curtains were drawn as a precaution against Allied bombing—though that is really more a habit than anything else. The Luftwaffe has been destroyed. American and British bombers are free to attack Berlin in broad daylight—which they do most days by nine in the morning, as the city's embattled residents hurry off to work.

There will be no stopping the Allies on the Western Front; of that, Hitler is certain. To the east, where the Russian superiority is eleven soldiers for every Wehrmacht fighter, the situation is even worse.

On this very day, January 30, 1945, Hitler's minister of armaments, Albert Speer, has sent Hitler a memo informing the Führer that the war is lost. Germany does not have the industrial capacity to churn out the tanks, planes, submarines, and bombs necessary to defeat the Allies. Nor does it have the manpower.

Nevertheless, Hitler has no plans to surrender. Nazi scientists are currently working on a new type of weapon known as an atomic bomb.* Once it is capable of being detonated, he can use it to wipe the Allied armies off the map. "On this day I do not want to leave any doubt about something else. Against an entire hostile world I once chose my road, according to my

---

*The Nazi plan to develop an atomic bomb began in January 1939, when German scientists Otto Hahn and Fritz Strassmann found a way to split a uranium atom, thus releasing vast amounts of energy. This was based on the theoretical work already done by the legendary Albert Einstein, who had immigrated to America. After the successful invasion of Poland in September 1939, the German Army Ordnance Office began work on a method of harnessing fission to form a nuclear explosive. There is evidence that the Germans built and tested a nuclear weapon in underground tunnels near the central German town of Ohrdruf. It was on a much smaller scale than the ones detonated by the Americans at Hiroshima and Nagasaki. In the end, even though Hitler waited in vain for the nuclear bomb that he hoped would win the war—or at least allow him to sue for peace on his terms—it did not come to pass. The majority of the scientists who worked on Hitler's nuclear effort were taken into custody by either the Americans or the Soviets. Rather than being transported to New Mexico to aid the American Manhattan Project, they were transported to a safe house in England. This is where they received news about the use of America's atomic weapons against Japan. They were allowed to return to postwar Germany in 1946.

inner call, and strode it, as an unknown and nameless man, to final success; often they reported I was dead and always they wished I were, but in the end I remained victor in spite of all. My life today is with an equal exclusiveness determined by the duties incumbent on me."

Hitler now makes his home in central Berlin, on the Wilhelmstrasse. He lives underground, in an elaborate bunker.* The blond-haired, blue-eyed Eva Braun still tends to him, though she often spends time outside the bunker and does not sleep there most nights. She remains calm, believing that Hitler's cruel genius can once again win the day. Living in an underground bunker is just one more precaution that is necessary in a time of war. Adding to the air of normalcy is that Hitler's beloved German shepherd, Blondi, and her new puppies make their home in the bunker as well.

Even though he fears that a direct hit from an Allied bomb will kill him, Adolf Hitler ultimately believes he will be saved. "However grave the crisis may be at the moment, it will, despite everything, finally be mastered by our unalterable will, by our readiness for sacrifice and by our abilities. We shall overcome this calamity, too, and this fight, too, will not be won by central Asia but by Europe; and at its head will be the nation that has represented Europe against the East for 1,500 years and shall represent it for all times: our Greater German Reich, the German nation."

Adolf Hitler has ninety days to live. He will never leave Berlin again.

---

*Hitler's bunker complex was much more than a simple air-raid shelter. It consisted of two levels: the upper *Vorbunker* containing a conference room, dining facility, kitchen, water storage room, and bedrooms for support staff, which numbered more than two dozen; and the *Führerbunker*, located some thirty feet below ground, with lavishly decorated rooms for Hitler and Eva Braun. A large oil painting of his personal hero Frederick the Great covered one wall. The entire complex was beneath a lavish garden, where Hitler emerged most days to walk Blondi.

15

———◆———

A RURAL ROAD IN POLAND
SPRING 1945
NIGHT

Helena Citrónóva is on a mission.

She is a twenty-five-year-old Slovakian Jew who survived Ausch-witz, thanks to her beauty, elegant singing voice, and guile. Helena was among the first women deported from Slovakia, on March 25, 1942. The women in the group were all between eighteen and twenty-two years old, and chosen for their youth. Their train chugged out of Poprad station at eight o'clock on that fateful spring evening, climbing slowly over the volcanic Vihorlat Mountains in the night to arrive in Auschwitz the fol-lowing morning.

Now Helena and her older sister, Rozinka, bed down in a barn, hop-ing for rest after a long day on the road. They are hungry and thirsty, but for now there is a roof over their heads and they are warm. Yet there is no safety in a war zone.

The Soviet liberation of Auschwitz has come at a time when the Red Army's immediate focus is on capturing Berlin. Its soldiers have little interest in providing care for the thousands of women and children the Nazis have left to die.

Helena and Rozinka are walking hundreds of miles to their home in the central Slovakian town of Humenné. Like so many others, they are marching away from the Germans as the Soviets are racing toward them. Each night, the barns and hedgerows of Germany and southern Poland are filled with refugees hoping for a few hours' sleep before they rise again to continue their journeys. Many have vague hopes of temporarily resettling in a major city such as Budapest. Not Helena and Rozinka Citrónóva. They have endured Auschwitz and deportment to another camp just a week before the Russians liberated Birkenau. Throughout their long captivity they have imagined the day they will once again walk through the front door and into the warmth and comfort of the house in Humenné where they were raised.

Now, as they try to sleep in the hay, the two women hear the soft breathing of their exhausted fellow travelers. Sleeping so close to strangers does not bother the sisters. They slept four to a cramped bunk while in Auschwitz. Sharing a stable feels far less claustrophobic.

Rozinka is the plainer of the two women. She is ten years older than Helena, but it is the loss of her two children in the gas chambers that has aged her. However, if not for Helena, she would not be alive at all.

Within Auschwitz-Birkenau there was a building where the clothing, suitcases, and other personal belongings of prisoners were taken after they'd been stripped upon arrival at the train platform. It was known as Canada. Laborers were allowed to steal clothing or food clandestinely as they searched through the piles of belongings for the gold, cash, and other valuables that would be sent back to Berlin to fund the Nazi war machine.

Helena was not originally assigned to Canada, but she quickly grasped the reality that her life would be easier if she could secure a spot in the sorting house. When a woman she knew who worked in Canada died, Helena switched uniforms with her and took her place the next day.

She was instantly found out. The kapo (as the Jewish informants who supervised their fellow prisoners were known) made it clear that she would be punished. This was no idle threat. The kapos could be incredibly harsh to their fellow Jews. In one instance, an Auschwitz kapo beat an inmate over the head with a shovel. Then, as the man fell to the ground, the kapo shoved the blade down into his throat, breaking his neck. He then pried the dead man's mouth open and hammered out his gold teeth.

So Helena had good reason to be scared that some sort of severe punishment awaited her.

Then, before the kapo could betray her, fate intervened. The date was March 21, 1944. Helena had been a prisoner in Auschwitz for two years. That day was also, coincidentally, the birthday of an SS guard named Franz Wunsch. Known to be an avowed "Jew hater," the twenty-two-year-old Wunsch was in charge of the Canada work detail. That day, he took the liberty of stopping the sorting process for a short time, and asked if anyone would sing for him. Recognizing the opportunity for what it was, Helena volunteered. Her voice soon wafted through the detritus of the sorting house, a stunning contrast to the sadness of ransacking dead people's clothing.

Wunsch was transfixed.

He immediately fell for the raven-haired Helena. Not long after, he took the bold risk of handing her a love note. Relations between guards and Jews were strictly forbidden, although they were a common occurrence. The guards took the risk for the sex. The prisoners took the gamble to save their lives.

But Helena was not interested—not at first. "He threw me a note," she will later remember. "I destroyed it right there and then. But I could see the word 'love'—'I fell in love with you.'"

Helena was appalled. "I thought I'd rather be dead than be involved with an SS man. For a long time afterward, there was just hatred. I couldn't even look at him."

But the smitten Wunsch was persistent. Every day, he would seek her out among the women at work in Canada. He would sneak her cookies, and took special interest in her welfare: the SS guard was trying to buy his way into her heart.

Then an incredible thing happened. Helena's sister, Rozinka, along with her two children, arrived at Auschwitz via a train from Slovakia. Wunsch noticed them.

"Tell me quickly what your sister's name is before I'm too late," he demanded of Helena.

"You won't be able to," she replied coolly. "She has two young children."

Wunsch was taken aback. "Children can't live here."

Finally, Helena gave him her sister's name. Wunsch then raced to the crematorium and, for show, beat Rozinka in front of her children, explaining to his fellow SS guards that she had disobeyed an order to work in Canada. The guards looked the other way as Wunsch dragged her off, leaving Rozinka's young daughter and infant son to die. Harsh as it was, Wunsch saved the woman's life.

Helena, however, now owed a debt to the SS guard.

"In the end, I loved him," Helena will recall of the affair that began that day. "But it could not be."

Franz Wunsch was sent to the Russian front as the war came to an end, along with many of his fellow guards. His last act of kindness was making sure that Helena and Rozinka each had a pair of warm fur-lined boots to help them survive the winter.

When the soldiers of the Soviet Sixtieth Army entered the camp on January 27, they were particularly taken with the plunder inside the building known as Canada. Almost a million articles of women's clothing and half as many men's garments still waited to be sorted.

But that job no longer fell to Helena and Rozinka. Their nightmare was over—at least for the moment. Working in Canada meant they had enjoyed better rations and regular access to water. They had not been beaten, and were extremely healthy compared to so many others in the camp. So they began walking home to Slovakia, eager to put as much distance between themselves and Auschwitz as possible.

But isolated country roads are never completely safe, even in peacetime. Now, as Helena and Rozinka sleep in the barn, their nightmares begin again. Soviet soldiers reeking of alcohol suddenly invade their small sanctuary. It is not one Red Army soldier, or even two, but an entire gang. They are thin from their long days of marching. Their clothes are threadbare. One by one, the women sleeping in the barn are wrestled to the ground if they try to run and then brutally raped, sometimes twice. "They were drunk—totally drunk," Helena later remembers. "They were wild animals."

As this goes on, Helena disguises her looks, messing her hair and covering her face in grime to make herself appear unattractive. The plain and matronly Rozinka helps shield her sister from the soldiers by pretending to be her mother. Some of those attacked show the Russian soldiers their camp tattoos, and cry out that they are Jewish, hoping it will make the Russians see them as undesirable. The soldiers' reply, delivered in terse German from those who have picked up a smattering of the language, is coarse: "Frau ist Frau"—"A woman is a woman."

Somehow Helena and Rozinka escape being raped. However, they must silently listen to the screams of those women being violated, and then the heart-wrenching silence when the act is completed.

The Russian soldiers are not satisfied with mere sexual conquest. They are animals, biting away chunks of women's breasts and cheeks and savagely mauling their genitals. Many strangle their victims after the act, silencing them forever. Perhaps they prefer murder to the personal shame of their victims glaring at them in hatred.

"I didn't want to see because I couldn't help them," Helena remembers. "I was afraid they would rape my sister and me. No matter where we hid, they found our hiding places and raped some of my girlfriends."

Russian soldiers raped millions of women during the course of the war.* A large proportion of these women will contract venereal disease from their attackers. Some of them will commit suicide afterward. Others will become pregnant but refuse to carry a rapist's baby to term and will find a way to abort the fetus. Many of those who give birth to these children of rape—*Russenbabies*, as they will be known—will abandon them. For some women, such as those in the barn, the liberation of Auschwitz was not the end of their suffering, but the beginning of a new kind of suffering.

"They did horrible things to them," Helena will recount decades later, from her new home in the Jewish nation of Israel, the image of

---

*Joseph Stalin specifically condoned rape as a reward for his soldiers. "People should understand it if a soldier who has crossed thousands of kilometers of blood and death has *fun* with a woman." The brutality will become systematic in the final days of the war. In the German city of Dresden, the Russians will gang-rape women in the streets, forcing husbands and fathers to watch. Afterward, the men will be shot. The Russians will claim that the rapes were retribution for atrocities committed during the German invasion of Russia, which does not explain the estimated one hundred thousand rapes in Austria, two hundred thousand in Hungary, and tens of thousands of others in Bulgaria, Poland, and Czechoslovakia. To this day, the Putin government in Russia denies that the Russian army committed mass rape, but the evidence contained in various eyewitness accounts is overwhelming.

kicking, biting, and clawing at a young Soviet officer to prevent herself from becoming a victim of rape still clear in her head.

"Right up to the last minute we couldn't believe that we were still meant to survive."

★   ★   ★

Many Auschwitz survivors find there is no shelter, even when they make it back to their hometowns. All throughout Eastern Europe, Joseph Stalin and the Russian military machine have taken advantage of the mass Nazi deportations of Jews to steal homes and farms and give them to the Russian people. This is just the start of a massive forced migration that will see millions of non-Soviets in Czechoslovakia, Hungary, Romania, Bulgaria, and Poland forced out of their homes. They will be left to resettle in the ruins of the Nazi occupation, in lands that will be without industry, farming, or infrastructure.

Like Helena and Rozinka Citrónóva, Linda Libusha is a Slovak who has survived Auschwitz. As she walks the streets of her beloved hometown of Stropkov, from where she was arrested and led away in March 1942, she believes the nightmare of the camps may be finally behind her.

But Linda doesn't recognize anyone during her stroll down the main street. It's as if everyone she ever knew has vanished. When she knocks at the door of the house in which she grew up, it is answered by someone she has never seen before, a heavyset man with a red Russian face. Over his shoulder she can see the same familiar rooms and hallways where she once played as a child—and where this foreigner now makes his home.

The Russian takes no pity on the death camp survivor.

"Go back where you came from," he says, slamming the door in her face.

16

George S. Patton is on the move.

Finally.

Sgt. John Mims drives Patton in his signature open-air jeep with its three-star flags over the wheel wells. The snows of the cruel subzero winter are melting at last. Patton and Mims pass the carcasses of cattle frozen legs-up as the road winds through Luxembourg and into Germany. Hulks of destroyed Sherman M-4s litter the countryside—so many tanks, in fact, that Patton makes a mental note to investigate which type of enemy round defeated each of them. This is Patton's way of helping the U.S. Army build better armor for fighting the next inevitable war.

It is a conflict that Patton believes will be fought soon. The Russians are moving to forcibly spread communism throughout the world, and Patton knows it. "They are a scurvy race and simply savages," he writes of the Russians in his journal. "We could beat the hell out of them."

But that's in the future, after Germany is defeated and the cruel task of dividing Europe among the victors takes center stage. For now, it is enough that the Third Army is advancing into Germany. Patton has sensed a weakness in the Wehrmacht lines and is eager to press his advantage.

It was four weeks ago, on February 10, when Dwight Eisenhower once again ordered Patton and his Third Army to stop their drive east and go on the defensive and selected British field marshal Bernard Law Montgomery to lead the massive Allied invasion force that will cross the strategically vital Rhine River. It is a politically astute maneuver, because while Montgomery officially reports to Eisenhower, the British field marshal believes himself to be—and is often portrayed in the British press as—Eisenhower's equal. Winston Churchill publicly fueled this portrayal by promoting Montgomery to field marshal months before Eisenhower received his fifth star, meaning that for a time Montgomery outranked the supreme commander of the Allied forces in Europe. Now Eisenhower's decision to throw his support to Montgomery's offensive neatly defuses any controversy that might have arisen over Eisenhower giving Patton the main thrust.

Stretching eight hundred miles down the length of Germany from the North Sea to Switzerland, the Rhine is the last great obstacle between the Allies and the German heartland. Whoever crosses it first might also soon know the glory of being the first Allied general to reach Berlin.

It is as if Patton's monumental achievement at Bastogne never happened.

"It was rather amusing, though perhaps not flattering, to note that General Eisenhower never mentioned the Bastogne offensive," he writes of his most recent discussions with Eisenhower. Then, referring to the emergency meeting in Verdun that turned the tide of the Battle of the Bulge, he adds, "Although this was the first time I had seen him since the nineteenth of December—when he seemed much pleased to have me at the critical point."

Even more galling, not just to Patton but also to American soldiers, is that Montgomery has publicly taken credit for the Allied victory at the Battle of the Bulge. Monty insists that it is his British forces of the Twenty-First Army Group, not American GIs, who stopped the German advance.

"As soon as I saw what was happening," Montgomery stated at a press conference, at which he wore an outlandish purple beret, "I took steps to ensure that the Germans would never get over the Meuse. I carried out certain movements to meet the threatened danger. I employed the whole power of the British group of armies."

What Montgomery neglected to mention was that just three British divisions were made available for the battle. Of the 650,000 Allied soldiers

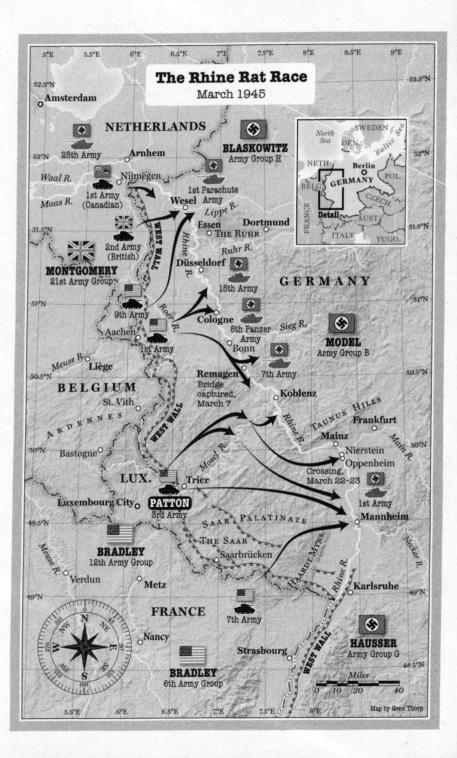

The Rhine Rat Race
March 1945

NETHERLANDS

Amsterdam

25th Army

Arnhem

Nijmegen

1st Army
(Canadian)

Waal R.

Maas R.

2nd Army
(British)

MONTGOMERY
21st Army Group

9th Army

Aachen

1st Army

Liège

BELGIUM

St. Vith

ARDENNES

Bastogne

Meuse R.

BLASKOWITZ
Army Group H

1st Parachute
Army

Wesel

Lippe R.

Essen   Dortmund
    THE RUHR

Ruhr R.

Düsseldorf

GERMANY

15th Army

Cologne

Bonn

WEST WALL

Rhine R.

Roer R.

5th Panzer
Army

Sieg R.

MODEL
Army Group B

7th Army

Remagen
Bridge
captured,
March 7

Koblenz

Rhine R.

TAUNUS HILLS

Frankfurt

Mainz

Main R.

Nierstein
Oppenheim

Crossing,
March 22-23

1st Army

Mannheim

Mosel R.

LUX.   Trier

Luxembourg City

PATTON
3rd Army

SAAR PALATINATE

THE SAAR

Saarbrücken

BRADLEY
12th Army Group

Verdun   Metz

Meuse R.

Nancy

FRANCE

7th Army

HAARDT MTNS.

Rhine R.

Karlsruhe

Neckar R.

Strasbourg

WEST WALL

HAUSSER
Army Group G

Miles
0 10 20 30 40

Map by Gene Thorp

North
Sea

SWEDEN

DEN.

Baltic Sea

NETH.

BELG.

Berlin

GERMANY

POL.

FRANCE

Detail

CZECH

AUST.

ITALY

YUGO.

who fought in the Battle of the Bulge, more than 600,000 were American. Once again, Bernard Law Montgomery used dishonest spin in an attempt to ensure his place in history.

Montgomery's stunning January 7 press conference did considerable damage to Anglo-American relations.* To Patton, it seems outrageous that Montgomery should be rewarded for such deceptive behavior.

Yet despite the fact that four American soldiers now serve along the German border for every British Tommy, Eisenhower has caved in to pressure from Churchill and selected Monty to lead the charge across the Rhine. Still, the reasons for this decision are practical as well as political: the crucial Ruhr industrial region is in northern Germany, as are Montgomery's troops. Theoretically, Monty is capable of quickly laying waste to the lifeblood of Germany's war machine.

Nevertheless, the decision makes George S. Patton furious.

On this chilly Tuesday morning, the cautious and finicky Montgomery is still ten days away from launching Operation Plunder, as the Rhine offensive is known. So Patton, sensing an immediate weakness in the German lines, has convinced Eisenhower to let him attack, two hundred miles to the south. The plan to invade southern Germany's Palatinate region came to Patton in a dream. It was fully formed, right down to the last logistical detail. "Whether ideas like this are inspiration or insomnia, I don't know," he writes in his journal. "I do things by sixth sense."

Patton's military ambitions for the assault are many, among them the devastation of all Wehrmacht forces guarding the heavily fortified Siegfried Line.[†]

Privately, however, he admits that not all his goals are tactical. The war is now personal. Patton has endured countless slights and setbacks.

---

*So much so that Winston Churchill was forced to give a pro-American speech in the British House of Commons to heal the wounds.

[†]The Siegfried Line was a four-hundred-mile-long defensive array of eighteen thousand bunkers and interlocking rows of pyramid-shaped concrete antitank obstacles nicknamed "dragon's teeth." The Germans referred to it as the Westwall, while the Americans continued to use "Siegfried," after a similar system of forts dating back to the First World War. Hitler built the Westwall between 1936 and 1938, anticipating by almost a decade the day when some great army—in this case, that of George S. Patton—would attempt to invade the Fatherland.

Many are of his own doing, but just as many are clearly not. Patton, at heart, is a simple man who wears his emotions on his sleeve. This makes him extremely poor at the sort of political posturing at which rivals such as Montgomery excel.

The man who lives for battle wants to be judged by his actions, not his words. The war will end soon. Patton would love nothing more than for the spotlight to shine on his accomplishments at least one more time.

Doing so at Bernard Law Montgomery's expense, of course, would make the experience all the richer.

"He advertises so damn much that they know where he is," Patton sneers of Montgomery, contrasting their leadership styles by alluding to the German high command's constant awareness of his rival's location. "I fool them."

At Patton's command, the Third Army romps through the Palatinate on what Col. Abe Abrams of the Fourth Armored Division calls the "Rhine Rat Race." They travel with ample supplies of metal decking and pontoons, allowing them to build temporary bridges across the Rhine—it is hoped, well ahead of Montgomery and his Twenty-First Army Group.

American armored divisions have already succeeded in crossing the Rhine, in the city of Remagen, eighty-six miles north of Trier. The incredulous Americans could not believe that the bridge remained intact, and crossed immediately. And while they were not able to advance beyond a small toehold on the Rhine's eastern shore, the symbolism of the Allied achievement struck such fear into the minds of the Nazi high command that Adolf Hitler ordered the firing squad executions of the four officers he considered responsible for not having destroyed the bridge.* The men were forced to kneel, and then were shot in the back of the neck. The final letters they had written to family and lovers were then burned.

---

*Adolf Hitler also fired the German army's commander in chief, Field Marshal Gerd von Rundstedt, because of the incident. His replacement, Field Marshal Albert Kesselring, immediately ordered a series of artillery and rocket strikes on the Remagen Bridge. It was eventually destroyed, on March 17, although not before the Allies had crossed ample men and supplies to the other side to secure the bridgehead. By the time the bridge collapsed into the Rhine, several pontoon bridges had been built across the river near its location, making the loss immaterial to the Allied advance. The bridge has never been rebuilt.

Hitler then ordered the great commando Otto Skorzeny to assemble a team of swimmers who would float down the Rhine and attach explosives to the Remagen Bridge. The mission failed when all of Skorzeny's amphibious commandos were discovered by sharp-eyed American sentries along the shore, and were either killed or captured.

The Allies still hold the bridge, but are unable to advance farther without the assistance of a greater fighting force.

George S. Patton understands the significance of Remagen. "Ninth Armored Division of the Third Corps," he writes in his journal on March 7, "got a bridge intact over the Rhine at Remagen. This may have a fine influence on our future movements. I hope we get one also."

But even if he can't find an intact bridge, Patton is determined to beat Montgomery across the Rhine.

He has just ten days.

★ ★ ★

Two weeks ago, the Third Army captured the ancient German fortress of Trier, attacking quickly and suffering few casualties. His victory complete, Patton now takes the opportunity to visit the conquered city.

Many are convinced that the Second World War will be the war to end all wars, but Patton knows better. As a reminder to himself that war is inevitable, he has been reading Julius Caesar's *Gallic Wars* each night before bed. The memoir recounts Caesar's battles in Gaul* and Germany from 58 to 51 BC. The words rise up off the page for Patton, and he feels a personal connection to the action.

As he drives to the decimated Trier, he studies the ancient highway carefully, absorbing its every nuance. It is not the sight of the swollen Moselle River that mesmerizes him, or even that of Allied engineers scurrying to corduroy† the muddy country thoroughfare before Allied vehicles accidentally tumble down the steep hillside and into the raging torrent.

No, it is the belief that he traveled this road two thousand years ago.

---

*Modern-day France, Belgium, Luxembourg, Switzerland, northern Italy, and regions of Germany west of the Rhine River.

†The placing of logs over a muddy road to improve traction.

Patton is convinced that he was a soldier and a great general in his many past lives. He once stood shoulder to shoulder with Alexander the Great and Napoléon. He crossed the Alps on an elephant while residing in the body of the Carthaginian conqueror Hannibal. Patton also is quite certain that he once fought for the great Caesar as a Roman legionary, marching into battle on this very same road from Wasserbillig to Trier. Even as a biting wind chaps his exposed face, Patton can "smell the coppery sweat and see the low dust clouds" of legionaries advancing on the Germanic hordes along the Moselle.

Patton has no problems meshing his Protestant faith with his belief in reincarnation. He simply believes that he has a powerful connection with the supernatural. This belief was reinforced by two very prominent occurrences during World War I. On one occasion, he found himself pressed to the ground during a battle, terrified to stand and fight. He believed that he saw the faces of his dead grandfather and several uncles demanding that he stop being a coward. The other instance took place in Langres, France, once occupied by the ancient Romans. Though he had never visited the city, Patton was able to navigate his way without the help of his French liaison officer. He gave the Frenchman a tour of the Roman ruins, including the amphitheater, parade ground, and various temples dedicated to a deity. He also drove straight to the spot where Caesar had once camped, and pointed to where the Roman leader had once pitched his tent.

Now, like Caesar in 57 BC, Patton has conquered Trier.

Over the week that it took to reduce the strategically vital city to rubble, the Germans fought tenaciously. Twenty Allied bombing raids pounded the Wehrmacht defenders, until it became only a matter of time before the Germans fled, and tanks from the American Tenth Armored Division rolled past the ancient Roman amphitheater on the eastern edge of town. The fact that this structure remains standing while all else has crumbled is not lost on Patton. "One of the few things undestroyed in Trier is the entrance to the old Roman amphitheater which still stands in sturdy magnificence."

Shortly after the conquest on March 1, Patton received a message from Allied headquarters. "Bypass Trier. It will take four divisions to capture it," read the order.

"Have taken Trier with two divisions," an acerbic Patton responded. "What do you want me to do? Give it back?"

One week later, Patton's plan to invade the Palatinate was approved by Eisenhower.

Following the old adage that it is better to seek forgiveness than to ask permission, Patton does not plan on asking for permission to ford the Rhine, should the opportunity present itself.

★   ★   ★

Patton's barbed sense of humor is not accidental. He is weary of the ineffectual leadership of General Eisenhower, who he believes consistently sabotages his success. He feels the same way about Omar Bradley, his immediate superior.

So Bradley's February 10 order to go on the defensive was soul crushing for Patton. He will be sixty this year, making him "the oldest leader in age and battle experience in the United States Army in Europe," by his own estimation. The war is winding down, but it has taken its toll on George Patton.

He has become so obsessed that he is now incapable of existing in a world without war. Even the total nudity of dancers at the famous Folies Bergère dance revue, seen on a mid-February leave in Paris, could not distract Patton from thoughts of the fighting. Nor did being recognized everywhere he went in the city, which is normally a salve for his ego.

After a case of food poisoning made him violently ill—and led to a growing belief that his life was being threatened by unknown forces— Patton hurried back to his headquarters near the front, unable to stay away from the war even one day longer.

He knows that his last battle is soon to come—at least in this lifetime. Thus Patton seeks to prolong his role in the fighting. "I should like to be considered for any type of combat command, from a division up against the Japanese. I am sure that my method of fighting might be successful. I am also of such an age that this is my last war, and I would therefore like to see it through to the end," Patton writes in a letter to the chief of the army, Gen. George Marshall, on March 13.

The mere thought that the fighting will soon end fills Patton with dread. "Peace is going to be hell on me," he writes to his wife, Beatrice. "I will probably be a great nuisance."

Patton wants to finish out the war on his own terms. That means go on the attack. "A great deal was owed to me," he wrote of one conversation with Omar Bradley, after it was suggested that the Third Army once again go on the defensive. "Unless I could continue attacking I would have to be relieved."

★ ★ ★

Dwight Eisenhower is quite confident that George Patton will never ask to be relieved. Yet he immediately follows up his February 10 order with a second command, allowing Patton to place his army on "aggressive defense." Ike knows that Patton will interpret this order as permission to launch a series of low-profile attacks.

Such dithering is an example of Eisenhower's greatest strength and his greatest weakness: compromise. He wants to make everyone happy, and believes that "public opinion wins wars." Very often it seems Eisenhower would rather make the popular decision than the right one. This is the manner in which he has behaved throughout his entire army career, and it has served him well. At the start of the war he was a colonel, leading training exercises at Fort Sam Houston, Texas. Now his penchant for compromise and diplomacy has allowed him to rise to prominence and power despite the glaring fact that he has never fought in battle, or even commanded troops in combat.

Eisenhower personally favors a "broad front" assault into Germany, much like the campaigns of Hannibal at Cannae in 216 BC and Gen. Ulysses S. Grant in the final days of the Civil War. By attacking Germany from both the north and south, Eisenhower can affect a pincer movement, trapping the Wehrmacht between the claws of his forces. Montgomery, however, prefers a single "full-blooded" thrust through the industrial Ruhr region of northern Germany. Naturally, Monty plans to be in charge, bringing the full weight of forty Allied divisions to bear on the Germans. Generals such as Patton will sit on the sidelines and watch.

At first Eisenhower privately mocked Montgomery's strategy, joking that the plan was a "pencil-like thrust." But Montgomery has worn him down. Monty is enormously popular in Britain, and many British people believe it is outrageously unjust, after all their suffering, that an American now commands all ground troops in Europe. Eisenhower has appeased Britain by placing Montgomery in charge of the Rhine offensive.

George Patton sees the underlying motives in Eisenhower's determination to remain popular. "Before long, Ike will be running for President," Patton tells one of his top generals. "You think I'm joking? Just wait and see."

Patton will be proven correct. On November 4, 1952, Dwight Eisenhower will be elected the thirty-fourth president of the United States.*

On a tactical level, it is clear that Eisenhower's broad-front strategy is the best possible method of attacking Germany. But in yet another example of attempting to make the popular choice, Eisenhower has temporarily discarded the strategy. Montgomery and Operation Plunder will be the focus of the Allied advance. But Montgomery's notorious caution on the battlefield, combined with the likelihood that his plan to attack through the industrial and heavily populated Ruhr region of Germany will mean bitter fighting and heavy Allied casualties, could very well spell disaster. So Eisenhower knows he needs Patton as a backup in case the Montgomery offensive doesn't work.

Thus, the war has once again become a personal competition between Patton and Montgomery—and once again, Monty seems to have the advantage.

Eisenhower is giving Monty and his Twenty-First Army Group all the manpower, ammunition, gasoline, and bridging supplies they need to cross the Rhine at the northern town of Wesel and push on to Berlin, while Patton and the Third Army stay south, content with destroying the Siegfried Line.

It looks like, this time, Montgomery will be the victor, making the decisive thrust across the Rhine and venturing the final three hundred miles to Berlin, and glory.

---

*He served two terms in office. His successor was a former U.S. Navy junior officer named John F. Kennedy, who served in the Pacific Theater during the Second World War at the same time as Eisenhower's running mate, Richard Nixon. Beginning with Eisenhower, every president for the next forty-two years served in World War II.

★ ★ ★

"If Ike stops holding Monty's hand and gives me the supplies, I'll go through the Siegfried Line like shit through a goose," Patton has promised a British newspaper reporter.

As the days tick down to Operation Plunder, Patton's army surrounds the Wehrmacht in southern Germany, capturing sixty thousand prisoners and ten thousand square miles of German countryside in two weeks. The Siegfried Line proves no match for the Third Army. Patton's forces are everywhere. Even in remote regions such as the Hunsrück Mountains hundreds of tanks and infantry units are seen rolling down roads long considered "impassable to armor."

"The enemy," notes one American soldier, is "a beaten mass of men, women, and children, interspersed with diehard Nazis."

Patton writes candidly to Beatrice about the condition of the German people. "I saw one woman with a perambulator full of her worldly

Beatrice Patton

goods sitting by it on a hill, crying. An old man with a wheelbarrow and three little children wringing his hands. A woman with five children and a tin cup crying. In hundreds of villages there is not a living thing, not even a chicken. Most of the houses are heaps and stones. They brought it on themselves, but these poor peasants are not responsible.

"I am getting soft?" Patton asks Beatrice rhetorically.

★ ★ ★

Predictably, Montgomery waits. The British commander is assembling the largest amphibious operation since D-day. His staff checks and rechecks every detail, from the perceived numerical superiority of Allied forces to the number of assault boats that will be required to cross the Rhine, and even to the tonnage of munitions that British bombers will drop on Wesel to set it ablaze and thus root out any concealed German resistance.

Meanwhile, Patton attacks. His Palatinate campaign will go down in history as one of the great strategies of the war. Even the Germans will say so. And their praise for Patton is evidence of their enormous respect for the general. "The greatest threat," a captured German officer reveals during his interrogation, "was the whereabouts of the feared U.S. Army." George Patton is always the topic of military discussion. "Where is he? When will he attack? Where? How? With what?"

Lt. Col. Freiherr von Wangenheim will go on to add, "General Patton is the most feared general on all fronts . . . The tactics of General Patton are daring and unpredictable . . . He is the most modern general and the best commander of armored and infantry troops combined."

Patton's tanks are riding roughshod over the rugged countryside. After the staggering setback at Metz six months ago, Patton has shown what he's made of at Bastogne and now at the Palatinate.

"We are the eighth wonder of the world," Patton says of the Third Army on March 19, congratulating himself on yet another success. "And I had to beg, lie and steal to get started."

Patton's forces capture the pivotal city of Koblenz, at the confluence of the Rhine and Moselle Rivers. He now has eight full divisions lined up along the western shore of the Rhine, the tank barrels aimed directly at the eastern bank.

All Patton needs is a place to cross.

★　★　★

The date is March 22, 1945. Two hours before midnight, under cover of darkness, a Third Army patrol paddles across the Rhine at Nierstein in flimsy wooden assault boats. The slap of their paddles stroking the swift waters goes unheard. They report back that no enemy troops are in the vicinity. When Patton receives the news, he immediately orders that bridging material be sent forward. By morning, hastily built pontoon bridges* span the river, and an entire division of Patton's army is soon across.

Patton calls Bradley, but instead of making the sort of bold pronouncement that would inform the Germans of his precise location, he sets aside his ego in a moment of caution.

"Don't tell anyone, but I'm across," Patton informs Bradley.

"Well, I'll be damned," Bradley responds. "You mean across the Rhine?"

"Sure I am. Sneaked a division over last night. But there are so few Krauts around here they don't know it yet. So don't make any announcement. We'll keep it a secret until we see how it goes."

It goes well—but only for a short time.

The sight of thousands of men marching across hastily built pontoon bridges is hard to conceal. The German air force discovers the Third Army's encroachment later that day. Disregarding Allied air superiority, the few Luftwaffe Messerschmitt fighters that have survived thus far in the war patrol low above the Rhine, searching for signs of soldiers, vehicles, and supplies. The pilots radio back what they see, then harass the intruders by dropping down to treetop level to strafe the Americans with lethal rounds of machine-gun and cannon fire.

But the German pilots are *too* bold, and in their determination to

---

*The U.S. Army had several types of temporary bridges that could be constructed quickly to cross a river. A pontoon bridge consisted of several floating barrels upon which steel tread was laid as a decking material. Such bridges could be built within hours. They were highly effective at moving men and matériel across a river, but also highly unstable due to the fact that they rested directly atop the river.

throw back Patton's invaders, all thirty-three Luftwaffe planes are blasted out of the sky by precision firing from the Third Army's antiaircraft guns. The German pilots are so low that bailing out and parachuting to safety is not an option. The American soldiers continue their march across the swift blue waters of the Rhine, cheered throughout the day by the sight of enemy planes exploding all across the horizon and falling into the river with a mighty splash.

It is clear that the Americans no longer need to proceed under radio silence.

Patton once again phones Bradley, on March 23, eager to make history at his rival Montgomery's expense. "Brad, for God's sake, tell the world we're across," he barks into the receiver. Bradley will later remember that Patton's already high voice "trebled" in happiness. "We knocked down thirty-three Krauts today when they came after our pontoon bridges. I want the world to know Third Army made it before Monty starts across."

★ ★ ★

Patton's swagger only increases the next day, as he takes his victorious celebration to a new level. He is driven to the front, close to where American troops pour across the Rhine at the small German town of Oppenheim. The broad, icy river is dull gray, reflecting the overcast morning sky.

Sergeant Mims eases Patton's jeep onto the temporary bridge, taking care to align the wheels with the wooden planks. Patton has thought carefully about how he will mark the occasion of crossing the Rhine and has a very special plan in mind.

At the bank of the river, he orders his driver to stop. "Time out for a short halt," he tells Sergeant Mims. Patton steps out of his jeep and walks along the wooden planks to the center of the bridge. "I have been looking forward to this for some time."

Walking carefully to the edge of the swaying bridge, Patton instructs army photographers to look away. However, his aide Charles Codman will be allowed to take a photograph to preserve the moment for posterity. Patton unzips his fly, faces downriver, and relieves himself.

General George Patton making good on his ambition to "piss in the Rhine"

"I didn't take a piss this morning when I got up so that I would have a full load," he brags as he begins to urinate.* Patton looks straight into the camera lens.

Upon reaching the far bank of the Rhine, Patton continues his celebration by once again stepping from his jeep and re-creating William the Conqueror's arrival in England nearly nine centuries earlier. It was William, the legendary invader from the Norman region of France, who famously fell flat on his face while leaping from his boat as it kissed the

---

*The desire to urinate on enemy soil was shared with British prime minister Winston Churchill, who visited Field Marshal Bernard Law Montgomery's lines in early March and made a point of relieving himself on the German homeland. Even as Patton was polluting the Rhine, Churchill was crossing the same river two hundred miles upstream, in Wesel, alongside Montgomery.

English shoreline. "See," he yelled to his men. "I have taken England with both hands."

Patton falls to one knee and then plants his hands deeply into the German soil. "Thus," Patton cries, "William the Conqueror," in an allusion appreciated but not completely understood by some within earshot.

George S. Patton and his Third Army are now across the Rhine and prepared to invade the German heartland. Just as he did nearly two years ago at Messina, the ever-competitive Patton has defeated his military nemesis, British field marshal Bernard Law Montgomery.

Patton will take particular pride in boasting of this accomplishment: "Without benefit of aerial bombardment, ground smoke, artillery preparation and airborne assistance, the Third Army at 2200 hours, Thursday, 22nd March, 1945, crossed the Rhine River.

"The 21st Army Group was supposed to cross the Rhine on 24th March, 1945," Patton will continue, "and in order to be ready for this 'earthshaking event,' Mr. Churchill wrote a speech congratulating Field Marshal Montgomery for his first 'assault' crossing over the Rhine River in modern history. The speech was recorded and through some error on the part of the British Broadcasting Corporation, was broadcast. In spite of the fact that the Third Army had been across the Rhine River for some thirty-six hours."

★ ★ ★

Looking east, Patton just needs to find a way to beat the Russians into Berlin.

"We are now fairly started on that phase of the campaign which I hope will be the final one," he writes to Eisenhower two days after crossing the Rhine. He couches his letter in respect, but his desire to remain in the fight is evident in the quiet demands of his conclusion.

"I know that Third Army will be in at the finish in the same decisive way that it has performed in all preliminary battle," Patton reminds Eisenhower.

17

BERLIN, GERMANY
APRIL 1, 1945
NIGHT

N obody stands as Adolf Hitler enters the conference room.
The Führer's entire body quivers as he assumes his usual place
before the war map table. Hitler's hands shake, his head nods uncontrollably, and he is bent at the waist, too weak to stand upright. The distant
thunder of Allied bombing shakes the concrete walls. Yet the Führer's eyes
shine brightly behind his rimless pale green spectacles, showing no fear as
he gazes down at the current location of his armies. Most of them, however,
are not real, though he is too deluded to know the truth. In his desperation
to end the war on his terms, Hitler imagines nonexistent "ghost" divisions as
he scrutinizes the map, and pictures thousands of Panzers in places where
there are none at all.

Meanwhile, private conversation hums as if the Führer has never
even entered the first-floor room. German officers and Hitler's secretaries
gossip and chitchat as if the most feared man in the world were not in
their presence.*

---

*Not everyone lived full-time in the bunker. People came and went as if going to work
at a regular job. Even Hitler left the bunker to travel through his private tunnel to the
Reich Chancellery. The usual contingent comprised soldiers; female secretaries
Gerda Christian and Traudl Junge; personal secretary Martin Bormann; SS adjutant
Maj. Otto Günsche; maintenance man Johannes Hentschel; veterinarian Fritz Tornow; nurse Erna Flegel; chief steward Arthur Kannenberg; Hitler's personal physician, Dr. Theodor Morell; Hitler's personal cook, Constanze Manziarly; and chief
valet Heinz Linge. Of these, only Morell, Linge, and Manziarly lived in the bunker
full-time, because Hitler depended upon them for immediate personal needs. Eva
Braun did not move in until mid-April.

An Allied bomb explodes nearby. Lights sway, flickering temporarily, then return to full strength. All talk ceases. The military officers know better than to appear afraid, while the secretaries train their eyes on Hitler, waiting for his response.

"That was close!" Hitler says to no one in particular.

Weak smiles fill the room, as yet another sign of defeat enhances the awkward sense of community. Just weeks ago such informality would have been an unforgivable lapse in protocol, but being fifty feet underground is taking its toll on Hitler's staff. They live like a cave-dwelling prehistoric Germanic tribe, in a world where the walls are made of hard rock. The cement corridors are narrow, painted the color of rust, and the ceilings low. The rooms are all painted a dull gray, and the walls weep as moisture seeps through the rock. They have their own water supply, thanks to a deep artesian well. A sixty-kilowatt diesel generator provides energy for the switchboard, lights, and heating. The air comes from up above, through a filter to ensure its purity.

Yet the bunker is hardly pleasant. There are three separate security checkpoints just to get in, and all entrances are manned by security guards carrying machine pistols and grenades. In this way, Hitler's headquarters is, in fact, a prison.

"The whole atmosphere down there was debilitating," one German soldier who served in the bunker will later remember. "In the long hours of the night it could be deathly silent, except for the hum of the generator . . . Then there was the fetid odor of boots, sweaty woolen uniforms, acrid coal-tar disinfectants. At times toward the end, when the drainage backed up, it was as pleasant as working in a public urinal."

The bunker's residents can hear the air-raid sirens at ground level, but rarely go up to the garden to feel the sun on their faces. The Führer has banned smoking in the bunker, but breathing dank air that is fouled all too often by the Führer's meteorism is an ordeal for all. As of late, the group has become so used to the sight of their Führer that even the lowest-level staffers no longer feel the need to cut short their conversations when he is in their presence.

Yet the informality belies the truth: everyone, with the exception of Adolf Hitler, is terrified. "You felt it to the point of physical illness," one German officer will later write. "Nothing was authentic except fear."

And yet Adolf Hitler is convinced that the war can still be won.

Aboveground, the Allies are bombing around the clock: the American Army Air Corps in the daylight and the British Royal Air Force by night. Berlin is a city in ruins. Of its 1,562,000 homes and apartments, one third have been completely destroyed. Almost 50,000 citizens have died, repaying the butcher's bill of the German bombings of London five times over. The people sleep most nights in cellars or subways. Still, despite the mayhem, there is an amazing sense of routine to life on the streets of Berlin: mail is delivered each day, the Berlin Philharmonic performs at night, and the subway runs on time. Bakeries open their doors each morning, ensuring that the beleaguered populace can purchase their daily *brot*. And despite the drone of RAF Lancaster bombers, the bars are jammed each night with Nazi bigwigs and those businessmen wealthy enough, and lucky enough, to have escaped military service. The gossip, as always, centers on the bombing: who died, who lost their homes, whose job no longer exists because their place of business has been reduced to rubble.

One quiet reality, however, pervades life in Berlin: the city is mostly female. Able-bodied men have been called away to war. The Russian army is now less than forty miles from Berlin; refugees pouring into the capital from the east, seeking to escape these brutal oppressors, tell horror stories of murder and rape. They talk of a pamphlet that has been distributed to the Russian troops through Joseph Stalin's propaganda ministry, directly threatening Germans of all ages, particularly women.

"Kill! Kill!" the leaflet reads. "Follow the precepts of Comrade Stalin. Stamp out the fascist beast once and for all in its lair! Use force and break the spirit of Germanic women. Take them as your lawful booty. Kill! As you storm onward, kill! You gallant soldiers of the Red Army."

While some wealthy Berliners are secretly making plans to flee the city and perhaps find sanctuary in Switzerland, most citizens are stuck. They cannot run. So they remain through the bombings, going about their business as best they can.

The turning point of the war between the Russians and Germans took place in the city of Stalingrad. The fierce battle lasted for five and a half months, and saw the death of 1.2 million Russian soldiers and civilians and 850,000 German dead or wounded. The fighting was often in close quarters, within the houses and buildings of the city itself. The

Germans were ruthless in their treatment of the Russian populace, murdering and raping with impunity.

Eventually, the German Sixth Army was cut off from supplies. German general Friedrich von Paulus implored Hitler to let his army withdraw. The Führer refused. This resulted in ninety-one thousand Germans being taken prisoner when the battle came to an end on February 2, 1943. Of that number, only six thousand survived the cruelty of their Russian captors and returned home alive after the war. From then on, the Soviet army steadily advanced westward, vowing to avenge the atrocities that the German army had inflicted upon the people of Russia.

The residents of Berlin will bear the brunt of this vengeance. They can only pray that the stories of rape and murder are mere rumors.

But those prayers will go unanswered.

★ ★ ★

On March 16, in a special ceremony, Hitler awarded Joachim Peiper and Otto Skorzeny the Oak Leaves to the Knight's Cross. But his two favorite soldiers are soon to fight no more. In Vienna, Peiper and his SS Panzer division have been defeated and disgraced in a last-ditch attempt to stop the Russian advance. Furious, Hitler has ordered that Peiper and his men remove from their uniforms the armbands bearing his name. Shortly after that, Peiper flees west and is captured by the Americans.

Skorzeny, a native of Vienna, hears that the Russians are about to enter the city and races there on April 10 with a team of commandos. He finds Vienna in flames, but otherwise dark. Instantly recognizing that the city will fall by morning, he and his commandos retreat. Their war is over. Skorzeny orders his men to hide themselves, while he escapes into the Alps, where he vacillates between committing suicide and fleeing Germany while he can still get out alive.

Like Adolf Hitler, Skorzeny is planning a way to end the war on his terms. In time, he will surrender to the Allies.

★ ★ ★

In the pale artificial light of the bunker, Adolf Hitler continues to stare, hour after hour, at his map table, waiting for some sign of hope that all will soon be well. "Think of Leonidas and his three hundred Spartans," he tells his personal secretary, the despicable Martin Bormann. "It does not suit us to let ourselves be slaughtered like sheep. They may exterminate us, but they will not be able to lead us to the slaughter."

Thus the Führer has begun a scorched-earth policy designed to deprive Germany's approaching conquerors of a form of sustenance. His "Nero Command" of March 19 states, "All military, transportation, communications, industrial, and food supply facilities, as well as all other resources within the Reich which the enemy might use either immediately or in the foreseeable future for continuing the war, are to be destroyed."

This is all Hitler can do: prepare for the end.

Hitler passes the time in the bunker, sleeping most days and then staying up until dawn most nights to scrutinize plans for battles that will never be fought. His palsied tremors make it impossible for him to turn the pages of a book, so he commands that his propaganda minister, Joseph Goebbels, read aloud to him from Thomas Carlyle's biography of Frederick the Great, the eighteenth-century Prussian warrior king who has always been an inspiration to the Führer.

Hitler specifically chooses Carlyle's book because it was the eminent Scottish historian who set forth the "Great Man" theory of history, which states that "the history of the world is but a biography of great men."

Leonidas was a great man.

Frederick was a great man.

Hitler considers himself a great man.

Reclining on the bed in his personal quarters as Goebbels sits in a nearby chair, Hitler is calmed by words that make a vivid comparison between Frederick's times and his own situation. It is a passage describing the winter of 1761/62, when all seemed lost during the Seven Years' War. Frederick had few allies at the time, and was also facing a multinational force that threatened to annihilate his Prussian troops.* Hitler is now himself facing Armageddon. Russian troops are poised to enter his capital city.

---

*Frederick's fortunes took a turn for the better when Britain stepped in as an ally, while Sweden and Russia withdrew their attacks, thus marking the end of the Seven Years' War. Prussia and Frederick the Great emerged from the conflict as a world power. It was his greatest triumph.

"The great king did not see any way out, and did not know what to do. All his generals and ministers were convinced that he was finished. The enemy already looked upon Prussia as vanquished," Goebbels reads. "If there was no change by February 15, he would give up and take poison."

Goebbels pauses. Hitler is utterly silent.

Then comes the advice Hitler is hoping for, delivered down through the ages from Frederick, through Carlyle. "Brave king, wait but a little while. The days of your suffering will be over. Behind the clouds the sun of your good fortune is already rising and soon will show itself to you."

Goebbels closes the book. He need read no further. Adolf Hitler, a man who believes in signs, knows that the universe is telling him not to give in.

The Führer begins to weep.

★ ★ ★

Just days later, Adolf Hitler receives yet another sign that Germany can still win the war. He summons all his top generals and ministers to the bunker to show them the news. "Here, you never wanted to believe it," he crows, distributing the report that he has just received.

The bunker erupts in cheers.

The news could not be more shocking: Hitler has prevailed over one of his biggest opponents.

American president Franklin Delano Roosevelt is dead.

18

---◆---

The president of the United States looks defeated. Sitting placidly near the French doors of his small vacation cottage, Franklin Roosevelt is trying to appear authoritative for the artist painting his portrait. He is failing.

Elizabeth Shoumatoff's paintbrush moves back and forth from palette to canvas, trying to capture the sixty-three-year-old president's image for posterity. But the task is difficult, as the president looks far older than his age.

FDR is exhausted from twelve years in office and the incredible burden of world war. Still, he soldiers on. His hands shake with a feeble palsy, forcing him to press his fountain pen firmly against the documents he is trying to sign as his portrait is being drawn.

Sitting in an alcove across the room, gazing adoringly at the president, is his longtime mistress, fifty-three-year-old Lucy Mercer Rutherfurd. Her husband, a prominent New York socialite nearly three decades her senior, has just died. But even while he was alive, Lucy and FDR carried on a thirty-year relationship. "He deserves a good time," his cousin Alice Roosevelt once remarked of their affair, "he's married to Eleanor."

It was British prime minister William Gladstone who said that the Eleventh Commandment for politicians is "Thou shall not get caught." The affair between Lucy Mercer Rutherfurd and FDR adheres to that

Lucy Mercer Rutherfurd

adage. Way back in 1918, Roosevelt promised his wife, Eleanor, that he would banish Lucy from his life—but that has not happened. Lucy is a tall, striking brunette with blue eyes and a flirtatious, fun-loving personality that is the polar opposite of Eleanor's prudish and critical one. Lucy is often by FDR's side when he travels outside Washington, and Secret Service agents clandestinely spirit her into the White House at the president's order.

Roosevelt arrived here at his beloved vacation home almost two weeks ago. This marks the forty-first time he has come to Warm Springs since taking office. When he boarded the *Ferdinand Magellan* for the overnight train ride from Washington down to Georgia, he was shrunken from weight loss. His face was pale and gray from exhaustion. His heart condition has worsened since his inauguration three months ago—in fact, FDR's health has declined so rapidly that Vice President Harry Truman is amazed that the president continues to take on so much work.

Suddenly, the artist Shoumatoff sees a crimson flush filling Roosevelt's cheeks. She has been struggling all morning with ways to make the president appear more youthful and robust, and is amazed at this instant change in his skin tone. The Russian-born painter reaches for the proper shade of red to capture this new ruddy glow.

What she does not know is that the president of the United States is in the early stages of a cerebral hemorrhage. Chronic hypertension brought on by years of smoking and lack of physical exercise has burst an artery in his brain. The surrounding tissue in his skull is now drenched in blood. There is no way to stanch the bleeding.

Roosevelt lurches, waving his right hand in the air. His left hand, like that entire side of his body, is now paralyzed. His face looks almost childish, as if the most powerful man in the world were lost and needed help finding his way.

"I have a terrific pain in the back of my head," he moans.

The president's eyes close. His head spills forward. FDR's trademark, that chin that so many cartoonists have drawn at a jaunty, uplifted angle, now settles atop his chest.

Roosevelt is immediately carried into his small bedroom by a butler and FDR's longtime valet, Arthur Prettyman. His blood pressure soars to 300 over 190. In a scene reminiscent of the death of Abraham Lincoln, a team of doctors soon arrives and begins to work feverishly to save him.

They fail.

At 2:15 p.m. Lucy Mercer Rutherfurd knows she must leave. She motions to Elizabeth Shoumatoff. "We must pack up and go," Lucy tells the painter. "The family will be arriving by plane, and the rooms must be vacant." She packs quickly, says good-bye to FDR one last time, and is out the door by 2:30.

At 3:35 p.m. the doctors labor no more.

FDR is gone.

★ ★ ★

Ninety minutes later, in Washington, Harry Truman walks into Speaker of the House Sam Rayburn's private office for a quiet glass of Old Grand Dad bourbon on the rocks. But Truman will have to hold off on that drink. An urgent message is waiting from White House press secretary Stephen Early, asking him to come to the White House as quickly as possible.

Truman leaves in such a hurry that he loses his Secret Service detail.* Once at the White House, he is led upstairs to the presidential residence, then immediately into Eleanor Roosevelt's study. Hundreds of framed photographs cover the walls of the enormous room. The First Lady sits on a chair, dressed in black, her face lit by the afternoon sun shining in through the two great windows. She was at a lunch, listening to a piano performance, when, like Truman, she received a call asking her to return to the White House.

She and her daughter, Anna, changed into black mourning dresses.† Eleanor then broke the news by cable to the Roosevelts' four sons, who are off serving in the military. Now she must break the news to the vice president that the man to whom she has been happily, and unhappily, married for forty years is dead.

Truman has no idea why he has been summoned. At first Eleanor gives nothing away. She was raised never to display emotion publicly, and is outwardly calm as he steps into the room. Her black dress provides the only clue as to what she is about to say. The First Lady walks to the vice president and tenderly places a hand on his shoulder.

"Harry," she informs him, "the president is dead."

Truman is shocked. "I had been afraid for some weeks that something would happen to this great leader, but now that this had happened I was unprepared for it," he will later recall.

---

*This is not unusual. Truman was in the habit of taking a long daily walk. Very often, he slipped out of the White House unnoticed and walked the five miles to the Marine Corps barracks and back. He believed that it was useless to worry about assassination, because if someone wanted to shoot him, they would find a way, regardless of Secret Service protection. This proved inaccurate on November 1, 1950, when two Puerto Rican nationals tried to sneak into a house where Truman was taking a nap. They were shot and killed by bodyguards. Truman was unharmed.

†Anna Roosevelt Boettiger was thirty-nine years old, and had recently moved back into the White House while her husband served in the military. The president put her to work, appointing Anna special assistant to the president. In this capacity, she soon learned many of the most well-kept secrets in the White House. It was Anna who had the unfortunate task of informing Eleanor Roosevelt about FDR's ongoing affair with Lucy Mercer Rutherfurd after the president's death. It was a number of years before Eleanor forgave Anna for her role in the deception.

Emotional as always, Truman fights back tears. The death of FDR is stunning, but not as much as the terrifying realization that he is now president of the United States.

"Is there anything I can do for you?" Truman asks, remembering his manners.

Eleanor Roosevelt looks hard at Harry Truman. "Is there anything *we* can do for *you?*" she says. "For you are the one in trouble now."*

★ ★ ★

Three thousand miles to the east, George Patton is just finishing his daily journal entries. The hour is late, but today has been extraordinary, and he needs to put every last detail on paper before going to bed. Finally, he closes his journal and puts down the pen.

Patton notices that his wristwatch needs winding. So he turns on the radio in the small truck trailer that serves as his field bedroom. He hopes to get the exact time from the British Broadcasting Corporation's evening broadcast.† Instead, he hears the shocking news that FDR is no more.

This is the wretched conclusion to what has been the most nerve-wracking day Patton has endured thus far in the war. Just after breakfast, he met with generals Dwight Eisenhower and Omar Bradley at his headquarters in an old Wehrmacht fort in Hersfeld, one hundred and sixty miles east of the Rhine. Together, they traveled to the town of Merkers, where Patton's army has just made an incredible find.

---

*America would be without a president for two hours and twenty-four minutes. Truman was not sworn in by Chief Justice Harlan Stone until 7:09 that evening. Part of the delay was waiting for Truman's wife, Bess, and daughter Margaret to travel to the White House. Another was the search for a Bible for the ceremony. Eventually, a cheap Gideon Bible was located in the office of chief usher Howell Crim, who made a point of dusting it before the ceremony.

†In a ritual that began in 1924 and still continues almost a century later, the BBC emits a series of "pips" at the top of each hour to denote the exact time. This is accomplished through the use of an atomic clock in the basement of the broadcast center. On the surface, this practice might seem to be an inordinate preoccupation with being punctual, but it actually saves lives. The "pips" are important for those sailors at sea who listen in to the BBC to set their watches, because exact time is vital to proper navigation, preventing them from sailing hundreds of miles off course.

The three men entered the mouth of a massive cave, where they boarded a flimsy wooden elevator that lowered them two thousand feet into a salt mine. The shaft was pitch black, so once the daylight above them narrowed to a pinprick during the descent, Patton could not see the other occupants of the car. Noting that the elevator was suspended from a single thin cable, he couldn't help but quip about their plight: "If that clothesline should break," he joked grimly, "promotions in the United States Army would be considerably stimulated."

"George, that's enough," shot back a nervous Eisenhower; "no more cracks until we are above ground again."

The purpose of their descent is of worldwide significance. Elements of Patton's Third Army accidentally discovered the Merkers mine while interrogating local citizens. The bombing of Berlin had forced the Nazis to smuggle their financial reserves out of the Reichsbank and to a place of safety. They chose this inaccessible salt mine. Literally hundreds of millions of dollars in the form of gold bars, currency, and priceless works of art were delivered the two hundred miles from Berlin to Merkers by train, then stored underground. As Patton, Eisenhower, and Bradley stepped off the darkness of the elevator and into the brightly lit cave, they found a surreal scene. Bags of gold and cash stretched as far as the eye could see. Hundreds of paintings and sculptures, including an Egyptian bust of Queen Nefertiti, lined the walls, along with paintings by Titian and Manet. In its way, the gathered wealth signifies the dissolution of the Nazi government. Without money in the capital city of Berlin, it can no longer wage war.

"In addition to the German Reichsmarks and gold bricks, there was a great deal of French, American and British gold currency. Also, a number of suitcases filled with jewelry, such as silver and gold cigarette cases, wristwatch cases, spoons, forks, vases, gold-filled teeth, false teeth, etc." Patton wrote in his journal.*

Patton suggests to Eisenhower that the gold be melted down into medals, "one for every son of a bitch in Third Army."

---

*The majority of the gold had been looted from the various nations conquered by Nazi Germany. Much of this was returned immediately after the war. The remainder was channeled into what was known as the Nazi Persecutee Relief Fund, which aided survivors of the Holocaust. This fund was exhausted in 1998.

222 ★ Bill O'Reilly and Martin Dugard

★   ★   ★

Later in the day, George Patton's mood abruptly shifts. The three generals lunch together and then go to tour the newly liberated concentration camp at Ohrdruf, eighty miles east of the Merkers mine. It was Patton's Fourth Armored Division—the first tanks into Bastogne and the first to reach the Rhine—that found the horrifying site. Unlike Auschwitz, where SS guards were so rattled by the approaching Russians that they fled before executing the inmates, many residents of Ohrdruf were either shot or marched off to the Buchenwald concentration camp. Many were so emaciated and malnourished that the bullet wounds in their skulls had not even bled.

Patton has seen death in many forms during his time in the military. He has seen men blown to pieces and seen others lose their entire faces to exploding shells. But nothing he has ever witnessed prepared him for Ohrdruf. "It was the most appalling sight imaginable," he will write in his journal.* A former inmate leads the tour, showing the generals the gallows where men were hanged for trying to escape, and the whipping table where beatings were administered at random. "Just beyond the whipping table," Patton later wrote, "there was a pile of forty bodies, more or less naked. All of these had been shot in the back of the head at short range, and the blood was still cooling on the ground."

At one point, Patton excuses himself from the tour and walks off to vomit against the side of a building.

"When our troops began to draw near, the Germans thought it expedient to remove the evidence of their crimes. They therefore used the inmates to exhume the recently buried bodies and to build a mammoth griddle of railway tracks laid on a brick foundation. The bodies were piled

---

*Eisenhower and Bradley were also deeply disturbed by what they saw. "The smell of death overwhelmed us," Bradley wrote in his memoirs. "More than 3,200 naked, emaciated bodies had been thrown into shallow graves. Others lay in the street where they had fallen. Lice crawled over the yellowed skin of their sharp, bony frames. A guard showed us how the blood had congealed in coarse black scabs where the prisoners had torn out the entrails of the dead for food." Ike's face "whitened into a mask," at the sight, in Bradley's description. Bradley then added, "I was too revolted to speak."

on this and they attempted to burn them. The attempt was a giant failure. Actually, one could not help but think of some giant cannibalistic barbecue," Patton wrote.

"In the pit itself were arms and legs and portions of bodies sticking out of the green water which partially filled it."

Writing those words should have been the end of the day for Patton, but the sudden news about FDR's death rates another journal entry. He thought highly of Roosevelt, and doubts that Truman will make much of a president.

Patton and Harry Truman actually fought together during World War I. Truman commanded artillery that protected his armored units in the Argonne Forest. But Patton does not know this. "It seems very unfortunate that in order to secure political preference, people are made vice presidents who were intended neither for the party nor by the Lord to be presidents," he writes in his journal before turning out the lights well past midnight.

★ ★ ★

Eight hours later, in the bathroom of his lavish suite at the Ritz Hotel in Paris, Wild Bill Donovan stands bare-chested, shaving. He arrived from London late last night and went to bed before FDR DEAD, the shortest wire service message in history, shocked the world. Right now, he does not yet know the bad news.

The spy in charge of the Office of Strategic Services last met with President Roosevelt less than a month ago, when FDR consented to give the full weight of his office to the formation of a new national spy organization. Donovan's future, and that of the fledgling CIA, seemed to be secure. Wild Bill has ordered many politically motivated assassinations—to him, murder is just one of many options in fulfilling a mission. But of late it has been just as important to pursue a policy of political gamesmanship. Donovan is good at that, and his hold on power seems to expand every day.

Donovan's suite will serve as his headquarters during his time in Paris. As with his London headquarters, at the equally luxurious Claridge's hotel, here aides and secretaries will stream in and out of the suite throughout the day, bringing Donovan cables and communiqués updating the actions of his ever-growing worldwide network of spies. So it is no surprise when J. Russell Forgan, the New York banker who now serves as the OSS London counterintelligence chief, races into the bathroom while Donovan is shaving.

For Donovan, the news that the president has died is nothing short of a calamity. He grabs a towel, wipes away his shaving cream, and immediately sends a condolence telegram to Eleanor.

Then Wild Bill Donovan sits down on the edge of his bed. It is a bed with a history, for it was used by Hermann Goering, head of the Luftwaffe, when he stayed in Paris during the Nazi occupation. Donovan knows this. But the Nazis are now the farthest thought from his mind. So is Franklin Roosevelt. Right now, the only thing on Wild Bill Donovan's mind is Wild Bill Donovan. His future appears in jeopardy. Without FDR to back him, his dreams of a postwar spy agency are now in peril.

Half-dressed and half-shaven, Donovan rests his head in his hands. "This is the most terrible news I've ever had," he moans.

Three hours later, he finally rises from the bed. His determination has returned.

19

———

HOUSES OF PARLIAMENT
LONDON, ENGLAND
APRIL 17, 1945
4:08 P.M.

onversation ceases as Winston Churchill rises to his feet. There is
Johnnie Walker scotch whisky on his breath, and he wears a bow tie
with his three-piece suit. The rotund prime minister's trademark half-
smoked, well-chewed cigar is nowhere to be seen as he stands somberly in
the center aisle of Britain's ornate House of Lords debating chamber, preparing to remember his late friend Franklin Delano Roosevelt. He was devastated when he received the news of FDR's death.

"I felt as if I had been struck a considerable blow," Churchill will write
in *The Second World War: Triumph and Tragedy*, the sixth volume of his
war memoirs. "I was overpowered by a sense of deep and irreparable loss."*

Standing five foot eight and weighing nearly three hundred pounds,
Winston Churchill is already a mythic figure in England. He is the son of
the legendary Randolph Churchill, a dynamic British statesman who died
at the age of forty-five never having fulfilled his goal of becoming prime
minister. It would be left to the eccentric Winston to fill that position,
although the journey was neither short nor easy. Winston was in a self-
described political wilderness for much of his career, and was considered
out of touch with political reality, thanks to his criticism of Nazi Germany
in the 1930s, a time when few British politicians were bothered by the rise
of Adolf Hitler. Once Churchill became prime minister in May 1940, at

---

*Joseph Stalin was informed by U.S. ambassador W. Averell Harriman, who made a
4:00 a.m. visit to the Kremlin to deliver the news. A visibly shaken Stalin took Harriman's
hand and held it for nearly a minute as he composed himself. The eternally suspicious
Stalin then suggested that FDR's body be autopsied for signs of food poisoning.

the height of the Nazi threat, he inspired the British people with fearless radio speeches that offered them hope at a time when they had none. When the Luftwaffe bombed London, Churchill was often seen in public, visiting bomb sites at great threat to his own life. Throughout his career, the one steadfast presence has been that of his wife, Clementine. They have been married for thirty-six years and have five children.

It is warm in London this April. "An excess of sunshine," in the words of one British meteorologist, now makes the air thick inside the century-old, un-air-conditioned chamber. Nevertheless, the 615 elected members of Parliament (MPs, for short) are almost all in attendance, seated in rows on either side of the aisle. Churchill's Conservative Party sits to his right, the opposition Labour Party to his left.

The MPs had more room to spread out before the war, but German bombers destroyed the House of Commons meeting room in 1941.* So now they pack into the smaller debating chamber, with its high ceilings and the boarded-up remains of the great stained-glass windows that were shattered by massive Luftwaffe *Betonbombes*.

The seventy-one-year-old Churchill is a creature of habit, rising each morning at 7:30 in his official residence at 10 Downing Street, just a half mile up the road from the Houses of Parliament. He works in bed until 11:00, whereupon he bathes, pours a weak Johnnie Walker Red scotch and water, and then works some more.† He sips Pol Roger champagne with

---

*The seating capacity was 802, which allowed more than enough room for the entire membership. At Churchill's insistence, the House of Commons was rebuilt in accordance with its original design between 1948 and 1950.

†Churchill was a close friend of the distiller Sir Alexander Walker. The prime minister favored hard alcohol, with beer being his least favorite beverage. However, he abhorred drunkenness, and was rarely known to drink to excess. Churchill's most famous drinking incident occurred just after the war, when the British Labour politician Bessie Braddock accosted him late one night as he left the House of Commons. "Winston, you are drunk. What's more, you are disgustingly drunk," she told him. To which Churchill replied, "Bessie, my dear, you are ugly. What's more, you are disgustingly ugly. But tomorrow I shall be sober, and you shall still be disgustingly ugly." Churchill borrowed the quote from the 1934 W. C. Fields movie *It's a Gift*. It's worth noting that despite exercising very little, if at all, and drinking so copiously, Churchill inherited a sturdy constitution. Well past his eightieth birthday, he could still boast of a very healthy blood pressure of 140 over 80.

lunch at 1:00 p.m. Whenever possible, this is followed by a game of backgammon with Clementine at 3:30. He takes a ninety-minute nap at 5:00 p.m. Arising, Churchill bathes a second time, works for an hour, eats a sumptuous dinner at 8:00 p.m., and smokes a post-dinner cigar with a vintage Hine brandy. After that, he goes back to his study for more work until well past midnight.

Unless he is traveling, this is how almost every day of Winston Churchill's life is structured, right down to the minute.

But today there is a different feel. Tonight will be the last time that American B-17s and British Lancasters will pound the German city of Dresden. Firebombs have already killed tens of thousands there. This was done with Churchill's full approval. One out of every 131 Londoners fell victim to German bombs, thus he has few moral qualms about punishing the German people.

What makes today special for Churchill is that it marks a personal and political crossroads. He must mourn the death of a very good friend whose company he compares with the joy one gets in drinking a fine glass of champagne, while also reckoning with the fact that this same friend betrayed him and the British people.

Conflicting emotions stir inside the prime minister as he begins his speech: "When I became Prime Minister, and the war broke out in all its hideous fury, when our own life and survival hung in the balance, I was already in a position to telegraph to the President on terms of an association which had become most intimate and, to me, most agreeable. This continued through all the ups and downs of the world struggle until Thursday last, when I received my last messages from him," Churchill says.

His voice is patrician and unmistakably English, and his tone is that of professor lecturing a classroom, allowing his fellow MPs a glimpse into what was long a private relationship.

One and all know that Churchill and Roosevelt were exceptionally close. What they do not know is that Roosevelt behaved very badly toward Churchill and England in the weeks leading up to his death. FDR was ineffectual in dealing with Joseph Stalin when the three met in the Black Sea resort of Yalta two months ago, allowing the Russians to dictate the future of postwar Europe at the expense of the British. It was Churchill who, during the early days of the war, relentlessly sought to build what he called the "Grand Alliance" between the three powers. To defeat Nazi Germany, he needed the industrial strength of the United States and the strategic power of Russia. But as time passed, Churchill was edged out of the alliance like an unwanted suitor.

Thus, the British Empire, which has ruled the globe since the voyages of Captain James Cook in the 1770s, is no more. Much of the world will soon be ruled by the United States and Russia.

Just as devastating to Churchill, a man who understands the powerful role symbolism plays in molding public opinion, the Americans are denying the British people their moment of glory. During the war, English cities have been bombed relentlessly, and homes set ablaze. The British Commonwealth has seen three million casualties in the deserts of Africa, in the jungles of Borneo, in the fields of Europe, and in the skies over their beloved Britain. Between 1939 and 1940 they stood with France against Nazi Germany. When France fell, England stood alone.

It was Roosevelt and America who came to their rescue. "There never was a moment's doubt, as the quarrel opened, upon which side his sympathies lay. The fall of France, and what seemed to most people outside this Island the impending destruction of Great Britain, were to him an agony, although he never lost faith in us."

Churchill now tells Parliament of the time FDR sent an emissary bearing a note "Written in his own hand. This letter contained the famous lines of Longfellow: 'Sail on, O ship of State, Sail on, O Union, strong and great! Humanity with all its fears, with all the hopes of future years, Is hanging breathless on thy fate!'"

Roosevelt did more than supply inspirational verse. He also "loaned" Great Britain ships, planes, tanks, and trucks.

"The bearing of the British nation at that time of stress, when we were all alone, filled him and vast numbers of his countrymen with the warmest sentiments towards our people," Churchill says to the members of Parliament.

The same Roosevelt of whom Churchill now speaks so warmly is the very politician who has just given Berlin to the Russians. All Allied forces on the Western Front, Field Marshal Bernard Law Montgomery's included, have been ordered to halt sixty miles short of Berlin, on the banks of the Elbe River.

The command came from Gen. Dwight Eisenhower, who now inexplicably sees Berlin as having no strategic value. Yet as Winston Churchill knows all too well, the order could not have been given without the approval of Franklin Delano Roosevelt. There are four million Allied soldiers in Germany right now, and three million of them are American. The people of the United States would find it unsettling to see a British commander get the glory of capturing the German capital, though Eisenhower sees no problem in allowing a Russian commander to know that very same sense of glory.

The British people will be denied that symbolic moment when Monty and his Tommies march into Berlin. There will be no victorious poses in front of Hitler's bombed-out Reichstag, allowing all of England to rejoice that their plucky island nation persevered in the face of long odds, and finally conquered the Führer's capital.

Making the betrayal sting even more is the fact that Churchill is half American. His mother, the beautiful Jenny Jerome Randolph, is from Brooklyn. His grandfather was editor of the *New York Times*. His ancestors came to America on the *Mayflower*, and a later generation wintered with George Washington at Valley Forge and waged a revolution against the British. Churchill is even distantly related to a Native American of the Iroquois nation. In this way, his forefathers were even more American than those of the late president.

Yet it is America that now commits the unconscionable act of deferring to Russia at the expense of Britain—in effect, killing England.

Winston Churchill is sad. Sad for his lost friend, sad for FDR's betrayals, sad for his nation, and, in the end, sad for the uncertainty that is to come. Churchill has already exchanged a number of cables with Harry Truman, and has yet to get a clear read on him.

After so many years of being wary of Nazi Germany, Churchill now sees the Russians as the world's greatest threat. The divide between the Communist worldview and that of Britain's is so great that Churchill will compare it to an "iron curtain," a phrase that will go down in history.

Churchill has been prime minister for five years. But unbeknownst to him, he will be voted out of office in just three months—rejected by the nation he loves, just as he was pushed aside by Stalin and FDR.

"For us, it remains only to say that in Franklin Roosevelt there died the greatest American friend we have ever known, and the greatest champion of freedom who has ever brought help and comfort from the new world to the old," Churchill concludes to a chorus of "Hear, hear" from MPs on both sides of the aisle.

The exhausted prime minister has spoken for twenty minutes. He then takes his seat. Winston Churchill could use a scotch. This has been a very long day.

20

George Patton and Winston Churchill are simpatico. They both believe that the Soviet Union is now the biggest threat to the world and to democracy. Patton is convinced that Churchill is the only man in power who knows what the world is "walking into."

For now, Patton keeps his comments to himself. Volatile words could get him fired—or even killed. Patton is a man of strong beliefs, and as he will tell the press in a few weeks, he is utterly sure of the Russian danger: "Churchill had a sense of history. Unfortunately, some of our leaders were just damn fools who had no idea of Russian history. Hell, I doubt if they even knew [that] Russia, just less than a hundred years ago, owned Finland, sucked the blood out of Poland, and were using Siberia as a prison for their own people. How Stalin must have sneered when he got through with them at all those phony conferences."*

This morning, Patton sits at his desk in one of the small trailers that form his mobile command center, thinking about his future. Unless he finagles a command in the Pacific, he knows that his career is all but done.

Still a powerful force, the Third Army was poised to wheel north to

---

*Quoted in statements to Third Army correspondents on May 8, 1945, at his head-quarters in Regensburg, Germany.

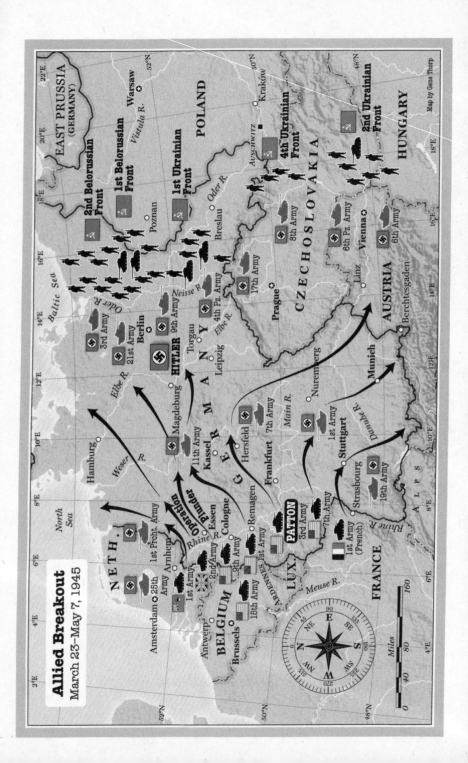

Allied Breakout
March 23–May 7, 1945

Map by Gene Thorp

capture Berlin, just as they made the hard left turn for Bastogne until Eisenhower stopped them.

Patton believes that letting the Russians have Berlin is folly. And he told Eisenhower this a few days ago. Americans should not only take Berlin, Patton said, but keep on pushing as far to the east as possible. In time, the entire world will come to realize that he is right.

But by then it will be too late. The Russians have already pushed through Austria and are now approaching Fortress Berlin from the south and east. Soon they will take total control of Eastern Europe—a stranglehold they will maintain for the next fifty years.

Fear of the Russians is spreading throughout Germany. Millions of civilian refugees flee toward the American lines—only to be turned back.* More than a half million German soldiers have raised their hands in surrender so that they will not have to face the Russians. In fact, so many Wehrmacht fighters are giving up that the Allies no longer accept all prisoners of war, because it is impossible to house and feed so many men. When the men of the once feared Eleventh Panzer Division attempt to quit the war, the Third Army will accept them as prisoners only under the condition that they bring their own food.

As Patton sips coffee in his headquarters, he knows that his future may lie as a civilian. He has once again appeared on the cover of *Time* magazine, and is at last getting the kind of public respect and glory he so desperately craves. Should Patton enter politics, he will be a formidable force.

But the war isn't over. For the first time in recent memory, the Third Army is not being ordered to go on the defensive. In fact, the opposite is true. Patton has just been given an additional three armored divisions so he can spearhead the final American attacks of the war in southern Germany.

"There was a big meeting yesterday and we got the ball for what looks like the final play," he writes to Beatrice. As a general, he is not

---

*There was great confusion about what was to be done with so many refugees. They had left their homes and farms. It was thought that they should be turned back, sent where they came from, and left to fend for themselves against the Russians, many of whom had been resettled in these very farms and homes. The refugees had no place to go and were unwelcome everywhere.

234 ★ Bill O'Reilly and Martin Dugard

subject to having his letters read by the military censors. Yet his wording is deft, nonetheless: he alludes to what is about to happen yet does not violate national security, lest this letter somehow fall into German hands.

His letter to his wife continues: "Sometimes I feel that I may be nearing the end of this life. I have liberated 'J.' and licked the Germans. So what else is there to do?"

The "J." to whom Patton refers is his son-in-law, thirty-eight-year-old Col. John Waters, who was captured in Tunisia two years ago.

★   ★   ★

On the surface, Task Force Baum, the "Hammelburg mission," was simply a daring attempt to rescue American prisoners of war. Shortly after crossing the Rhine in late March, Patton received word that the POW camp near the German town of Hammelburg held three hundred U.S. soldiers—many of them officers. Its location was sixty long miles from Patton's army. Among them was Col. John Waters, the husband of Patton's beloved daughter Beatrice.

After conquering the Polish town of Szubin, Russian soldiers had discovered the remains of a hastily abandoned POW camp. The Allied prisoners had been marched three hundred miles west in the dead of February to prevent their falling into Russian hands. Prison records showed that Waters was once incarcerated there.

Patton will later insist that he did not know Waters was incarcerated in Hammelburg. Yet the truth is he was informed of this fact by the American Military Mission in Moscow on February 9. Furthermore, on the eve of the attack, Patton specifically wrote to Beatrice, "Hope to send an expedition tomorrow to get John."

Patton's staff questioned his plan to rescue the prisoners, stating that Patton needed at least thirty-five hundred men to liberate the POW camp, rather than the mere three hundred who were being deployed. Even the hero of Bastogne, Lt. Col. Abe Abrams, thought the mission so foolish that he turned it down, giving the command role to Lt. Harold Cohen. But Cohen didn't want it, either. He told Patton that he was incapacitated by hemorrhoids. Patton called Cohen's bluff, ordering that he be taken into the next room and examined by a doctor. Only when the hemorrhoids were confirmed did Patton give the lead role to Capt. Abra-

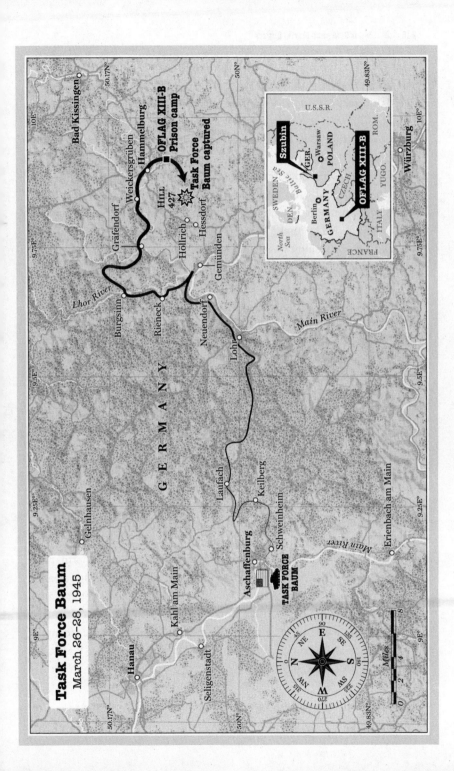

ham J. Baum, the twice-wounded twenty-three-year-old son of a Brooklyn blouse maker.

Baum and his rescue force were already exhausted from the Rhine crossing. They were handed just fifteen maps for fifty-seven vehicles. It was possible that Task Force Baum would not even find Hammelburg, let alone the POW camp.

Yet Patton, normally such a meticulous planner, ordered the rescue mission to proceed. Gen. Douglas MacArthur had received a great deal of media exposure for liberating thousands of Allied POWs in the Pacific, and Patton hoped to "make MacArthur look like a piker."*

German opposition was heavy, and soon half the task force lay dead or dying.

But the Americans got through. Less than twenty-four hours after setting out, Task Force Baum miraculously arrived at the gates of Oflag XIII-B, as the camp was known. Seeing gray uniforms, they began firing at what they mistakenly believed to be German guards. Instead, the uniforms belonged to Serbian prisoners of war being interned at the camp. The German commandant, Gen. Günther von Goeckel, took pity on the Serbians and requested that a contingent of American prisoners march out the gates and tell their rescuers to cease firing. Meanwhile, von Goeckel and the remaining German guards fled. They no longer had any interest in defending the camp.

At 6:15 p.m., Patton's son-in-law Colonel Waters marched out the front gate carrying a white flag of surrender. Several American officers and a lone German officer were by his side. Waters was noticeably gaunt from more than forty pounds of weight loss. He walked slowly, intending to tell Captain Baum to stop firing.

Waters never made it. A German guard in a camouflage uniform, not knowing that a truce had been arranged by the camp commandant, steadied his rifle atop a fence post and took careful aim. The bullet entered John Waters's right hip and exited through his left buttocks. He collapsed to the ground, where he lay until he could be carried back into the camp. There, fellow POW and chief surgeon of the Yugoslavian Army, Radovan Danic, quickly removed the bullet.

*Quoted by Martin Blumenson, Patton's staff historian for the Third Army.

As Task Force Baum stormed the gates to the camp, cheered by hundreds of American prisoners, one thing became quite clear: Col. John Waters wasn't physically capable of going anywhere.

Captain Baum soon found himself faced with another dilemma: instead of three hundred POWs, there were well over a thousand. The task force simply didn't have enough vehicles to carry every single prisoner back to freedom. The convoy needed to turn around and race back to the American lines under cover of darkness before the Germans could counterattack.

An estimated seven hundred prisoners soon draped themselves atop tanks and halftracks, gorging themselves on K-rations the task force had brought along for just that purpose.* Those well enough to walk followed along behind the column.

The Germans counterattacked at sunrise the next morning. The strength of the Nazi reprisal was terrifying. Swiftly and efficiently, they destroyed the American column and began rounding up the POWs for their return to Oflag XIII-B. Many who were not prisoners of war before the rescue attempt now found themselves in German captivity. Wehrmacht soldiers used dogs to hunt down the Americans now scattered across the countryside. Captain Baum was burned when a rocket hit his tank, and suffered a gunshot wound to the groin, yet he managed to evade the Germans for almost twenty-four hours before being captured and led into captivity.†

Nine days later, the American Fourteenth Armored Division liberated the POW camp. Patton's initial raid, which had cost thirty-two men their lives, was all for naught.

George Patton immediately visited his son-in-law at a hospital in Frankfurt, where Colonel Waters had been taken to recuperate from his wounds.

---

*The K-ration was a boxed meal containing breakfast, lunch, or dinner. A full box typically consisted of tinned food, crackers, cigarettes, matches, and dessert.

†Later in life, Baum will devote himself to the creation of the Israeli state. The Jewish tank commander will also exchange holiday cards with camp commandant von Goeckel. He will become good friends with John Waters, who went on to become a four-star general. However, at the time, he was furious that Patton had risked so much for just one man.

Upon seeing Patton, the colonel burst out, "Did you know I was at Hammelburg?"

It was the first question out of Waters's mouth, because he well knew that many considered him to blame for a horrible waste of American lives. Thirty-two Americans had been killed, and almost three hundred more wounded or taken prisoner. In addition, sixteen tanks, twenty-eight halftracks, twelve jeeps, and a medical vehicle known as a Weasel were destroyed.

"Not for sure," came the answer from his father-in-law.

★ ★ ★

Patton has sworn a professional oath of honor that does not allow lying, cheating, or tolerating those who do so. Covering up the real reason for Task Force Baum was not the first of George S. Patton's untruths. One lie, in particular, broke his wife Beatrice's heart and almost cost him his marriage, and may now be coming back to haunt him. For the beautiful young woman with whom he was secretly unfaithful has once again entered his life.

The year was 1935. The place was Hawaii. Jean Gordon was visiting the Patton family on her way to the Orient. A willowy unmarried young woman who spoke fluent French, she was the daughter of Beatrice Patton's half sister, and thus the general's niece by marriage. She also served as maid of honor at the wedding between Patton's daughter Beatrice and John Waters. Patton was old enough to know better, a career soldier and the father of three children who had long enjoyed the love of a wife who understood his unusual temperament. Beatrice was a remarkable woman in her own right, capable of making conversation in German, French, Spanish, and Italian. She had written a book, and had a passion for music and drama. And her ferocious passion for her husband was such that, on one occasion, she physically attacked an officer who had disparaged her beloved Georgie. Patton had to pry her off the man when she knocked him down and was banging his head on the tile floor.

When the eighteen-year-old Jean began flirting with her husband, Beatrice was unaware. George Patton was flattered. So it was that when Beatrice Patton fell ill shortly before a planned journey from one Hawai-

Jean Gordon in her Red Cross uniform

ian island to another, Jean went in her place. There was no chaperone to prevent what occurred next.

When a heartbroken Beatrice learned of the tryst, she told her daughter Ruth Ellen, "It's lucky for us that I don't have a mother. Because if I did, I'd pack up and go home to her now."

That might have been the end of it, because for all intents and purposes the relationship between George Patton and Jean Gordon seemed to have run its course.

But in the summer of 1944, Jean arrived in England as a Red Cross volunteer and wasted no time in reconnecting with Patton. When Beatrice learned that Jean was in England, she wrote to her husband that she was aware that Patton's former lover had returned to his side, but Patton denied spending time with the young woman. Still, once the Third Army began its drive across France, Jean managed to get assigned to the task of Red Cross "donut girl" for the troops, visiting them and providing them with donuts, hot coffee, and conversation. She became a regular at Patton's headquarters, where she often spoke fluent French with the general.

Infatuated, Patton confided to a West Point classmate, "She's been mine for twelve years."

On March 31, 1945, Beatrice wrote to her husband wondering why Jean Gordon was still in Europe. Patton replied, "I am not a fool. So quit worrying."

When, soon after, Patton learned that Jean Gordon was also having an affair with a young officer serving in a safe headquarters position, the general, as competitive as ever, ordered the young man transferred to frontline combat.

★   ★   ★

Late on the afternoon of April 17, Patton flies to Paris. His son-in-law has been moved to a nearby hospital, and he sits with Waters for a long discussion. The controversy surrounding the Hammelburg incident seems to be blowing over. Dwight Eisenhower reprimanded Patton, but little else is being done. It appears there will be no further repercussions.

Patton sits for breakfast the next morning with his old West Point classmate Gen. Everett Hughes. The two men are very close, and it is to Hughes that Patton confides his relationship with Jean Gordon.

The waiter hands Hughes a copy of the American military newspaper *Stars and Stripes*. Hughes smiles at an announcement printed in the paper, but says nothing as he hands the newspaper over to Patton.

Patton suddenly grins broadly as he reads the news that President Harry Truman has just nominated him for the rank of four-star general. He leans back in his chair as those all around him in the dining room who've already read the news wait to see his response.

"Well, I'll be goddamned."

★   ★   ★   ★

The biblical David was also a great general. He was said to be "a man after God's own heart," despite the fact that he slept with his best friend's wife, lied about the act, and then ordered the husband sent to the front lines so that he might be murdered in battle.

Yet David ultimately paid a steep price for his behavior, losing a son at a very young age and eventually losing his entire kingdom.

Like David, George Patton knows himself to be a flawed yet God-fearing man. His recent bouts of duplicity have also cost more lives than the duplicities of King David. But as Patton flies back to his headquarters in a plane newly decorated with insignia denoting his four-star rank, it appears that he will not endure the divine punishments that befell David. In fact, Patton has weathered the storm unscathed.

But as the devout general well knows, David once thought the same thing, too.

★   ★   ★   ★

Patton's single-engine L-5 Sentinel propeller plane flies low over the German countryside, en route to his headquarters. It is the quickest way to travel from one place to another, allowing the general to visit several of his units each day. Suddenly another aircraft drops down on him like an avenging angel. Guns blazing, the Spitfire fighter bears the markings of the British Royal Air Force, and attacks head-on.

Patton's L-5 is an American-made plane. Yet with its wings mounted above the fuselage and the slow speeds caused by its fixed landing gear, the L-5 also bears a distinct resemblance to the German Fi-156 Storch.

Tracer bullets fly past the right side of Patton's L-5. The small plane has no weaponry, and thus no chance of fighting back. The Spitfire misses on the first pass, almost colliding with the L-5 as it roars past, but is soon banking high into the sky and coming around behind them for another strafing run.

It is either a case of mistaken identity or a bold attempt to murder George Patton in broad daylight.

Patton reaches for his camera. He snaps several pictures of the RAF plane, even as his pilot takes desperate evasive measures that make the Spitfire miss them a second time. Patton is so terrified that he forgets to take the lens cap off the camera. His aircraft is no match for the Spitfire, which was so famously effective at defeating German Messerschmitt fighter planes during the Battle of Britain.

But the pilot who has been assigned to fly General Patton on this April morning is extremely good at his job. He pushes the stick forward, pressing the L-5 down almost right against the earth. Just one slip of his fingers and the plane will nose into the ground.

The Spitfire comes in low and shoots again. The shots miss, and the careless Spitfire pilot realizes too late that his angle of attack places him too low to the ground. A split second later, the British fighter plane crashes into the German soil.

"It flew so close to the ground that it could not pull out and crashed," Patton writes in his journal that night. "The planes in this group had RAF markings on them, and I believe they were probably a Polish group flying for the RAF. Why there were out of their area, I don't know."

George S. Patton has lived to fight another day. "Four other planes were circling over us, but did not engage in the attack."

Patton must now contemplate an obvious nagging question: Was the Spitfire attack an accident?*

---

*The name of the attacker has never been verified, nor has the nationality of the pilot. Although the plane had Polish markings, there were no Polish Spitfires in that part of Germany on April 20.

21

The man who will be dead in ten days is marking his fifty-sixth birthday.

Adolf Hitler's mistress, Eva Braun, is in the mood to dance, but the Führer merely slumps on the blue-and-white couch in the sitting room of his underground bunker. He stares into space, paying no attention to the playful Eva or to the sleek blue brocade dress hugging her thighs. She knows that the prudish Hitler doesn't like her to dress provocatively, but on this occasion Eva does as she pleases.

The two of them, along with three of Hitler's female secretaries, sip champagne. It is the end of what has been another long and depressing day for the Führer.

Adolf Hitler once dreamed of establishing Berlin as the world's most cosmopolitan city, even though its citizens have long considered him to be an unsophisticated bore. Back in the days when Germany held free elections, the people of Berlin were almost unanimous in rejecting Hitler and his National Socialist German Workers' Party. Even now, thirteen years later, Berlin is considered the least Nazi of all cities in Germany. To spite its inhabitants, Hitler had planned to rename the city Germania during the grand postwar rebuilding, thus wiping Berlin off the map forever.

The advancing Russians know nothing about Germania. And they are also not waiting until the end of the war to wipe Berlin off the map.

Eva Braun

The armies of Joseph Stalin have the city almost completely surrounded. It is just a matter of time before it falls.

Per tradition, Hitler was joined in the bunker for his birthday celebration this morning by the Nazi Party's most elite membership: SS leader Heinrich Himmler, Reichsmarschall Hermann Goering, and chief of the operations staff Gen. Alfred Jodl, among them.

But now these killers are gone—for good. They have paid their respects to Hitler and are running for their lives, desperate to get out of Berlin and save their own skins, planning eventually to adopt new identities.

Only the most faithful followers remain. Martin Bormann, Hitler's private secretary, continues to prove his loyalty by remaining in the bunker. Hitler is glad. It has been said that Bormann is so threatening that he can "slit a throat with a whisper." A testimony to his character comes from none other than Hitler, the most callous of men. The Führer deems Bormann to be utterly "ruthless."

Bormann is now upstairs on the top floor of the bunker, hard at work despite the late hour and the approaching danger.

There is still time for Hitler to find a way out of Berlin. The Soviets are closing in, but some roads remain open. As recently as yesterday, the Führer was planning to escape to his Eagle's Nest retreat, high in the mountains of southern Germany. He even sent some members of the household staff ahead to prepare for his arrival. But he has since changed his mind, deciding to stay in the bunker, hoping against hope that the phantom divisions seen only by him will somehow repel the Russians.

As he does so often, Hitler takes solace in thoughts of Frederick the Great, who suffered a devastating defeat at the Battle of Kunersdorf in 1759. If Frederick could lose and then regain power, perhaps the Führer can find some miraculous way to do the same.

At last, Hitler announces he is going to bed. He looks awful as he stands to walk the five steps into his bedroom: face pale, back stooped, eyes bloodshot from fatigue, and his entire body shaking. He is beyond medical help. His cocaine eye drops were administered this morning, but tomorrow he is sending Dr. Morell away, explaining that "drugs can't help me anymore."

With those words, Hitler admits defeat. There will be no Germania. The Führer can hear Russian artillery falling on Berlin, the explosions resounding through the city, thundering closer and closer to the lovely park known as the Tiergarten, to the Reichstag, and then, inevitably, shaking the ground directly above him in the Reich Chancellery park. Hitler doesn't know if the bunker's thick roof can handle a direct hit, but he likes his chances inside his underground fortress better than on top, out in the open. Earlier today, he walked up the steps into the garden and spoke to a collection of young boys from the Hitler Youth, who had distinguished themselves in the face of Russian tanks. With the rumble of artillery as a backdrop, Hitler reviewed the rows of assembled young soldiers, his frail body all but swallowed up inside his brownish green overcoat. Despite his obvious palsy, he shook each and every young man's hand. Then he exhorted them to save Berlin. "Heil Euch," he barked as distracted words of praise before descending once again into the bunker—"Hail to you."

The ceremony marks the last time Adolf Hitler will ever see the light of day.

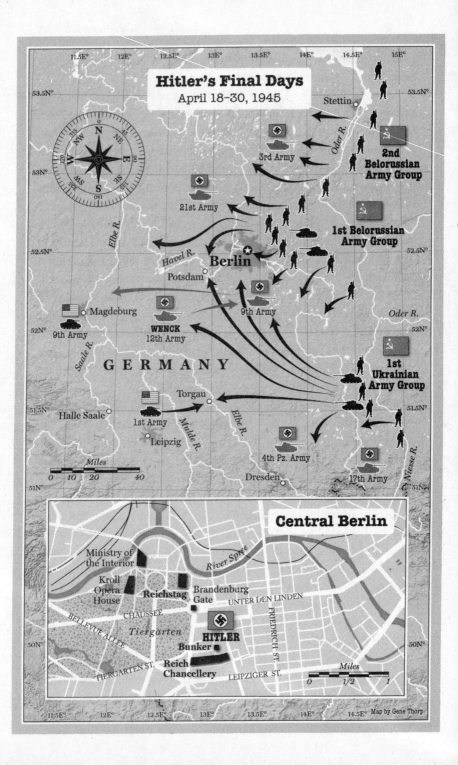

Hitler's Final Days
April 18–30, 1945

Stettin

Oder R.

3rd Army

2nd Belorussian Army Group

21st Army

1st Belorussian Army Group

Berlin

Havel R.

Potsdam

9th Army

Oder R.

Magdeburg

WENCK
12th Army

9th Army

Saale R.

1st Ukrainian Army Group

GERMANY

Torgau

1st Army

Mulde R.

Elbe R.

Elbe R.

Halle Saale

Leipzig

4th Pz. Army

17th Army

Neisse R.

Dresden

Miles

0 10 20 40

Central Berlin

Ministry of the Interior

River Spree

Kroll Opera House

Reichstag

Brandenburg Gate

UNTER DEN LINDEN

BELLEVUE ALLEE

CHAUSSEE

Tiergarten

FRIEDRICH ST.

HITLER
Bunker

TIERGARTEN ST.

Reich Chancellery

LEIPZIGER ST.

Miles

0 1/2 1

Map by Gene Thorp

That was hours ago. Now Eva Braun helps him to bed, assisting him as he changes out of his uniform and into his plain white nightshirt. Thanks to years of living nocturnally, his body is "bright white," in the words of one secretary.

Eva does not get in bed with her beloved Adolf. Instead, she steps back into the sitting room, closing behind her the door dividing the two rooms.

Now that the Führer is asleep, it's time to party.

"Eva Braun wanted to numb the fear that had awoken in her heart," Traudl Junge, one of the secretaries sipping champagne in Hitler's sitting room, will one day remember. "She wanted to celebrate once again, to dance, to drink, to forget."

Eva beckons the three young women to follow. The group climbs the steps to the second floor. They sweep through the bunker, rounding up everyone, uptight Martin Bormann among them. "Even fat Theo Morell came up from the safety of his bunker, in spite of the constant thunder of artillery fire," Junge will later write.

The party marches through the secret underground tunnel connecting the bunker with the Reich Chancellery, where Hitler keeps a small apartment. The paintings have been removed from the walls and the furniture moved down into the bunker, but there is still a gramophone in the room, and one very special record: "Blood-Red Roses Speak of Happiness to You."

Eva Braun knows the words of the song by heart. She and Adolf Hitler have been listening to this record by the Max Mensing Orchestra over and over again. The Führer enjoys classical music and even the solos of Jewish pianist Artur Schnabel, but the dance orchestra sound of "Blood Red Roses" is *their* song.

Champagne bottles are uncorked. The record player is turned up loud. Eva Braun whirls around the room, alone or with anyone who will dance with her. Blond and vivacious, she is the life of the party.

A distant explosion makes the room shake. The party ceases, but only temporarily. So Eva Braun dances on, "In a desperate frenzy, like a woman who has already felt the faint breath of death," Traudl Junge will remember. "No one said anything about the war. No one mentioned victory. No one mentioned death. This was a party given by ghosts."

★ ★ ★ ★

Three days later, Gen. Walther Wenck, commander of the German Twelfth Army, is up past midnight in his headquarters, a gamekeeper's home known Alte Holle, or "Old Hell." Located in a thick forest thirty miles west of Berlin, it is an ideal hiding place from Allied reconnaissance planes.

The phone rings. Wenck answers and learns that Field Marshal Wilhelm Keitel, Adolf Hitler's arrogant chief of staff, will soon be paying him a visit.

Walther Wenck is a fine officer. At forty-three, he is the youngest man in the Wehrmacht to hold a general's rank. As such, he bears the nickname the "Boy General." Currently, Wenck has taken it upon himself to house and feed a half million war refugees who have fled Berlin. He does this without informing his superiors. Rather than drawing up battle plans, Wenck spends his days "like a visiting priest," checking in on the children and sick to make sure they have food and medicine.

In truth, the general is physically incapable of doing much else. Just two months ago, he was fighting the Russians on the Eastern Front, near the Oder River. His duties required him to direct his troops by day, then drive back into Berlin each evening to brief Hitler himself in the bunker. The pace was exhausting, and Wenck got little sleep. On February 14, while making the one-hundred-mile drive back to his headquarters after one such meeting, Wenck elected to take the wheel when his chauffeur collapsed from fatigue.

It was late at night. Wenck himself soon fell asleep. The car plowed into a bridge parapet. Wenck's chauffeur pulled the unconscious general from the wreckage and smothered the flames that were on the verge of engulfing his body. Wenck survived but suffered a skull fracture and five broken ribs. He was relieved of his frontline command, but with the Russians advancing so quickly, he was not afforded the luxury of a lengthy hospital stay. Instead, now wearing a corset and enduring the occasional blinding headache, he enjoys the quiet of the forest while guarding against an Allied attack that will never come.

The Russians encircle Berlin without any accompanying pincer movement by the Americans or British, so Wenck's Twelfth Army stands down west of Berlin. The general is preparing to surrender to the Allies rather than let his men fall into Russian hands.

True to form, Keitel shows up at Wenck's headquarters in his best uniform, complete with field marshal's baton.

"The battle for Berlin has begun," Keitel says somberly. Wenck loathes the man.

The field marshal then divulges a terrible secret: Wenck's army is Berlin's only hope. He orders the Twelfth to ignore the Americans who are approaching from the west and immediately turn in the opposite direction to save Berlin.

It is 12:45 on the morning of April 23.

★ ★ ★ ★

At that very moment, eleven hundred miles east in Moscow, Joseph Stalin has already foreseen the fall of Berlin. He now signs a directive known as Stavka 11074, dictating that the First Belorussian and First Ukrainian armies divide the city between them. Of his top generals, it will be Marshal Georgy K. Zhukov, the shaven-headed hero of Stalingrad and the Battle of Moscow, who will get the honor of hoisting the Soviet flag atop the German Reichstag.

Stalin's power is at its pinnacle. He is thinking far beyond the last days of the Third Reich. The Soviet dictator is sure that a new war will soon begin, and equally sure of Communist victory.

But, for now, he has ordered that no brutality be spared the Germans. He wants maximum suffering inflicted. With that thought in mind, he prepares for sleep.

★ ★ ★ ★

Gen. Walther Wenck has no time for sleep. If he disobeys Keitel, he will be relieved of his command and most likely shot. Any hope of saving his men, who call him Pappi, as a term of endearment, will be lost. Yet if he follows the field marshal's order, his army will be destroyed by the Russians and the refugees to whom he now devotes his days will be left to suffer whatever horrors the Red Army wishes to impose upon them.

There is no good outcome for Wenck. Yet Field Marshal Keitel demands an answer right now.

"Of course," Wenck tells him. "We will do as you order."

But Gen. Walther Wenck is lying.

★ ★ ★ ★

Some 2.5 million Russians ring Berlin, outnumbering German soldiers three to one in men, tanks, aircraft, and artillery. The city's inner limits are defended by teenage Hitler Youth, the Volkssturm people's militia, and units of elderly Home Guardsmen. Few of them are battle-tested.

It will be a slaughter. Hordes of approaching Red Army soldiers, many of whom have marched a thousand miles to see their nation's flag raised over the capital of Germany, are eager to brutalize its citizens.

Forty thousand Russian artillery guns hammer the city around the clock, filling the streets with rubble and setting homes ablaze. In time, the Russians will drop more tonnage of explosives on Berlin than the American and British air forces combined.

Berliners no longer pretend that life is normal. Thousands of refugees leave the city each day, hoping to find safety in the countryside. They walk, push their belongings in carts, and choke the roads in vehicles that are often abandoned when gasoline runs out. They sleep in churches, forests, abandoned railway cars. Everyone travels west. Only a fool would travel east.

For those who choose not to leave Berlin, the nightly ritual of sleeping in cellars and underground stations has become revolting. The rancid odor of excrement and unwashed bodies makes these fetid spaces appalling. Of course, the wealthy are somewhat immune to these problems for now. For instance, the family who owns the tony restaurant Gruban-Souchay enjoy a fine life in their cellar, complete with a French chef and countless bottles of champagne, which substitute for water when it comes time for brushing teeth.

Aboveground, roving gangs of Nazi thugs and SS units travel from house to house, searching for Wehrmacht deserters and then hanging them from lampposts. Signs bearing the word *traitor* are pinned to the offenders' chests, and their bodies are left to swing freely as a warning to others who might wish to quit the war prematurely.

At the notorious Lehrterstrasse Prison, Nazi fanatics finish their dirty work. A special Gestapo contingent known as the Sonderkommando pretends that it is freeing political prisoners. As the men depart their cells, however, they are forced at gunpoint to kneel. Armed Gestapo agents then fire bullets into the back of their necks.

There is no gas. There is no electricity. There is little food. (The only item that remains a normal part of daily life in Berlin is beer. Citing its "essential" nature, the government has ordered eleven local breweries to remain open.) German women kneel in the streets butchering workhorses that have been killed by Russian shelling. Other citizens seek food by trekking to the city's rail yards and breaking into freight trains, searching for canned goods and anything else that will fill their bellies.

Uniformed Hitler Youth members walk into grocery stores and demand food at gunpoint. "You are a godless youth, using American gangster methods," one woman screams at her nephew after she watches him terrorize a shopkeeper into giving him a hidden cache of food.

"Shut up," the Hitler Youth sneers. "It's now a matter of life and death."

In some parts of Berlin, shopkeepers give away everything on the shelves, not wanting their supplies to fall into Russian hands.

Throughout the city, department stores are being looted—among them, the cavernous Karstadt, on the Hermannplatz. Late on the afternoon of April 25, as otherwise law-abiding citizens steal boots and heavy jackets, an explosion brings the building crashing down. It is not the Russians who destroy Karstadt and kill innocent civilians, but the SS. They have hidden a fortune worth twenty-nine million German marks in the basement, and they do not want the Russians to get it.

The worst, however, is yet to come. Many of the Russian invaders are professional soldiers with civilized manners and bearing. But far more of them are barbarians, men who grew up in the remote Eurasian steppes, those vast wild plains far from the big city lights of Moscow. These illiterate and unkempt hordes wear fur hats and carry knives in their boots. Many have never seen a flush toilet. They chug vodka by the tumbler and believe that the women of Berlin are their just reward for years of fighting. Their leader, Joseph Stalin, agrees.

George S. Patton does not refer to these crude invaders as Russians.

Instead, he prefers "Mongolians," in reference to Genghis Khan and the Mongol hordes who ravaged eastern Europe six centuries ago—for many of these men are their direct descendants.

Now the barbarians are coming to stay.

★ ★ ★ ★

A week passes. Russian troops advance street by street, slowly taking control of the city. The outmanned young boys and old men enlisted as a last line of German defense now tear off their uniforms and armbands, frantically changing back into civilian clothing to avoid being murdered. Those who choose to stand and fight are now retreating into the heart of the city. An attempt to blow up vital bridges to stall the Russian advance ends in tragedy when an underground railway tunnel is mistakenly detonated. Inside are thousands of civilians and wounded soldiers trying to avoid the aboveground artillery. They drown as the four-mile-long tunnel floods with water.*

Nazi leaflets litter the city, dropped from one of the few remaining Luftwaffe aircraft. "Persevere!" they read. "General Wenck and General Steiner are coming to the aid of Berlin."

Wenck is certainly trying, although not in the way that Nazi officials had hoped. He has turned the Twelfth Army back toward Berlin, surprising Russian forces near the suburb of Potsdam. But the Germans are vastly outnumbered and can soon go no farther. Rather than fight onward, Wenck orders his troops to open a corridor from the city that will allow refugees and elements of the German Ninth Army to follow him back to the safety of the American lines. "It's not about Berlin anymore," he tells his army as they turn their backs on the German capital. "It's not about the Reich anymore." In time, Wenck will lead hundreds of thousands of German civilians and soldiers westward across the Elbe, where he will surrender to American troops.† The Russians chase Wenck's

---

*An estimated eighty thousand Russians died in the Battle of Berlin. Civilian casualties are difficult to place, but it is estimated that between eighty thousand and one hundred thousand citizens of Berlin were killed.

†Walther Wenck was arrested as a prisoner of war and held by the Americans until 1947. He died in 1982, following an automobile crash. He was eighty-one years old.

long columns of civilians and soldiers all the way to the American lines, shooting at them right up until the moment they cross the Elbe.

But even if General Wenck had succeeded in reaching Central Berlin, there would have been no stopping the Russians. Berlin is a city with 248 bridges, and only 120 have been destroyed as the Soviets penetrate closer and closer to the *Führerbunker*. With every new block they capture, the Russians pause and take what they believe to be theirs. The stories of their savagery will become legendary: the two Russian soldiers who rip a nursing infant from his mother's breast, calmly place the child in his carriage, and then take turns raping the mother; the soldiers who silence an eighty-year-old woman by stuffing a stick of butter in her mouth before violating her. Incredibly, countless women in maternity wards throughout Berlin, some about to go into labor and some who have just given birth, are raped. Horrified screams echo up and down hospital corridors as heartless Russians have their way.

Everywhere, there are suicides: the mother so ashamed by her rape that she ties two shopping satchels full of bricks to her arms, hugs her two infant children, and jumps into the Havel River with them clutched in her grasp; the woman gang-raped all night long who staggers home in the morning to find that her own mother has hanged her three children to protect them, and then hanged herself; the distraught woman sees no other choice but to slash her own wrists.

"The Germans were worse than this in Russia," a German woman is told when she complains about the atrocities to a Russian officer. "This is simply revenge."

★ ★ ★ ★

The date is April 30, shortly before 2:00 p.m. The Führer is saying farewell. His staff lines up in the corridor outside his bedroom. Wearing a dark gray uniform jacket and creased black pants, Hitler shakes each hand and whispers a personal message to the two dozen secretaries, soldiers, and doctors who have tended to him during his three months in the bunker. They have all sworn an oath of loyalty to the Führer, but he now releases them from that bond, giving them permission to leave the bunker immediately and flee to the American lines, should they choose.

All the while, Eva Braun stands at the Führer's side wearing a black dress with pink roses framing the square neckline. She has chosen this dress specifically, for it is Hitler's favorite. Her blond hair is washed and perfectly coiffed.

After the Führer speaks with Traudl Junge, Eva pulls the secretary close and whispers in her ear, "Please do try to get out. You may yet make it through."

Eva Braun, of course, is not leaving. She has just sworn the ultimate loyalty oath to the Führer: yesterday they were married. These same servants gathered to celebrate the wedding of Adolf Hitler and Eva Braun. Glasses of champagne were filled; only the Führer did not partake. The mood was outwardly joyous, but there was a somber tone to the proceedings. Marriage is normally a time of hope for the future. But everyone assembled knew that Adolf Hitler and Eva Braun would soon kill themselves.

Gen. Walther Wenck and his Twelfth Army will never save Berlin. The Soviet army is close by. Their advance units are just five hundred yards away from the *Führerbunker*, and they now shell the compound from their positions in the Tiergarten, the sprawling park in the heart of the city where Eva Braun once delighted in afternoons of target practice with her pistol. Many of the trees are now mere splinters. Yet those still standing bear the first blooms of spring—signs of life that contrast sharply with the nearby Reichstag building and Kroll Opera House, both battered and pocked by artillery.

Adolf Hitler has been talking of suicide for the last ten days, pragmatically stating that the only other option is to become a Russian prisoner—and for the Führer, that grisly fate is no option at all. Eva Braun, of course, would be a similar trophy if the Russians took her alive, so she, too, must die by her own hand. Earlier today she chose not to have a dentist examine a sore tooth, laughing that it soon wouldn't matter anyway. And she surprised Traudl Junge just a few hours ago by giving her a silver-fox fur coat. Eva's initials were sewn onto the lining, inside the well-known symbol of good luck: a four-leaf clover.

Hitler plans to kill himself with a cyanide pill. Until recently he was frightened that it would not work. So he ordered that a similar pill be tested on his beloved dog Blondi, the German shepherd who has been by his side for almost the entire war. Sgt. Fritz Tornow, the Führer's dog handler, pried open her jaws. Then Dr. Werner Haase, the professor who devised Hitler's own unique suicide technique, used a pair of pliers to place a pill of prussic acid* in the dog's mouth.

Blondi is a large dog, originally chosen by the Führer as a symbol of German pride because she closely resembled a wolf. She trusts her master, and was docile as she allowed Haase to press the jaws of the pliers together, breaking the capsule and spilling the acid onto her tongue.

Blondi died instantly.

Dr. Haase immediately called for Hitler, so that he might see for himself the pill's effectiveness. The Führer was speechless at the sight of Blondi lying motionless on the floor. He took one look and went directly to his bedroom.

Now it's his turn.

After dismissing the staff, Hitler and Eva retire to his sitting room and close the door. Eva Braun sits down on one end of the blue-and-white couch in the corner, still wearing her black dress with roses framing the neckline. She rests her head on the couch's arm and curls her legs up under her, as if lying down to take a nap.

The solemnity of the moment is broken by a frantic banging on the room's steel door. A sobbing Magda Goebbels, wife of propaganda minister Joseph Goebbels, demands to see the Führer and begs him not to end his life. Magda and her husband recently moved into the bunker's top floor with their six children. Only three days ago, Hitler gave her his own Golden Party Badge† as a thank-you for her years of fervent support. Now Hitler allows Magda into his sitting room one last time, says a few quiet words of good-bye, then forces her to leave, closing the metal door behind her. He does not lock it, however, for the Führer has given

---

*The liquid form of cyanide. Also known as hydrocyanic acid.

†A special medallion given to the first one hundred thousand people who joined the Nazi Party. Each was numbered in the order in which the individual became a member. Hitler's bore the number 1, making his gift to Magda Goebbels a most treasured memento.

strict instructions about what must be done with his body once he is gone. "Wait ten minutes," he orders SS major Otto Günsche, his military adjutant.

Hitler has been carrying his Walther 7.65 mm pistol for the past few weeks, and now he chambers a round. History does not record the final words between him and Eva Braun. They have known each other for sixteen years. She has seen him rise to power, just as she more recently has witnessed his physical decline.

Eva is curled up like a cat on the right side of the sofa. Adolf Hitler takes a seat on the other end, pistol in hand. Eva's own revolver rests on a nearby table, next to a vase of flowers.

She goes first, sliding the cyanide pill out of the small brass lipstick-size vial and placing it between her teeth. She rests her head on the armrest and bites down on the capsule.

To prevent the possibility of failure, Eva is now meant to place her small handgun to her temple and finish the job. This is the policy outlined by the suicide professor Dr. Werner Haase. But Eva has already made it clear she will not shoot herself: "I want to be a beautiful corpse," she insisted to Hitler.

The bunker sitting room immediately smells of almonds, a scent commonly associated with hydrocyanic acid. Eva Braun's body loses the ability to absorb oxygen. Her heart and brain, the two organs that need air the most, shut down in an instant. Sadly, it is a death far quicker than that suffered by the millions of Jews her new husband sent to the gas chambers. For the Zyklon B gas that was used in the death camps is also a form of hydrocyanic acid.

Seconds later, still curled in the fetal position, Eva Braun is dead.

The Führer then places his capsule between his teeth. At the same time, he points the business end of the Walther at his right temple. He bites down on the capsule and pulls the Walther's trigger a split second later.

His body sags to the side, until his torso hangs limp against Eva Braun's. The Führer's pistol drops to the floor next to his foot. Blood pours from his shattered skull, dripping off the couch and forming a great crimson puddle on the floor.

Ten minutes pass. Major Günsche enters. The bodies are wrapped in blankets and taken aboveground. Hitler's dying fear was that his corpse might become an exhibit in a Russian museum, so the bodies are doused with forty gallons of gasoline and incinerated.*

Adolf Hitler, the man who murdered millions, has claimed his last victim.

---

*The Soviets confirmed the identity of the bodies within two weeks but, for years, pretended to know nothing about Hitler's fate. At the Potsdam Conference in July 1945, Joseph Stalin made a point of pretending that Hitler was alive and on the run. Stalin, a master at creating uncertainty, believed that the ghosts of Nazism would enhance his power.

22

George Patton is smoking a cigar. He has once again been trying to kick the habit, but the boredom of his new job as military governor of Bavaria requires the distraction. With the fighting in Europe over, Patton now works alone in the commandant's office of this former SS officer training school thirty miles south of Munich. On this beautiful spring afternoon, he can see the Alps rising in the distance.

The magnificent Bavarian headquarters is just one of the perks Patton enjoys now that Germany has been defeated. Rather than sleep on an air mattress in the cramped mobile trailer he has called home for much of the last nine months, the general lives in a manor house built on the shores of a shimmering blue mountain lake. "This is the handsomest villa I have ever seen," he remarked in a letter to his brother-in-law Frederick Ayer just yesterday. Patton has a bowling alley, a swimming pool, and two boats at his disposal. "If one has to occupy Germany," he added, "this is a good place to do it from."

May in Bavaria should be an idyllic time for Patton, yet he is anxious, longing for just one more battle. The Third Army was still at full strength in May 1945, soon to begin the process of transitioning men and matériel back to the United States.* Patton spends his days lobbying to fight in the Pacific. He is still "hopeful of having a chance to fight the Japanese," as he wrote in two letters to well-connected friends in Washington yesterday, knowing that they would pass along the word to others who might arrange such a posting. But a command in the Pacific is now unlikely. His monumental ego and that of the massively self-important Pacific Theater commander Gen. Douglas MacArthur would surely clash.

Yet Patton is not one to avoid conflict. He is still fuming over an order from Dwight Eisenhower in the waning days of the war that prevented the Third Army from advancing into Czechoslovakia to assist the people of Prague. Instead of allowing Americans to come to their aid, by halting Patton's tanks Eisenhower made it possible for the Russian army to enter Prague. As in Berlin, the Russians did not come in peace, and were soon suppressing the locals in the same horrific manner.

Even weeks later, Patton still seethes about the absurdity of Eisenhower's order. He believes Ike to be a fool. Patton has been wary of Russian duplicity as far back as November 1943, when he noted in his diary that "It will be just as bad for us to have Russia win the war as it will be for Germany to do so. To be a success and maintain world peace, the U.S. and the U.S. alone should destroy Germany and Japan and be ready to stop Russia."

Patton has met with Russian generals and officials several times since the war ended. Each time, they have plied him with alcohol, his Russian counterparts trying to get him drunk, hoping he would embarrass himself. But Patton is onto the game, constantly adding water to his whisky, and drinking the Russians under the table.

---

*Priority for going home was based on a system of points accrued by months in service, time in combat, number of children under the age of eighteen, and whether the individual had been awarded a medal such as the Bronze Star or Purple Heart. As for the Third's job in Germany after the war, days were spent making sure that displaced people did not travel into the American occupation zone, patrolling a "frontier" between the American and Russian lines by erecting signs and barricades to prevent the flow of individuals traveling from east to west, and sealing off Germany to prevent intelligence officials and other high-ranking members of the Nazi Party from escaping the country.

The Red Army is relentless in its quest to control as much of Europe as possible, with Stalin taking full advantage of Dwight Eisenhower's timidity. The Russians are seizing more land, and more people are coming under their occupation.

Patton is incensed. "You cannot lay down with a diseased jackal," he recently insisted to a group of journalists. "Neither can we ever do business with the Russians."

When Undersecretary of War Robert Patterson visited the Third Army, Patton openly lobbied for at least 30 percent of all American troops to remain in Europe, "Keeping our forces intact. Let's keep our boots polished, bayonets sharpened, and present a picture of force and strength to these people. This is the only language they understand and respect. If you fail to do this, then I would like to say to you that we have had a victory over the Germans but have lost the war."

Even Patton's nemesis, British field marshal Montgomery, agrees: when accepting the surrender of German soldiers, he ordered his troops to stack the Wehrmacht rifles in such a way that they could easily be redistributed should the Germans and British need to defend themselves against a Russian advance.

Yet the Harvard-educated undersecretary Patterson thinks Patton is delusional. He advises Eisenhower, army chief of staff Gen. George C. Marshall, and President Harry Truman to continue to view the Russians benevolently.*

In time, of course, Patton's predictions will come true, and the world will have to live with the consequences of American gullibility.

---

*The fifty-four-year-old Patterson was a native of Glens Falls, New York, who had been awarded the Distinguished Service Cross for bravery during World War I. He later practiced law and served as a U.S. District Court judge before accepting the position of undersecretary of war when FDR offered it to him in 1940. Patterson became a favorite of Harry Truman, who elevated him to secretary of war on September 27, 1945. Patterson served two years before returning to the law. His firm of Patterson Belknap Webb & Tyler still exists in New York City. Patterson died on January 22, 1952, when the plane he was flying in from Buffalo to Newark crashed into a house while trying to land. He was rushing to get home and at the last minute had traded in his rail ticket for the plane ticket.

★ ★ ★ ★

The Soviet threat is not the only thing troubling Patton. He personally has undergone a series of strange near-death "coincidences." First there was the attempt a few weeks ago by the Spitfire to shoot down his airplane. The British had loaned many of those airplanes to the Polish air force, and it was originally believed that it was a Polish pilot who attacked Patton's L-5. But it turns out that the only Polish Spitfire wing in that part of Germany at the time was stationed far to the north, on the Baltic coast. The Spitfire has a combat range of 395 miles, making it impossible for the Polish fighters to make the round-trip flight from their base in Nordhorn to the location where Patton was fired upon, nearly three hundred miles south.

Records also show that no Polish aircraft went missing, and no Polish pilots were killed on the date of the attack—even though the Spitfire in question had Polish markings.

A Russian pilot, however, could have been the culprit.

Winston Churchill had been kind enough to give Joseph Stalin's air force one thousand Mark IX Spitfires to fight the Nazis. The planes were everywhere over the skies of Germany.

Two weeks after the air attack, Patton was riding in the passenger seat of his open-air jeep when a German peasant's ox cart nearly smashed into his vehicle. A long pole tipped with a sharpened farming blade protruded from the front of the cart. "We were nearly killed," Patton wrote of his near decapitation in his journal. "The pole missed us by inches."

Army intelligence agents have warned Patton that his life may be in danger. NKVD, the Russian security force in charge of political assassinations and espionage, is thought to be tracking his movements.* Whether it is the Russians or crazed Nazi sympathizers who have visions of assassinating him, Patton is taking no chances. His security detail has been strengthened, and he now carries a loaded revolver with him at all times.

As night approaches, Patton takes a break from writing letters in his

---

*Narodny Komissariat Vnutrennikh Del, translated as the "People's Commissariat for Internal Affairs."

office near Bad Tölz as Gen. Hobart "Hap" Gay, Patton's longtime chief of staff, enters through the open door. "General," he says to Patton, "there's a Russian brigadier out in my office who says he has instructions to speak with you personally."

Patton removes the Montecristo Especial cigar from the corner of his mouth. "What the hell does the son of a bitch want?"

"It's about river craft on the Danube," Gay replies vaguely.

"Bring the bastard in," Patton replies. "You and Harkins come with him."

Patton depends greatly on the wisdom of both Gay and Col. Paul Harkins, who have been at his side for years. In fact, it was Harkins who six months ago at Verdun nodded to Patton and confirmed that the Third Army was poised to quickly wheel north to save Bastogne.

The English-speaking Russian general enters Patton's office, followed closely by Gay and Harkins. The Russian snaps to attention as Patton rises.

What follows is a lengthy protest against the behavior of the American army. Many Germans fled the Russians by crossing the Danube River into what is now known as the "American Zone." Among them were boatmen who made their living ferrying people across the river. The Russians feel that these men and their boats rightfully belong to Mother Russia. "General Patton," the general concludes. "The Fourth Russian Guards Army demands that you, General Patton, return these craft to Russian control."

Patton does not immediately respond. He calmly places his Cuban cigar in an ashtray, slides opens his desk drawer, and removes his Smith and Wesson .357 Magnum revolver.

Patton looks hard at the general. He then picks up the revolver and smashes it down hard on the desk. His face goes red. "Gay, goddamnit! Get this son of a bitch out of here. Who in the hell let him in? Don't let any more Russian bastards into this headquarters. Harkins! Alert the Fourth and Eleventh and Sixty-Fifth Divisions for an attack to the east."

The Russian general's face instantly goes pale. Terrified, he says nothing as Gay leads him from the room. Harkins, as ordered, picks up a telephone and gives the command to commence attacking the Russian lines.

The general hurries away from Patton's headquarters.

Gay and Harkins quickly return to Patton's office to report on the situation. They fear that Patton may have just started a new war.

But the general is all smiles. He reclines in his desk chair, once again puffing on his cigar. "How was that?" he asks with a grin.

Patton doesn't wait for an answer. "Sometimes you have to put on an act, and I'm not going to let any Russian marshal, general or private tell me what I have to do. Harkins, call off the alert.

"That's the last we'll hear from those bastards."

But even George Patton knows that is not true.

★ ★ ★ ★

On June 13, it is George S. Patton who is effectively silenced. He receives news that he has long dreaded: his combat career is over. Gen. Courtney Hodges's emotional meltdown and his ineffective leadership of the American First Army during the early days of the Battle of the Bulge have been forgotten. Gen. Douglas MacArthur has chosen Hodges instead of Patton to join him in the Pacific Theater for the fight against the Japanese army.

George Patton has fought his last battle.

23

———— · ————

President Harry S. Truman wants a word with Joseph Stalin.

As diplomatic negotiations end for the afternoon, he maneuvers around to where Stalin sits. The two men, alongside British prime minister Winston Churchill, have spent the day discussing the postwar future of Germany. A small group of advisers from each nation is also seated at the ten-foot-wide circular table in this century-old palace just outside Berlin. The high-ceilinged room is stifling, smelling of stale cigarette smoke, and ten degrees too warm, thanks to the summer sun shining in through the unopened windows.

The Potsdam Conference, as it will be remembered, is the first time that the new Big Three are meeting since the death of Franklin Roosevelt. Joseph Stalin plays the role of entitled host, behaving as if Potsdam were now part of Russia. The tablecloth and chairs at the negotiating table are bright Russian red. Outside, in the gardens, the Russians have even planted bright red flowers in the shape of the Communist star.

As with the last meeting between Allied leaders, in Yalta, Stalin has every intention of steamrolling his guests into acceding to his demands. The ongoing American policy of accommodating the Soviets, rather than containing their growing power, plays right into his hands.

Churchill is bitter. Joseph Stalin has not only taken full control of Eastern Europe, but is widely viewed as a hero by the rest of the Continent. There is growing speculation that voters in France, Scandinavia, Italy, and even England will favor Communist candidates in their next elections. Indeed, even as Churchill watches Harry Truman casually rise from the table and then pull Stalin aside for a brief chat, the people of Britain are at the polls selecting a new government. Churchill will fly home tomorrow to hear that he is no longer prime minister.

Harry Truman does not have that kind of a problem. He's America's leader until at least 1948. He is a reluctant president, and considers the White House a "jail." But Truman is also moving quickly to put his own stamp on American politics by replacing FDR's cabinet and trusted advisers with men he considers loyal to him.

Truman possesses one presidential trait that Franklin Roosevelt lacked, and that is the poker player's ability to tell when another man is lying to him. FDR's administration was filled with men such as Wild Bill Donovan, who gained access to the president through flattery and self-promotion. Harry Truman has no time for panderers who put their own interests before those of the American people. When one of Roosevelt's most powerful advisers, Secretary of the Treasury Henry Morgenthau Jr., threatened to resign if he wasn't allowed to attend the Potsdam Conference, Truman immediately called his bluff.*

Morgenthau stepped down three days ago. His plan will not be implemented.

Truman is fiercely independent. In his lifetime, he has been a soldier, farmer, bank clerk, railroad worker, owner of a men's clothing store, judge, and senator. He once dreamed of being a concert pianist, and still makes time to play. He waited until he was thirty-five to get married, but his devotion to his wife, Bess, is such that he regularly writes her long letters whenever they are apart. Upon his arrival in Potsdam, the Secret Service overheard an army officer make the mistake of telling Truman he could "arrange anything you like while you're here—anything in the way of wine and women."

---

*At the heart of the dispute was the Morgenthau Plan, a strategy to decimate postwar Germany by destroying its industrial strength and forcing the nation to return to its agrarian roots, soon to produce only beer, grain, and textiles. This would unknowingly have played into Russian hands, because by reducing Germany's industrial output the nation would not be able to attack Russia again.

An appalled Truman chewed out the officer, telling him that "I married my sweetheart. She doesn't run around on me and I don't run around on her. And I want that understood. Don't ever mention that kind of stuff to me again."

This traditional American president who dotes on his wife now grabs the elbow of Joseph Stalin, a man whose infidelities and brutality drove his wife to suicide. The two world leaders stand apart from the other attendees at the Potsdam Conference, but remain near the negotiating table. For those who can't hear what the two men are saying, it would appear that they are simply making small talk. In fact, what Truman is about to tell Stalin will forever change the relationship between the United States and Russia. Truman, the smooth-talking "Missouri horse trader," is determined to send a clear message: America is the true power broker at this meeting.

The president looks dapper in his double-breasted suit and his bow tie. Stalin and the Russian contingent are all clad in drab Soviet military uniforms. The Russian dictator is a man just as comfortable with hiding his emotions as Truman.

Choosing to leave his own interpreter behind, Truman speaks directly to Stalin, letting the young Russian interpreter V. N. Pavlov translate his very important message.

Winston Churchill stands five feet away, next to his foreign minister, Anthony Eden. Both have already been told the news. They silently watch Stalin, to gauge his reaction.

Stalin is known to remain expressionless in negotiations, so as not to give away his true emotions, but Truman knows there is more than one way to bluff in a poker game. "After long experimentation," he tells Stalin in his typically direct way, "we have developed a new bomb far more destructive than any known bomb, and we plan to use it very soon unless Japan surrenders."

Stalin's face is impassive, pretending not to comprehend the full weight of Truman's words. "I am glad to hear it," the Russian responds. "I hope you make good use of it against the Japanese."

The discussion over, the two engage in small talk for a few minutes before Truman makes his way back over to the U.S. delegation.

Churchill is flabbergasted by Stalin's lack of comprehension, and will later write, "If he had the slightest idea of the revolution in world affairs which was in progress his reactions would have been obvious. Nothing would have been easier than for him to say, 'Thank you so much for telling me about your new bomb. I of course have no technical knowledge. May I send my expert in these nuclear sciences to see your expert tomorrow morning?' But his face remained gay and genial, and the talk between these two potentates soon came to an end."

The British and Americans have been cooperating on the special bomb since 1939. Just eight days ago, in the vast desert of New Mexico, this new "atomic" weapon was successfully detonated. The explosion was equal to twenty kilotons of dynamite, and sent a bulbous cloud nearly eight miles into the sky. The sand beneath the blast was instantly turned into a layer of green glass ten feet deep, and the shock waves could be felt one hundred miles away. The man who directed the bomb-making project, a theoretical physicist named Robert Oppenheimer, made one simple remark to others who observed the explosion: "It worked."

Yet Oppenheimer also realized that this device brought an entirely new form of evil to mankind. "I am become Death," he thought to himself, "the destroyer of worlds."*

Truman had been waiting for confirmation of the blast results, and received them while on his way to Potsdam. The coded message detailing the bomb's success was handed to him upon his arrival: "Operated this morning. Diagnosis seems satisfactory, and already exceeds expectations," it read. With those words, Truman instantly has the power to assert American demands at the Potsdam Conference. No fighting force on earth possesses such a weapon, and he can threaten to use it on whoever stands in America's way. Here at Potsdam, Truman uses the bomb as leverage to gain assurances that the Russians will join the war against the Japanese. The president also opposes Russian demands that the German people pay for the rebuilding of postwar Europe, with the bulk of those reparations going directly to the Soviet Union.

Yet Stalin is not afraid. Unbeknownst to Truman, he knows all about

*Oppenheimer is quoting from the *Bhagavad Gita*, a Hindu scripture.

the atomic bomb, thanks to his extensive global intelligence network.* He has deliberately prepared for this moment, determined not to give away any hint of emotion that will reveal the depth of Russian espionage in America.

It does not matter that America is an ally. The Russians spy on anyone who is a threat, considering no act of intrigue to be off limits. Stalin believes that "atomic bombs are meant to frighten those with weak nerves." Besides, his scientists are hard at work on an atomic bomb of their own. In four short years, the Russians will detonate a giant fireball.

Simply put, Joseph Stalin is determined to rule the world.

No American president, or American general, will stand in his way.

★   ★   ★   ★

The outcome of the Potsdam Conference is harsh: in keeping with an earlier agreement at Yalta, Germany will be divided into occupation zones governed by the Allies. Truman also secures a firm commitment from Stalin to join the war against Japan. But after meeting Stalin in person, Truman realizes that the dictator is not the friend to America that FDR believed him to be. Thus begins Truman's policy of taking a hard line against the Russians, and the start of the Cold War that George S. Patton has long predicted.

★   ★   ★   ★

The sun shines brightly over Germany as George Patton stands at attention. The fingertips of his right hand are firmly pressed to his polished helmet in salute. Dwight Eisenhower stands to his right, also saluting the American flag as it is raised over Berlin for the first time. President Harry Truman stands to Patton's left with his hand over his heart. Next to him stands Gen. Omar Bradley.

Per a 1944 agreement between the Allies known as the London Protocol, Berlin is now the territory of the four occupying powers: the United States, Great Britain, the Soviet Union, and France. Each nation governs

---

*There are some who believe that Robert Oppenheimer, who had known Communist leanings and whose wife was once a member of the Communist Party, was among those providing nuclear secrets to the Russians. In fact, the Soviet spy's name was Klaus Fuchs.

*General Eisenhower, General Patton, and President Truman
at the Berlin flag-raising ceremony*

a portion of the city. Russia still controls the areas of Germany surrounding the city, making Berlin a rubble-filled island. "You who have not seen it," Patton said of the German capital, "do not know what hell looks like."

Patton was invited to Potsdam as a visitor to the conference, and from there traveled by car with the president and his fellow generals to Berlin for the flag raising ceremony. He has grown despondent in the past few months, undone by the fact that his fighting days are over. He plays squash and rides horses in the Bavarian countryside to keep himself in shape, and has even tried giving up cigars, but to no avail. By all outer appearances, he looks fit and healthy. But the reality is that he is bored, spending his days attending ceremonies, reviewing troops, saluting the

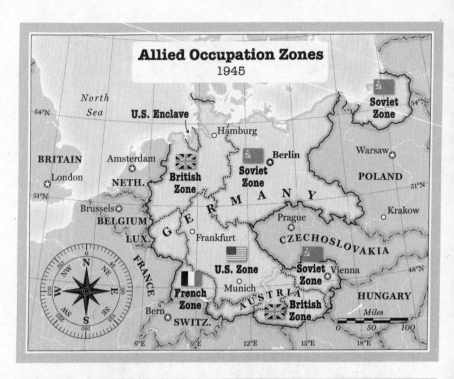

Allied Occupation Zones
1945

North Sea

54°N

BRITAIN

London

51°N

NETH.
Amsterdam

BELGIUM
Brussels

LUX.

FRANCE

Bern

SWITZ.

6°E   9°E

U.S. Enclave

Hamburg

British Zone

G E R M A N Y

Frankfurt

French Zone

Munich

U.S. Zone

Soviet Zone

Berlin

Prague

CZECHOSLOVAKIA

Soviet Zone

AUSTRIA

British Zone

Vienna

12°E   15°E   18°E

Soviet Zone

54°N

Warsaw

POLAND

Krakow

51°N

48°N

HUNGARY

Miles
0   50   100

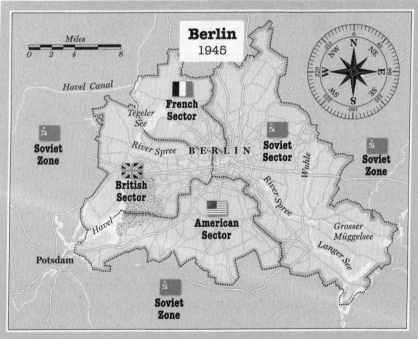

Berlin
1945

Miles
0   2   4   8

Havel Canal

Tegeler See

French Sector

River Spree

B E R L I N

Soviet Sector

Wuhle

Soviet Zone

British Sector

Havel

American Sector

River Spree

Grosser Müggelsee

Langer See

Soviet Zone

Potsdam

Soviet Zone

flag, and pinning medals on those whose wartime commendations have finally come through. Without a war to fight, Patton is lost.

To make matters worse, the new president dislikes Patton. Back in 1918 the two men fought in the great Battle of Meuse-Argonne, and Patton surely appreciated the precision artillery support provided by Truman's Battery D, even though he didn't know Truman personally. A colonel in those waning days of World War I, he outranked Captain Truman, but now the tables are turned.

"Don't see how a country can produce such men as Robert E. Lee, John J. Pershing, Eisenhower, and Bradley," Truman will write in his journal, "and at the same time produce Custers, Pattons and MacArthurs."

Truman's scathing opinion of the general is based solely on a first impression. He has not taken the time to get to know Patton, and the two will never engage in a meaningful discussion of any kind.

Truman just doesn't like him.

The two men are polar opposites.

Patton has swagger; Truman is humble.

Patton is tall and athletic, a larger-than-life military hero. The diminutive, bespectacled Truman, on the other hand, looks like the bank clerk he once was.

Patton was born into wealth, and then married into even more money. Truman has been handed nothing in his life—nothing, that is, except the presidency.

In Patton, Truman sees a braggart who struts around like a peacock in his showy uniform, with the polished helmet and bloused riding pants.

Truman dresses simply, and avoids putting on airs. He detests Patton's flashy style. Despite the many pressing international obligations on his mind as the flag is being raised over Berlin, Truman takes time to covertly count the number of stars adorning Patton's uniform—and is appalled to find them adding up to twenty-eight.

With the Second World War now at an end, the president has little need for a general who believes it his birthright to speak his mind, especially when it creates international discord.

The official American policy toward the Germans is that anyone previously connected with Nazi Germany is ineligible to help the nation rebuild. The Russians agree; in fact, this is a cornerstone of the Potsdam discussions. But Patton dissents. He speaks fearlessly about the lunacy of "denazification," telling the press that it is "no more possible for a man to be a civil servant in Germany and not have paid lip service to Nazism than it is for a man to be a postmaster in America and not have paid at least lip service to the Democratic Party or the Republican Party when it is in power."

Patton disagrees with official American policy. One disturbing element of which is that former German soldiers be used as forced labor in Russia, France, and the United Kingdom. These men, Patton feels, should be used to rebuild their own country. Germany's hospitals are no longer functional, its sewer systems don't work, the roads and bridges have been bombed, and there are millions of former POWs and displaced persons who will need shelter and food once winter comes.

So with words that put him directly at odds with the policies of his president, Patton tells a reporter that German labor is the solution to rebuilding Germany—whether or not someone was once a Nazi. He says, "My soldiers are fighting men and if I dismiss the sewer cleaners and the clerks[,] my soldiers will have to take over those jobs. They'd have to run the telephone exchanges, the power facilities, the street cars, and that's not what soldiers are for."

In his own way, Patton is still fighting battles. Even as he quietly begins making plans to leave the military, he wages an ironic war in favor of the German people. "The Germans are the only decent people left in Europe. It's a choice between them and the Russians. I prefer the Germans."*

The Russians interpret this stance as an attempt to shield former SS members, perhaps to use them against the Russians in a future war. They have lodged a formal complaint with Omar Bradley suggesting just that, noting that Waffen SS fighters who surrendered to the Third Army in Czechoslovakia during the month of May have not shown up on the lists of individuals turned over to the Russians for repatriation. Soviet spies now fill Bavaria, hunting these men down.

The Russians win again. On June 13, while Patton is on tour in

---

*Patton admired the discipline of the German military and the German work ethic.

America selling war bonds,* his headquarters is informed by cable that the Third Army must immediately account for any German forces in its region. At the same time, army chief of staff George Marshall orders that Patton's phones be tapped, and even takes the extraordinary measure of requesting that a psychoanalyst from the navy's Medical Corps observe one of the general's press conferences to see if Patton is suffering from a nervous breakdown.

Marshall, himself, likes Patton, but his top commander, Eisenhower, has written to him that Patton is a "mentally unbalanced officer." Ever since the Knutsford incident in 1944, when Patton inadvertently slighted the Russians while speaking to a group of British women, Ike has come to believe that Patton suffers from seizures and bouts of dementia. This serious charge, and Patton's habit of speaking out in favor of the Germans, has convinced Marshall to investigate Patton's mental health.

The powerful Wild Bill Donovan also loathes Patton. Donovan and the OSS have been working with the Russians ever since he visited Moscow in December 1943. The American and Russian spy agencies are now exchanging information and helping one another on espionage projects within Germany, including spying on George Patton.

In fact, OSS agent Duncan Lee, an Oxford graduate and descendant of Confederate general Robert E. Lee, is assigned to deliver to Donovan "the monthly confidential report of the military governor in the U.S. occupation zone of Germany." This includes an OSS accounting of Patton's personal movements and wiretap recordings.

Wild Bill Donovan's future is uncertain now that Franklin Roosevelt has died. Harry Truman keeps his distance. With the war over, the OSS may be dissolved. Donovan will do whatever it takes to keep his spy agency intact, including undermining the Truman administration's increasingly hard-line stance against the Russians by sharing secrets about Patton.

But Donovan himself is being deceived.

The spy war in Germany between Russia and the United States is

---

*Although Patton was received as a hero when he returned to the United States in the summer of 1945, his affair with Jean Gordon caused considerable animosity between him and his wife. "Beatrice gave me hell," Patton told his friend Gen. Everett Hughes upon his return to Bavaria. "I'm glad to be in Europe."

ratcheting up. It is, as American intelligence officer James H. Critchfield
will later write, "the largest, most concentrated and intense intelligence
warfare in history." However, Donovan does little to stop the Russian
influence within the OSS. Since the summer of 1944, his security office
has made it known to Donovan that forty-seven OSS agents are either
Communists or Russian sympathizers. Wild Bill also knows that Joseph
Stalin has been planting Russian spies within the OSS since 1942.

What Donovan does *not* know is that Duncan Lee, his executive
secretary and the man who knows all his secrets, is a traitor. Lee is working for the Russian spy agency NKVD, as a double agent. Among invaluable nuggets of information Lee has provided the Soviets over the course
of the war was advance warning of the D-day landing date and the exact
location of the atomic bomb research in Tennessee. That the Russians
would use such a prized asset, Lee, to gather information about George
Patton speaks volumes about their eagerness to see him silenced.

In May 1945, Donovan gains shocking information about Patton, of
which the general himself is totally unaware. Stephen Skubik, a special
agent in the U.S. Army Counterintelligence Corps, speaks fluent Ukrainian, and is tasked with developing undercover sources of Slavic ethnicity to report to American intelligence. On May 16 he met with Ukrainian
nationalist leader Stepan Bandera, who will one day assist the Americans
and British in spying on the Russians.* Bandera specifically told Skubik
that "Soviet High Command has been ordered by Marshal Stalin to kill
U.S. Army General George Patton."

Stalin's reasons are simple: Patton defied Russian authority when he
invaded Czechoslovakia back in May, during the waning days of the war.†

---

*Bandera will himself be assassinated by the Russians in 1959, as noted in the Cen-
tral Intelligence Agency journal *Studies in Intelligence* 19, no. 3.

†On May 4, Patton received approval from Dwight Eisenhower to invade Czechoslovakia. At this point in the war, the Third Army comprised eighteen divisions and more than
half a million men, making it the largest U.S. force in history. The Third Army swept
into western Czechoslovakia, quickly capturing vast regions of the nation and accepting
the surrender of thousands of German prisoners who did not want to fall into Russian
hands. On May 6, Eisenhower ordered Patton to halt—which he did, albeit very reluctantly. However, elements of the Third Army did not receive the order. In the ancient city
of Rokycany, just east of Plzeň, there was conflict when the American and Russian
armies linked up, very nearly starting the new war for which Patton had long argued.

But rather than being shocked by Skubik's news, Donovan orders him to arrest Bandera so that he can be returned to the Russians, thereby silencing the man who is warning about an attempt on Patton's life.

"I was disappointed with my first visit to OSS," Skubik will later write with a great deal of understatement.

But the investigation is not over for Stephen Skubik. A few weeks later he meets with Professor Roman Smal-Stocki, an academic and former Ukrainian diplomat, who is on the verge of being expelled from Germany and sent back into Russian hands. Smal-Stocki informs Skubik that "the NKVD will soon attempt to kill General George Patton. Stalin wants him dead."

Finally, in the middle of the summer, Special Agent Skubik interviews yet another Ukrainian, Gen. Pavlo Shandruk, who fought with the Nazis in the waning days of the war and is now desperately trying to avoid being sent back to Russia. He offers the United States some vital intelligence that he hopes will allow him to remain in the American Zone. "Please tell General Patton to be on guard," Shandruk tells Agent Skubik. "He is at the top of the NKVD list to be killed."

Wild Bill Donovan and Special Agent Skubik soon meet again. And once more, Skubik tells him of the threats. But Donovan dismisses them, saying they are "just a provocation."

★ ★ ★ ★

Back in Berlin, Patton stands at attention on this crisp morning, watching the Stars and Stripes hoisted over the city he once longed to conquer. Today, Patton is harboring a dangerous secret. Although American undersecretary of war Robert Patterson proclaimed on May 31, 1945, that all Allied POWs had been returned, Patton knows that a top-secret policy instituted by Gen. George Marshall, then tacitly approved by Franklin Roosevelt and Harry Truman, effectively abandons all American and British POWs who fell into Russian hands at the end of the war. The Russians are using them as leverage in negotiations with the Allies to ensure that all Soviets who have fled to the West will be returned.

Patton believes that the man to his left, President Truman, has allowed more than twenty thousand American POWs to remain in Russian hands. As a military man, Patton will do whatever it takes to see these men released—even wage war. But he is conflicted, because he

276 ★ Bill O'Reilly and Martin Dugard

understands that Truman's motivations for allowing these Americans to be held hostage is to ensure that the Russians join in the fight against the Japanese and then, once the war is over, join a new organization to be known as the United Nations, in order to ensure future world peace.*

Patton is becoming more and more certain that the only way he can speak freely about these issues is to leave the military.

Armed with top-secret knowledge and his usual defiant attitude, George Patton has made himself a target—and he knows it.

A few weeks ago, before leaving his daughters in Washington, Patton said something that disturbed them greatly: "Well, I guess this is good-bye. I won't be seeing you again."

Patton's daughters were shocked. "It's crazy," they protested. "The war is over." To which Patton mysteriously responded, "My luck has run out."

---

*The Russians denied the Americans and British access to many of the POW camps they had liberated, and also denied that they held any Allied POWs. Truman, and Roosevelt before him, allegedly knew otherwise, but did not want to create strife with Stalin. Thus it is believed that many American and British soldiers died in Russian captivity because their release was not demanded.

24

IG Farben Building
Frankfurt am Main, Germany
September 28, 1945
4:30 p.m.

The man with eighty-five days to live is about to be fired.

George S. Patton has been summoned, with prejudice, to meet with his boss Dwight Eisenhower. The same foul autumn rains that stymied Patton one year ago in Metz now make flying impossible, so Patton has driven seven and a half hours to the massive industrial office complex that now serves as Ike's headquarters. Patton spent the journey through the bombed-out ruins of Germany preparing a plan of attack, thinking of the words he must speak to save his career once again. "The ride reminded me of a similar one," he will write in his diary tonight, that "I took from Knutsford to London . . . when I was strongly under the impression I was going to be relieved and sent home—if not tried."

The IG Farben Building rises palatial and scrubbed in the midst of a decimated Frankfurt am Main. Olive-drab American army bulldozers prowl the streets all day long, pushing rubble to the side of roads. The local Germans eke out a living as best they can, collecting debris to make fires for cooking and warmth, sleeping each night in whatever shelter they can find. "Frankfurt resembles a city," one visitor will write of the destruction, "not so much as a pile of bones and smashed skulls resembles a prized steer."

But Ike's headquarters is an island of luxury in this decimation, a beige fortress where the curving stairwells are made of marble, elaborate fountains burble soothingly, and senior American officers can enjoy a meal of venison, ice cream, and red wine—all served by German servants. Visitors need a special pass just to get in the door. When they do, they find the hallways filled with clerks and junior officers who spend their days pushing paper and counting down the hours until they can rotate stateside. The more quick-witted Germans label Eisenhower's headquarters "G.I. Farben Haus."

This same grand complex was also the site where the cyanide-based Zyklon B gas, which was used to exterminate millions in the Nazi death camps, was developed. For that reason, the more cynical residents of this city call the structure *Das Pharisäer Ghetto*, the "Ghetto of the Pharisees."*

Fresh-cut roses are delivered each day to Capt. Kay Summersby and other women serving in U.S. military offices. Summersby's secretarial desk sits just outside Eisenhower's vast office. She wears red lipstick, and her auburn hair is pinned back to reveal her high forehead. Summersby's brown Women's Army Corps uniform is tailored to accentuate her figure. Despite the relaxed working environment, she keeps her jacket on at all times, and her tie firmly knotted. Eisenhower's headquarters is a "luxurious" space, she will write, adding that "several tennis courts could have fitted into Ike's office."

Summersby hears the footfalls of George Patton's trademark riding boots coming down the hallway, and snaps to attention as General Patton enters the office for the long-delayed meeting. Soon she hears Eisenhower raising his voice loud enough to be heard through the thick wooden door. This is not typical behavior for Ike, and Summersby is shocked. The meeting between Patton and Eisenhower borders on the volcanic.

The relationship between Summersby and Eisenhower is far more congenial. They have been together for three years now and are closer than ever. Summersby could have returned to her home in England, but she does not want to leave Eisenhower. However, in just a month, Ike is slated to return to America, where he will replace George C. Marshall as army chief of staff.

Summersby wants to go with him.

---

*This is a reference to the smooth-talking religious officials whom Jesus of Nazareth condemned for their lies and air of self-importance, noting that their acts and their beliefs differed greatly.

She isn't demanding that Eisenhower leave Mamie, his wife of almost thirty years. She would be content to serve as a member of his staff at the Pentagon. After all this time as part of what Eisenhower calls his "immediate wartime family," she finds the thought of returning home alone to England devastating.

Their relationship is an open secret. It was quietly condoned during time of war, and even now, Summersby stays in a special house reserved for female officers, which Eisenhower visits most nights for supper and a few rubbers of bridge. Such an esteemed presence at the dinner table can hardly be kept under wraps. But now, unbeknownst to Summersby, great effort is being taken to make sure that the relationship comes to an end.

Army censors have already doctored the official photograph taken at the German surrender ceremony on May 7. The signing took place in a redbrick schoolhouse in Reims, France. In the original photograph, Summersby stands just behind a grinning Eisenhower, who holds up the two

General Eisenhower at the German military surrender

pens used to sign the surrender documents. Ike is making a V, for "Victory," with the pens.

In the censored version of the photograph, Eisenhower is still all smiles, but Kay Summersby's image has vanished. No other person was edited out of the picture.

The doctored photograph is just the first sign that the affair is doomed. Ike already knows it. Gen. George Marshall has threatened to expose Eisenhower if he requests a divorce.* Unbeknownst to Summersby, her name will not be on the list of those approved to travel home with Ike. No other member of his staff will be left behind.

★ ★ ★ ★

George Patton thinks Eisenhower is "very nasty and showoffish" when Kay Summersby is around. But the shouts that Summersby hears coming from Eisenhower's office are hardly for her benefit. Patton tries to appear calm, but he squirms in his seat as the evidence against him is presented. He has made a mess of things with the media yet again, going on the record as stating that being a member of the Nazi Party is no different from being a member of the Republican or Democratic Party. "To get things done in Bavaria, after the complete disorganization and disruption of four years of war, we had to compromise with the devil a little. We had no alternative but to turn to the people who knew what to do and how to do it," he told a small gathering of the press one recent morning in his office, defending his use of former Nazi officials in the rebuilding of Germany.

With war at an end, the journalists who remain in Europe are hungry for any story they can find. Reporters from the *New York Times, Chicago Daily News,* and *New York Herald Tribune* were overheard plotting

*The source of this innuendo is Harry Truman, speaking to a biographer in 1974. Marshall's reasons were as much personal as political. It was widely held that Eisenhower had a great political future after the war, but Americans did not look kindly on candidates who were divorced—particularly one who left his wife for a foreigner several years younger. Marshall, in effect, believed he was saving Eisenhower from making a great mistake.

to "get" Patton by tripping him up with loaded questions that would lead him to make the same sort of ill-advised comments to the press that he made at Knutsford.* The *Philadelphia Bulletin* saw nothing newsworthy in Patton's quote, and did not run the story. And the piece was originally buried on the back pages of the Chicago paper. Yet the *New York Times*, *Stars and Stripes*, and the *New York Herald Tribune* made much of Patton's remarks. Eisenhower was irate when he received word, erupting in what Kay Summersby will later describe as "the granddaddy of all tempers. General Patton had made his last and final mistake."

Now Patton must explain to Eisenhower how he could have been so careless with his words.

After past missteps, Patton appeared contrite in Eisenhower's presence. He humbled himself to save his career. But Patton does not do that now. He is dressed in a simple uniform without his pistols. He believes that supplication will be unnecessary. Some well-chosen flattery and reminders of their longtime friendship should be enough to get Patton out of this jam with Ike.

But the truth is Patton no longer has a career worth saving. He is restless and bored. His behavior borders on depressive some days, with the best remedy being a hunting expedition or time on horseback.

Patton desperately misses the war. He longs to arm the Germans and lead them against the Russians. It is a war that should have begun even before Berlin fell, Patton believes. He's not afraid to stand up to the Russians, as he proved at a September 7 parade in Berlin, to celebrate the end of the war against Japan. More than five thousand American, Russian, French, and British soldiers stood in formation on the bright afternoon, on the broad Unter den Linden Boulevard, near the partially demolished columns of the landmark Brandenburg Gate. Patton stood on the review stand alongside the Russian general Georgy Zhukov, both men squinting in the strong sunlight as the troops marched past in review.

---

*Raymond Daniell of the *Chicago Daily News* would later attempt to apologize to Beatrice Patton for his part in this scheme, and for his anti-Patton bias. She refused to accept his apology.

It is Zhukov who put the greatest pressure on Dwight Eisenhower to ensure that Patton hand over all German POWs to the Russians—particularly those elite SS units whom the Russians believe Patton is hiding from them. Eisenhower has already aligned himself with Zhukov, slighting Patton, Montgomery, and every other American and British general by stating in June that "The war in Europe has been won and to no man do the United Nations owe a greater debt than to Marshal Zhukov."

The Russian general is used to such supplicant behavior. During the war, he ordered his troops to shoot any of their comrades who ran from the Germans, and any Russian village that was thought to have collaborated with the Nazis was burned to the ground. Zhukov is so feared that other Russian generals have been known to tremble in his presence.

Patton does not tremble.

"He was in full dress uniform much like comic opera and covered in medals," Patton later wrote to Beatrice of Zhukov. "He is short, rather fat and has a prehensile chin like an ape but good blue eyes."

As Russian tanks rolled past the reviewing stand, Patton noticed Zhu-

Marshal Georgy K. Zhukov with General Eisenhower

kov gloating over the new Soviet IS-3 model tank.* Looking up at his American counterpart, the Russian general delivered a taunt: "My dear General Patton," he crowed. "You see that tank? It carries a cannon which can throw a shell seven miles."

Patton's face remained impassive, his tone calm and sure. "Indeed? Well, my dear Marshal Zhukov, let me tell you this: if any of my gunners started firing at your people before they had closed to less than seven hundred yards, I'd have them court-martialed for cowardice."

Patton's aide Maj. Van S. Merle-Smith will later state that he had never before seen "a Russian commander stunned into silence."

Yet in his publicly stated belief that the Russians are America's new enemy, and should be treated as such, Patton stands alone. Indeed, American troops are either going home or being sent to the Pacific to fight the Japanese, leaving fewer and fewer GIs to fight "the Mongols," as Patton calls the Russians—not that the Truman administration has any intention of doing such a thing.

Among those departing is Sgt. John Mims, Patton's driver for the last four years. The two have traveled thousands of miles together, and Mims's caution at the wheel has kept Patton from being injured, despite navigating battlefields and avoiding artillery shells. "You have been the driver of my official car since 1940," Patton writes in a farewell commendation to Mims. "During that time, you have safely driven me in many parts of the world, under all conditions of dust and snow and ice and mud, of enemy fire and attack by enemy aircraft. At no time during these years of danger and difficulty have you so much as bumped a fender."

Another driver will soon be assigned to the general, but Mims can never truly be replaced, and Patton is so upset about his leaving that he originally fought to keep him in Europe. Only when he was reminded that Mims has a young wife at home did Patton relent and sign the travel orders.

But even more disturbing to Patton is that all his peers are going home to bigger and better jobs. While Patton spends his days reluctantly getting rid of the Nazi presence in Bavaria, Ike will soon be army chief of staff, Gen. Omar Bradley is already in Washington heading up the new

---

*Named for Joseph Stalin. In the Cyrillic alphabet, IS is the close equivalent to his initials.

Veterans Administration, and, of course, Gen. Courtney Hodges is off to fight in the Pacific.

It seems there is no place for George Patton in a peacetime army. The one job he really wanted, that of commandant of the War College at the Carlisle Barracks in Pennsylvania, has been given away to Gen. Leonard T. Gerow, a close friend of Eisenhower's who helped plan and lead the D-day invasion.

As their turbulent meeting stretches on, Dwight Eisenhower finally calms down a bit and gets to the main point: shockingly, his plan is to take away the Third Army from George S. Patton.

With this decision, Eisenhower can effectively terminate the press furor over Patton's remarks and place someone in charge of the Third Army who will be less sympathetic to the Nazis.

"Your greatest fault," Eisenhower tells Patton, "is your audacity."

The words are meant to sting, but both men know that Patton considers audacity his greatest asset.

Then the meeting takes another turn. Instead of simply relieving Patton of active command, Eisenhower suggests instead that Patton assume control of the Fifteenth Army.

It is a face-saving solution, meant to ensure that Patton does not return to America in disgrace. Yet to a fighting man such as Patton, the notion is absurd. The Fifteenth is a paper army, tasked with the job of writing the war's history.

But Patton has no choice. As he walks out of Eisenhower's office, he finds the same reporters who published the stories leading to his downfall now waiting in the corridor for news of his fate.

Eisenhower tells them nothing. Patton also says nothing. He would normally have stayed and had dinner and drinks with Ike; instead, Patton rushes to the train station across from the IG Farben Building to catch a 7:00 p.m. train back to Bavaria.

The humiliation slowly sinks in: Patton's beloved Third Army has been wrenched from his grasp. One of the greatest fighting forces in the history of war will now be commanded by another man. Under Patton's leadership, that spectacular assemblage of men, tanks, and big guns led the liberation of France, rescued Bastogne, crossed the Rhine, and would have freed all of Eastern Europe if Eisenhower had not halted Patton's advance.

"I've obeyed orders," Patton tells an aide over dinner on the long nighttime train ride. "I think that I'd like to resign from the Army so that I could go home and say what I have to say."

But powerful people do not want this to happen. George Patton knows too much—and saying what he knows would be a disaster.

He must be silenced.

25

---·---

JOSEPH STALIN'S PRIVATE VILLA
SOCHI, RUSSIA
OCTOBER 17, 1945
AFTERNOON

Joseph Stalin is down but not out.

The sixty-six-year-old Russian dictator is taking a rare vacation at his favorite hideaway. At his direction, the lavish mountain home has been painted forest green, so that it is completely camouflaged within a grove of cypress trees.* Despite this cloak of invisibility, Stalin is on guard as he strolls alone in the palm-tree-lined courtyard. Trademark pipe clenched firmly between his teeth, he is obsessively contemplating his future—and that of the Soviet Union.

"The Boss," as Stalin is known, desperately needs time away from Moscow. The fresh air and quiet of this retreat one thousand miles due south of the Russian capital are more than a mere tonic to the overworked despot. Unbeknownst to the Americans and British, Stalin suffered two minor heart attacks at the Potsdam Conference, which he concealed from the public. Despite the ailments, Stalin was able to continue negotiating the future of Europe.

---

*In addition to camouflaging the villa's exterior, Stalin added several curious security details to it. He ordered that the drapes be short, so that he could see the feet of anyone trying to hide behind them. There were no rugs, so that Stalin could hear any approaching footsteps. Also, the backs of the sofas were bulletproof, and designed to be high enough so that Stalin's head was not visible when he was seated.

The stress of the war, combined with years of working sixteen hours a day while puffing on a pipe filled with strong tobacco, is taking a savage toll on Stalin's body. He is afraid that any sign of weakness might lead to an attempt to oust him from power. Only his personal physician, Vladimir Vinogradov, knows the full extent of his health problems. But even at leisure, Stalin is a workaholic and finds vacationing to be a nuisance. Now, as he takes two months away from the Kremlin, spending his days in gardening and long walks, he still receives dozens of reports from Moscow each day.

And these reports trouble him deeply.

Stalin's absence is causing a furor. TASS, the official Soviet news agency, has simply explained that "Comrade Stalin has departed for vacation to rest," but few in Moscow or around the world believe there is not more to the story. Foreign diplomats and the international press scurry to learn the truth about what's happening in Sochi, as rumors fly.*

There are rumors that Stalin will soon quit his job, to be replaced either by Marshal Georgy Zhukov or perhaps by foreign affairs commissar Vyacheslav Molotov. "Stalin may leave his post," the *Chicago Tribune* is reporting. "The ambitious aspirations of Marshal Zhukov to become a dictator have full backing of the army, while Molotov is backed by the Communist Party."

Stalin considers such rumors as a *poruganiie*—a desecration not only of his reputation but of the power to which he clings so dearly. Two men who learned the hard way how ruthlessly Stalin deals with those who attempt to usurp his power were Marxist revolutionary Leon Trotsky and his son Lev Sedov. Trotsky was once a trusted commissar of foreign affairs, just as Molotov is now. But the bond between Stalin and Trotsky was broken when their ideologies about the true nature of communism began to differ. Eventually, Trotsky was forced to flee Russia, taking up residence in Mexico. There he openly criticized Stalin, believing that he was safe from the long arm of the NKVD.

Trotsky was wrong.

---

*At the 2014 Winter Olympics in Sochi, Stalin's dacha served as a hotel. Rooms rented for seven thousand rubles—approximately two hundred dollars—per night.

In August 1940, NKVD agent Ramon Mercader attacked Trotsky in his home, plunging the sharp tip of an ice axe deep into the former revolutionary's skull. Miraculously, Trotsky initially survived the blow, only to die one day later in the hospital.

Trotsky's assassination mimicked that of his thirty-two-year-old son, Lev Sedov, two years earlier. At the time of his death, Sedov was on the NKVD execution list because he was arranging an international Communist conference in Paris that would celebrate his father's, rather than Stalin's, vision of communism.

Sedov suffered an acute attack of what appeared to be appendicitis in late January 1938. His symptoms mysteriously disappeared, then reappeared a few weeks later. Immediately, his best friend, an anthropologist named Mark Zborowski, informed Russian intelligence that Sedov had checked into a small Paris hospital known as the Clinique Mirabeau.

Unbeknownst to Sedov, Zborowski was an NKVD agent.

A few days after emerging from surgery, Sedov was in good spirits. He joked with his wife, Jeanne, and for several days was thought to be enjoying a normal recovery. But when his wife came to visit him on February 14, 1938, Sedov appeared listless.

"You know what they did to me last night?" he asked his wife. Suddenly, Sedov stopped talking, apparently unable to finish his thought. Two days later, to the horror of his wife, he died. An examination found strange purple bruising on his abdomen. Sedov was autopsied twice, but Parisian medical authorities ruled that he'd died from natural causes.*

The NKVD chiefs were relentless in their zeal to develop untraceable poisons. Beginning with Genrikh Yagoda; his successor, the reprehensible Nikolai Yezhov; and then the even more heinous Lavrentiy

---

*In 1964, CIA analysis cast suspicion on Sedov's death. It pointed out that the autopsies did not probe for evidence of poisoning, such as traces of microbes that might have been injected, nor did they include a thorough search of the nervous system and the skin, to make sure that the location of all injection marks was consistent with medical procedures. Sedov's successor in Trotsky's Communist movement, a German named Rudolf Klement, was murdered by NKVD agent Alexander Korotkov on June 13, 1938. His headless body was found floating in Paris's Seine River.

Beria, the ruthless spymasters pushed Soviet scientists to experiment with deadly toxins.*

The research was done at a top-secret laboratory known as the Kamera ("the Chamber"), where poisons of all kinds were tested on Russian political prisoners. The goal of the scientists working at the Kamera was to concoct an odorless, tasteless poison that would go undiscovered in case of an autopsy.

"We set ourselves the task of developing in the laboratory poisons so that they could be consumed using wine, drinks and food without modifying the taste or color of the food and drink," one Russian official would testify at Yezhov's secret trial in 1940.† "It was also proposed that we invent fast-acting and slow-acting poisons but they had to have no visible impact on the body so that the autopsy on someone who had been poisoned would be unable to detect that the person had been poisoned."

The Kamera came into being during Stalin's reign of terror. Various poisons were used to silence enemies of the state. Now, as he endures his necessary time away from Moscow, Stalin has plenty of enemies in need of silencing. He lives like a monk as he plots the future. After spending each day in the gardens, the Boss spends his nights reading hand-carried reports from Moscow. He receives no visitors, and communicates with the outside world only through the occasional telephone call. Among the dossiers he receives each day are reports from Beria apprising him of the findings of the many NKVD surveillance teams hidden throughout occupied Europe. Stalin is already making plans to replace Zhukov as deputy minis-

---

*Known as the Bloody Dwarf, Yezhov rose to power by arranging the arrest and execution of Yagoda. He then went on an unparalleled terror spree, killing an estimated six hundred thousand men and women in just two years. The killing was systematic, with security officials given murder quotas that, if not met, resulted in their own executions. Beria, Yezhov's successor, almost became one of Yezhov's victims. However, he cleverly aligned himself with Stalin, and Yezhov's influence soon waned. The Bloody Dwarf was arrested on April 10, 1939, and soon confessed to anti-Soviet activities and homosexual behavior. He was executed on February 4, 1940. His nickname then changed to the Vanishing Commissar, because his image was soon removed from all official photographs until it was as if he had never existed at all.

†Testimony of Semyon Zhukovsky, head of the Twelfth Department of the NKVD. File number 975026 in the archives of the Soviet Senior Military Prosecutor's Office.

ter of defense, and to humiliate Molotov before firing him as commissar of foreign affairs. As to relationships with the Western Allies, the time away from Moscow is giving Stalin an even greater resolve. "It is obvious that in dealing with such partners as the U.S. and Britain we cannot achieve anything serious if we begin to give in to intimidation or betray uncertainty," he messages his top advisers in Moscow. "To get anything from this kind of partner, we must arm ourselves with the policy of *stoikosti i vyderzhki*"— "tenacity and steadfastness."

The dacha in which Joseph Stalin now rests was built in 1934. Since then, he has personally signed the death warrants of forty thousand people—among them, political rivals, military officials, troublesome intellectuals, and personal enemies. Anyone who dares cross Joseph Stalin soon finds himself dead. All it takes is the stroke of a pen—and perhaps a lethal dose of untraceable poison.

★   ★   ★

Two thousand miles northwest of Stalin's dacha, George S. Patton is restless. Many thoughts run through his mind now that it is no longer occupied by war. Patton understands that he is a famous person throughout the world, and that his future might lie in political activism—he'd rather be "outside the tent pissing in, than inside the tent pissing out," in his own words. In a way, speaking out about controversial issues would give the general an opportunity to wage rhetorical war. Above all, Patton remains a warrior, but his battlefield may be changing.

And that prospect is not lost on his enemies, one of whom is currently resting in South Russia.

Another is dealing with captured Nazis at Nuremberg.

26

The crowd rises to its feet in Courtroom 600 as the Nuremberg war crimes trials get under way. Twenty of Nazi Germany's most brutal leaders sit in the dock under a bank of hot floodlights so bright that each of the prisoners has been given sunglasses.* Behind them, a row of white-helmeted American military police stand at crisp attention. The eight judges, two each from the United States, Britain, Russia, and France, take their seats at the front of the room. The proceedings begin with a reading of the twenty-four-thousand-word document listing the atrocities for which these men are being tried: the murder of one million Russians at Leningrad, the death of 780 Catholic priests at Mauthausen concentration camp, the machine-gunning of British POWs who were recaptured after their "Great Escape" from Stalag Luft III, and much more.

The litany of grisly indictments will take two full days to recount, and the Nazi prisoners soon grow bored. Some, such as Hitler's former deputy führer Rudolf Hess, actually fall asleep.

Former Luftwaffe commander Hermann Goering wears headphones

---

*In all, twenty-four political and military leaders of the Third Reich were tried at Nuremberg. Martin Bormann was tried in absentia. Twelve will be sentenced to death by hanging, seven will be given time in prison, three will be acquitted, one will commit suicide four days after the trial begins, and one will be declared medically unfit for trial.

The Nuremberg courtroom

to listen to an interpreter repeat what is being said. Arrogantly, he smirks as an accounting of his war crimes and tales of the art treasures he looted are read into the official court records. The formerly obese *Reichsmarschall* wears a simple gray uniform that hangs off him; he has lost seventy pounds since being taken prisoner. Goering is eager to speak in his own defense. Across the courtroom, he can see the deputy prosecutor, an American who has interviewed him for weeks. They have come to know each other quite well—so much so that Goering has confided stories about the sex lives of Germany's greatest generals, and other salacious gossip, to his new friend, who speaks fluent German.

That prosecutor is none other than Wild Bill Donovan, the sixty-two-year-old major general, Medal of Honor winner, and chief of the OSS. The war may be over, but Donovan still has scores to settle. That is why he is here today. Many of his spies died at the hands of the Nazis, who also murdered countless innocent civilians as revenge for successful

Hermann Goering with Hitler in Berlin

OSS operations. Donovan is relentlessly anti-Nazi, and began laying the groundwork for these trials as far back as October 1943, when he coaxed President Roosevelt into setting up a postwar apparatus for trying war criminals. It was two months later, in the spirit of Allied cooperation, that Donovan flew to Moscow and began forging a relationship between the OSS and the NKVD.

But things have gone horribly wrong for Donovan in recent months. He has been undone by sordid and unfounded rumors that he is having an affair with his daughter-in-law—a rumor that most displeased the prudish Harry Truman when it reached the Oval Office.*

In a separate incident, a fifty-nine-page report leveling charges of gross mismanagement and incompetence within the OSS was manufactured by Donovan's rivals and also found its way to President Truman.

---

*The rumor was untrue, and some believe it was generated by FBI director J. Edgar Hoover.

Now, even as the heat from the courtroom spotlights makes his pale, broad face flush a light crimson, Wild Bill is desperately clinging to what little authority he has left. A power struggle with chief Nuremberg prosecutor Robert Jackson has not ended in his favor, and the fiery Donovan has decided that he will soon leave the trials rather than be a subordinate.

Even worse, as of October 1, his agency is no more. President Truman has shut down the OSS.

But Donovan knows that the United States needs a global spy network. So even though he is not technically America's top spy any longer, he still maintains a close relationship with the leaders of the Russian NKVD and with British spymaster William Stephenson.*

It was with British help that Donovan undertook what was known as Operation Jedburgh, in which teams of British, French, and American commandos parachuted into Nazi-occupied Europe and conducted the espionage that laid the groundwork for D-day. The men selected to be "Jedburghs" were trained in firearms, sabotage, and close-quarters fighting.

In early 1945, while staying at Claridge's, his favorite London hotel, Donovan met with a Jedburgh soldier named Douglas Bazata. The thirty-four-year-old Bazata was a red-haired former U.S. Marine with a fondness for tweaking authority by calling colonels "sugar" rather than "sir." He was also a top marksman and was once the unofficial heavyweight boxing champion of the Marine Corps.

As he sat down for lunch, Bazata was curious: "You have an additional mission for me? You can trust me totally. I am the servant of the United States, of the OSS and General Donovan."

"Douglas, I do indeed have a problem," Donovan admitted. They were at a corner table, where they could not be overheard. "It is the extreme disobedience of General George Patton, and of his very serious disregard of orders for the common cause."

"Shall I kill him, sir?" Bazata was eager to please Donovan, but also cautious. He had met Patton before and liked the general.

---

*The forty-eight-year-old head of British intelligence is widely considered to be the model for Ian Fleming's fictitious spy, James Bond. It was Stephenson who convinced FDR that Donovan should head the OSS.

"Yes, Douglas. You do exactly what you must. It is now totally your creation."*

★ ★ ★ ★

Weeks ago, Donovan sent his personal papers relating to the Nuremberg Trials back to his home in Washington. But it is not yet time for him to return from Europe. There is something else he must do.

Between the last week of November and the middle of December, when his plane finally touches down at LaGuardia Field in New York, Wild Bill Donovan will roam the continent. With no assignment or agency, he has no reason to report his whereabouts to anyone.

But one thing is clear as the morning of December 9 dawns cold and damp over central Germany: Wild Bill Donovan and Douglas Bazata are on a mission, and it may very well alter George Patton's future.

---

*Bazata was held in high esteem by members of the OSS. No less than William Colby, a former OSS agent who went on to become head of the Central Intelligence Agency, made a point of depicting Bazata's heroism in the 1978 book *Honorable Men*. Bazata's obituary in the *New York Times* on August 22, 1999, was specific in recounting his work behind enemy lines in France. However, for three decades after the general died, Bazata remained silent about his alleged role in Patton's death. These quotes come from a letter he wrote to a friend on August 2, 1975. He later confirmed these claims in a 1979 article in *Spotlight* magazine.

27

PATTON'S HEADQUARTERS
BAD NAUHEIM, GERMANY*
DECEMBER 9, 1945
6:00 A.M.

The man with twelve days to live has awakened.

His longtime orderly, African American sergeant William George Meeks, draws the bedroom curtains in George Patton's mansion on the Höhenweg Road. Morning light floods the room as the general stirs and says good morning. The weariness that rimmed his blue eyes the last year of the war is gone. He still has the spot on his pale pink lips from smoking one too many cigars, but he has once again kicked the habit—at least temporarily. Patton has also lost weight through diet, exercise, and giving up tobacco, and looks more athletic than he has in years. He is a rejuvenated man, completely ready for whatever the future might bring.

The morning wake-up is a routine that Patton and Meeks have followed throughout the war, but now that routine is soon to end. George S. Patton is going home to America. Official army orders are directing him

---

*In addition to being the location of Patton's headquarters, Bad Nauheim was also the site of Hitler's Adlerhorst command post. Also, Franklin Delano Roosevelt's father used to travel there to take the waters for his heart condition. Finally, Bad Nauheim was host to Elvis Presley during his short stint in the army between 1958 and 1960. The gate to the city's castle is depicted on the cover of Presley's 1959 No.1 hit record, "A Big Hunk o' Love."

to return home, where he has arranged to take thirty days' leave and celebrate Christmas with his family. After that, he plans to leave the military.

Meeks will return to America with Patton, soon to settle into civilian life in Georgia. Tomorrow morning, the two men will travel by car to Paris, then on to the coast of France, where they will board a U.S. Navy battleship for the five-day Atlantic crossing. Patton has been allowed one hundred and sixty-five pounds of luggage, which Meeks has already packed. Meeks has just finished laying out Patton's clothes for his last day in Germany, but there is soon to be a change in wardrobe.

Sergeant Meeks informs Patton that last night's dinner guest, the general's close friend and commander of the Seventh Army Maj. Gen. Geoffrey Keyes, has been called back to his headquarters on urgent business.

Patton is disappointed. Keyes is one his few friends remaining in Europe, and was a stalwart armored commander on whom Patton depended greatly during the Sicilian campaign. Patton has nothing to do today, and was hoping a morning of conversation with Keyes would help allay the boredom and restlessness that has accompanied the end of the war.

Patton's mansion is surrounded by a dense forest. Rattling around all day with nothing to do holds no appeal for him. So before going downstairs to his waiting breakfast, Patton orders Meeks to assemble a hunting party. There are fields a hundred miles south in Mannheim, where the pheasant hunting is very good, and Patton has spent an occasional Sunday there since taking command of the Fifteenth.

Meeks knows exactly what to do.

★ ★ ★ ★

"Get the limousine ready," Meeks orders. "The General and General Gay are going hunting."

As the intercom once again goes silent, PFC Horace Woodring quickly rises from bed and obeys the order. The handsome, lantern-jawed Kentucky native is Patton's new driver. He likes the job so much that he has just enlisted for an additional year so that he can continue to drive the general. The nineteen-year-old son of a dairy farmer, Woodring has always had a passion for speed. He grew up racing stock cars and flying stunt planes. But if not for the fact that he suffered frostbite and was deemed incapable of remaining in the infantry, he wouldn't have been assigned to the motor pool. Twice the crime of having relationships with local German women has seen him busted down from sergeant to private, but Patton has taken a shine to his new young driver.

"Woodring is the fastest," Patton marvels of the man he calls Woody. After three years of the overly cautious John Mims at the wheel, Patton revels in Woodring's daredevil driving. "He's better than a Piper Cub to get you there ahead of time," says the general.

Today will be Woodring's last day as Patton's military driver. However, Patton has hinted that he would like to hire him as his personal chauffeur after they both leave the service.

The summons to go hunting is unexpected. As with most Saturday nights, Woodring was out on the town carousing the evening before. But he knew better than to overdo it, just in case the general should call. Now is such a moment. Woodring will be driving Patton and his longtime chief of staff, Gen. Hap Gay.

Woodring pulls on his uniform, making sure to dress warmly for a day outside. Patton's house is across the street from where his household staff sleeps. The "limousine" is parked on the street, due to lack of garage space. It is a dull green 1938 Cadillac Model 75, one of four cars Patton makes use of since assuming command of the Fifteenth. The vehicle's interior is spacious, with six feet of legroom between the backseat and the window partition separating the driver's compartment from the back. Woodring normally spends hours making sure that all Patton's vehicles are spotless inside and out, knowing that despite their somewhat informal relationship Patton will have no trouble chewing him out if the car is the slightest bit unkempt.

The morning is exceptionally cold. Woodring waits ninety minutes before Patton steps outside with Gay; their breaths are visible in the frigid morning air. Both men are dressed in thick military coats and gloves. Heavy boots add two inches to Patton's six-foot-two-inch height, making the general even more imposing than usual. With nothing else to do these past two months, he has spent the time traveling throughout Europe, riding and hunting whenever he could. Patton turned sixty just four weeks ago, and celebrated with a lavish party thrown by his staff at Bad Nauheim's Grand Hotel.

Never at a loss for words, even at this early hour, Patton walks to the sedan and jokes with Woodring, who holds the door open while the two men take their seats in the back. A jeep driven by another of Patton's aides, Sgt. Joe Scruce, pulls into line behind them. The rifles for today's hunt are loaded in Scruce's car, along with a hunting dog.

Patton gives Woodring directions to the hunting ground but first orders the driver to go to the ruins of a first-century Roman fort near Saalburg. Shortly before 9:00 a.m. the caravan pulls out, leaving behind the forest-lined road.

Few local Germans possess a vehicle, so there is very little traffic on the autobahn this morning. This allows Woodring to indulge his penchant for speed. At Bad Homburg, he exits onto a side road that Patton has suggested, then carefully navigates his way up a hill to the site of the ruins.

Woodring is not surprised when Patton insists on getting out of the warm car and exploring the site up close. The general's boots are not waterproof and are soon soaked as he climbs through the snow and frozen mud. Upon returning to the Cadillac after a half hour, he moves up to the front passenger seat so the car's heater can warm his sodden feet.

Woodring enjoys defying authority whenever he can. So when the Cadillac comes upon a military checkpoint on the country road known as Route 38, he initially attempts to race through without stopping. The four stars on the car's license plates should tell the military policemen all they need to know. But suddenly an MP stops Patton's vehicle. "The guy must be crazy," Woodring mumbles as he gets out of the Cadillac.

But Patton is only a few steps behind him. Rather than punish the sentry, who has drawn the unfortunate job of manning this lonely post on a frozen Sunday morning, Patton pats him warmly on the back. "You are a good soldier, son. I'll see to it that your CO is told what a fine MP you make."

On his way back to the warmth of the front seat, Patton makes a decision that will change everything. He spies the hunting dog in the other car. "The poor thing is going to freeze to death in your goddam truck," he yells to Sergeant Scruce, referring to the hunting dog.

"Woody," Patton orders his driver, "go and bring that dog inside the car. He looks cold."

With the hunting dog safely in the front seat, Patton returns to his perch in the back.

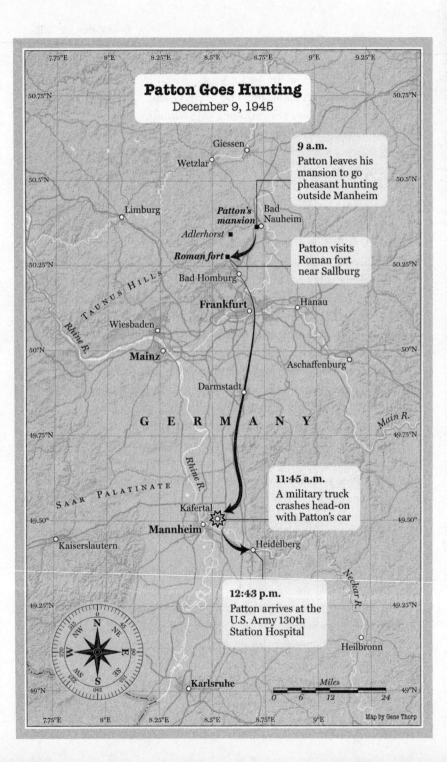

Patton Goes Hunting
December 9, 1945

Giessen
Wetzlar

9 a.m.
Patton leaves his mansion to go pheasant hunting outside Manheim

Patton's mansion
Bad Nauheim

Adlerhorst ■

Roman fort ■

Patton visits Roman fort near Sallburg

Limburg

TAUNUS HILLS

Bad Homburg

Frankfurt

Hanau

Rhine R.

Wiesbaden

Mainz

Aschaffenburg

Darmstadt

G E R M A N Y

Main R.

Rhine R.

SAAR PALATINATE

Kafertal

11:45 a.m.
A military truck crashes head-on with Patton's car

Mannheim

Heidelberg

Kaiserslautern

Neckar R.

12:43 p.m.
Patton arrives at the U.S. Army 130th Station Hospital

Heilbronn

Karlsruhe

Miles
0   6   12   24

Map by Gene Thorp

The journey, now in its third hour, continues. Patton is in no hurry to go hunting, and relaxes as Woodring is forced to stop for a freight train. The Cadillac is at the back of a long line of U.S. military vehicles.

The landscape is now far different from the wooded stretch where Patton's journey began. Bad Nauheim was untouched during the war. But now Patton sees vivid reminders of the war's destruction. Countless disabled trucks, jeeps, and tanks line the road. Just before Woodring stopped for the train, Patton got a glimpse of a Polish displaced persons camp housing thousands of people who now lack a country. He has visited many of these facilities and witnessed firsthand the filthy living conditions the residents must endure. As they wait for the long train to pass, Patton sits on the edge of his seat, as if poised to leap out of the vehicle. He peers out the window at the destruction, and simply tells Gay, "How awful war is."

At 11:45, the crossing bar goes up as the train disappears.

Woodring slowly accelerates.

Six hundred yards in the distance, on the side of the road, two U.S. Army "deuce and a half" (2.5 ton) vehicles are parked on the shoulder. As Patton's limousine approaches, the trucks pull onto the highway.

★ ★ ★ ★

Behind the wheel of the first truck, Tech Sgt. Robert L. Thompson is a little drunk. He is a nervous man whose thick glasses give him an intellectual appearance. He wears his olive-drab uniform cap at a jaunty angle. His pants are bloused into his boots, and he wears a thick army-issue coat and gloves.

Thompson stayed up all night drinking beer with a couple of military buddies. He will later tell investigators that they spontaneously commandeered a Signal Corps deuce and a half for a few hours of joyriding through the German countryside.

But in fact there is evidence that Sergeant Thompson has stolen the truck. With the war over, and the black market providing a lucrative way to make a few extra bucks, there is a very good chance that this vehicle will never be returned to the Signal Corps. Stealing an army vehicle, of course, is a strict violation of regulations. Another violation is in Thompson's two pals riding in the cab with him, both of them apparently hungover.

Army rules strictly state that only two soldiers may ride in the front seat of army trucks.

But Tech Sgt. Robert L. Thompson will go completely unpunished for the violations. Soon he will vanish without a trace, as will the official accident report detailing the destruction he will cause.

★ ★ ★ ★

Sergeant Scruce's jeep overtakes Patton's limousine. Scruce is the only one in the hunting party who knows the way to the special fields outside Mannheim where Patton likes to hunt; Woodring will follow Scruce the rest of the way.

Woodring is driving just twenty miles per hour. George Patton is looking out the right-side window of the limo, while Hap Gay stares out the left. No one has time to react when Robert Thompson abruptly swerves hard to the left, driving his vehicle directly into the path of Patton's Cadillac. His motives for making the abrupt turn are unclear—there is no driveway or road in the direction he is pointing the heavy army truck. "To this day," Woodring will remember years later, "I don't know where the truck was going." The sudden turn comes without warning, and both Gay and Woodring will later note that Thompson did not signal before taking the action.*

PFC Horace Woodring, for all his years behind the wheel, cannot avoid the collision. He slams hard on the brakes, bracing for impact, and grips the steering wheel tightly with two hands. "He just turned into my car," Woodring will later tell the military police, who will soon evaluate the evidence and conclude that the collision was simply an accident. "I saw him in time to hit my brakes, but not in time to do anything else. I was not more than twenty feet from him when he began to turn."

---

*Thompson will try to cover his tracks regarding the "borrowed" truck by telling investigators that at the time of the accident he was turning into a quartermaster depot to return the vehicle, but in fact the depot was much farther down the road. There was a redbrick building to Patton's right, with a broad driveway that might have been Thompson's intended path. He will later change his story to say that he was turning onto a side street. But that is suspicious. The closest street to Thompson's vehicle was fifteen feet north of the accident. In effect, Thompson did not know where he was going.

In the truck, Sgt. Robert Thompson makes no attempt to brake. Instead, he steps on the gas.

As the truck's front bumper crashes into the Cadillac, Woodring hears the thump of flying bodies in the compartment behind him. General Gay, remembering that the best way to avoid injury when falling from a horse is to completely relax his body, does just that. He falls to the floor behind Woodring, uninjured.

In the right backseat, George Patton is thrown forward, his head slamming violently into the steel partition between Woodring's driver's compartment and the backseat. His nose breaks. He feels a sharp pain in the back of his neck, but no sensation in his lower body. Instantly, George Patton knows he is paralyzed.

Ever the leader, Patton immediately checks on his men. "Is anyone hurt?"

After being assured that Gay and Woodring are fine, Patton says in a weak voice, "I believe I am paralyzed."

He sits slumped in an upright position. Hap Gay has his right arm

General Patton's car after the accident

around him, directing Patton's head to his shoulder. "Work my fingers for me, Hap," Patton commands Gay.

After five long minutes, an MP named Lt. Peter K. Babalas of Boston, Massachusetts, happens on the scene. He opens the rear door to the Cadillac and is shocked to find himself staring at George S. Patton, still being supported in an upright seated position by General Gay. "My neck hurts," Patton tells the lieutenant.

A distraught Private Woodring is outside the car surveying the damage, and standing guard until an ambulance arrives. Radiator fluid leaks on the ground, the car's right fender is crumpled, and the engine has been dislodged from its mount. But the rest of the Cadillac is untouched. The windshield is not even cracked. "Do you realize who you hit?" Woodring screams at Thompson, who has stepped down from the truck. Woodring is close enough to smell the liquor on the private's breath. "This is General Patton and he is critically injured."

Thompson grins drunkenly. "General Patton," he says to his companions. "Do you believe it?"

Others have now been alerted to the crash and race to the scene. Members of the 290th Engineer Combat Battalion soon arrive with an ambulance and a doctor.

Meanwhile, blood pours from the top of Patton's head, where a flap of skin extending from the bridge of his nose to the peak of his forehead has peeled back from his skull as if he has been scalped.

"I'm having trouble breathing, Hap," Patton tells his chief of staff. Gay turns to look at Patton with his good eye. In 1922, Gay was blinded in one eye in a polo match and has fooled army doctors about his condition ever since. Now he stares at Patton out of his left eye and studies his bleeding friend.

"Work my fingers for me," Patton commands Gay once more. "Take and rub my arms and shoulders and rub them hard."

Gay does as he is told.

★ ★ ★ ★

At 12:43 p.m., George Patton's ambulance arrives outside the brand-new U.S. Army 130th Station Hospital. Patton has not spoken a word throughout the twenty-five-minute ride from Mannheim. His face is growing pale, and his feet are extremely cold—although he himself cannot feel them.

★ ★ ★ ★

There is no medical staff waiting to rush Patton into surgery, no crack team of spinal specialists assembled to deal with this life-threatening traumatic injury. For some reason, no one at the hospital answered the radio call from the accident site. So it is just a sleepy Sunday afternoon in Heidelberg, where the Neckar River flows slow and green past the legendary Philosophers' Walk.

When the ambulance arrives, all this changes.

Patton mumbles something as a young doctor leans over him.

"Is there anything you want, sir?" the doctor asks.

"I don't want a damned thing, Captain," Patton tells him. "I was just saying Jesus Christ, what a nice way to start a vacation."

George S. Patton is wheeled into an examining room, and eventually Allied authorities are given the top-secret information that one of America's great heroes is incapacitated. Two days later, his wife, Beatrice, and a spinal cord specialist arrive in Germany to be at his side. Doctors believe the strong general will survive his injuries and might be able to regain some mobility.

At the very least, he should be able to travel soon.

They are wrong.

28

George Patton's body is wheeled down to a makeshift morgue in the hospital basement. The room was a horse stall back in the days when this building was a German cavalry barracks. It might have made more sense simply to keep Patton in Room 110, where he died, but the humiliation of his body being stored in a stall is nothing compared to the grisly spectacle that will unfold if a photograph of the dead general's body is splashed across front pages of newspapers worldwide. Hiding Patton in the basement is the best way to avoid the horde of journalists that has descended upon this tiny military hospital. Sergeant Meeks makes the concealment complete by bringing Patton's personal four-star flag to the hospital, where he shields the general's body by draping the flag over his corpse.

There will be no autopsy, at the demand of Beatrice Patton. The doctors quietly insist, but she will not bend on this issue. Beatrice cannot bear the thought of her beloved Georgie being carved up. Instead, she mourns him by making plans for Patton's funeral. There are many issues that need to be confronted immediately. For instance, the hospital has no morticians, and thus no one capable of preparing the body for burial. There are also no caskets, so one will have to be flown in from London. Finally, there is the matter of where George Patton will be laid to rest.

Beatrice wants him buried at West Point, where he can be surrounded by soldiers for eternity.

The army says no. Of all the thousands of Americans who have died on foreign soil during the Second World War, not a single man has been shipped home for burial, due to the cost. Vast cemeteries in Europe and Asia now hold the American dead. As distinguished as Patton might be, allowing him to be buried anyplace other than Europe would set a dangerous precedent.

"Of course he must be buried here," Beatrice Patton says when she is informed of this policy. "I know that George would want to lie beside the men of his army who have fallen."

Christmas is just days away. The decision is made to bury Patton before the holiday, rather than wait until afterward. He is laid to rest at the American Military Cemetery in Hamm, Luxembourg. Neither Gen. Dwight Eisenhower nor President Harry Truman attends. One German newspaper, the *Süddeutsche Zeitung* of Munich, will write eloquently

Pallbearers carrying Patton's casket in Luxembourg

about their former enemy's burial: "In spite of the pouring rain, thousands lined the streets from the central railroad station along the tracks to the cemetery, in order to render this last homage to the dead general. Hundreds of people walked from the capital to attend the burial ceremonies. Representatives of nine countries and highest-ranking officers of the American troops stationed in Europe followed the coffin . . . While the gun carriage with the coffin was on its way from the railroad station to the cemetery, a French battery fired a seventeen-round volley of salute. During the burial, a military band played the Third Army March. After a brief religious service, the coffin was lowered into the grave."

Patton once wrote, "I certainly think it is worth going into the army just to get a military funeral. I would like to get killed in a great victory and then have my body born [sic] between the ranks of my defeated enemy, escorted by my own regiment, and have my spirit come down and revel in hearing what people thought of me."

George Patton did not suffer the death he once longed for. But his body has been borne through the streets of a defeated Germany, and on this day he has had his military funeral.

Afterword

---·---

If you have read *Killing Kennedy,* you know that Martin Dugard and I are not conspiracy theorists. We write from a factual point of view with no agenda.

But the death of General George S. Patton presents a disturbing picture if one fully accepts history's contention that his demise was simply the result of an accident.

We begin with Sgt. Robert Thompson and his two friends, who were responsible for plowing into Patton's car. Shortly after the accident, Thompson claims to have been flown to England by army intelligence for his own safety, due to the number of American soldiers who worshipped Patton and would perhaps have wanted to cause Thompson physical harm. However, just four days after the collision, Thompson mysteriously makes his way back to Germany. There, he is interviewed by American journalist Howard K. Smith. In the wire service story Smith files on December 13, Thompson claims that Patton's driver was speeding and at fault.

Thompson also asserts that he was alone in the truck when it struck Patton's limo, but Gen. Hap Gay and PFC Horace Woodring swear there were two other people in the truck with Thompson. Indeed, a report dated December 18, 1945, by the Seventh Army provost marshal specifies that a German civilian employee of the 141st Signal Company of the First Armored Division (Thompson's company) named Frank Krummer was in the truck at the time of the accident. The name of the other passenger was not mentioned.

But that report, like every other document relating to the accident, has disappeared. So the veracity of Thompson's story was never officially challenged. His version of events was not vetted by the military police. He was not arrested or detained for anything having to do with the accident.

Robert Thompson soon vanishes from the historical record, surfacing only after he dies in Camden, New Jersey, on June 5, 1994. Frank Krummer also disappears. And if there was a third occupant of the vehicle, his name remains unknown to this day.

★　★　★　★

Despite Patton's rank and fame, the military police documenting the accident treated it as nothing more than a fender bender. The crime scene investigation was conducted by Lt. Peter K. Babalas, the MP who arrived first on the scene. Military police from his 818th MP Battalion at Mannheim questioned both drivers, made notes about the damage to both vehicles, and wrote up a standard accident report. Though Patton's driver testified that "the driver and his passengers were drunk and feeling no pain," Sgt. Robert Thompson's blood alcohol levels were never tested and he was never charged with driving under the influence. Thompson's possession of the Signal Company's truck also went unquestioned, despite the fact that he was almost sixty miles north of his duty station, with no apparent reason for being in Mannheim on an otherwise quiet Sunday morning. His assertion that at the time of the accident he was turning into a quartermaster's depot to return the truck does not hold up, as the depot was still several hundred yards down the road. George Patton, in fact, commented about the depot when Woodring drove past it.

Thompson's drunkenness, negligence, and apparent larceny went unquestioned. In fact, the first MP on the scene attempted to arrest Private Woodring, Patton's driver. It was only through the intercession of Gen. Hap Gay that the MP let Woodring go free.

The case was then declared closed. There was no formal inquest, no attempt to speak to Patton in the hospital about his version of events, and no inquiry after his death. Sgt. Robert Thompson's military records, which might have detailed any further actions that were taken against him, were burned on July 12, 1973, when fire swept through the National Personnel Records Center in St. Louis, Missouri, destroying nearly eighteen million official military personnel files.

Incredibly, Lieutenant Babalas's report has also vanished. A 1953 request for a copy of the report by the Gary, Indiana, *Post-Tribune* received an official response from the army noting that, first, the "Report of investigation is not on file;" second, "Casualty Branch has no papers on file regarding accident"; and third, "There is no information re the accident in General Gay's 201 [personnel] file."

★ ★ ★ ★

Seeking more information about the death of his friend, Gen. Geoffrey Keyes, commander of the Seventh Army, immediately launched a probe of his own into the accident. But Keyes's report, too, went missing. In fact, the only report that remained in circulation was a curious document that was allegedly written in 1952 and signed by PFC Horace Woodring, Patton's driver. When asked about it in 1979, Woodring swore that he had never made any statements or signed his name to any such report. He believed the paperwork was completely fabricated.

Attempts by the authors of this book to find the official accident report were unsuccessful. If it does exist, it is well hidden.

★ ★ ★ ★

In 1979, OSS Jedburgh Douglas Bazata made the astounding assertion that he was part of a hit team that lay in wait for Patton's limousine. He claimed that after the crash, he fired a low-velocity projectile into the back of Patton's neck in order to snap it. When Patton did not die immediately, Bazata said, the general was murdered in the hospital by NKVD agents using an odorless poison. Bazata also swore that Wild Bill Donovan paid him ten thousand dollars plus another eight hundred dollars in expenses for his role in Patton's death.

But many believe that Bazata's story is far-fetched. No projectiles were ever found, and surely Woodring and Hap Gay would have seen any assassination team. However, Bazata held to his story. On September 25, 1979, he described Patton's assassination to four hundred and fifty former OSS agents gathered for a reunion at the Washington Hilton.*

Bazata does have some credibility. He was heavily decorated for his service as a Jedburgh, winning the Distinguished Service Cross, four Purple Hearts, and France's Croix de Guerre with two palms.† After the war ended and he left the army in 1947 as a major, Bazata led a flamboyant life. He remained in France, where he studied wine making and had a successful career as a painter, with the Duchess of Windsor and Princess Grace of Monaco each sponsoring a showing of his work. Bazata himself was the subject of a painting by the eccentric artist Salvador Dalí, who put the former Jedburgh on canvas dressed up as Don Quixote. The British art critic Mark Webber, writing in 1969, noted that Bazata had "lived a life eventful enough for a dozen novels."

Among the former OSS members gathered in the ballroom of the Washington Hilton when Bazata made his claims to have killed Patton, there was much conversation. Some believed him. And even after the astounding claim, Bazata was hired to work for the U.S. government, during the Reagan administration, as special assistant to Secretary of the Navy John F. Lehman Jr. Upon his death in 1999 at the age of eighty-eight, Bazata was the subject of a lengthy obituary in the *New York Times*

---

*This was reported in the *Washington Star*.

†This is the citation for Bazata's Distinguished Cross: "The President of the United States of America, authorized by Act of Congress, July 9, 1918, takes pleasure in presenting the Distinguished Service Cross to Captain (Infantry) Douglas D. Bazata, United States Army, for extraordinary heroism in connection with military operations against an armed enemy as an organizer and Director of Resistance forces serving with the Office of Strategic Services, in action against enemy forces from 27 August 1944 to 6 October 1944. Captain Bazata, after having been parachuted into the Haute Saone Department of France, organized and armed Resistance Forces, numbering 7,000; planned and executed acts of sabotage against rail and highway markers in order to divert German convoys onto secondary routes, leading them into well prepared ambushes and causing them to lose many men and motor vehicles. All of these tasks were performed in civilian clothing. Captain Bazata's services reflect great credit upon him and are in keeping with the highest traditions of the armed forces of the United States."

that made no mention of the claims that he'd killed Patton, which were widely known.

However, in 1974 a work of fiction entitled *The Algonquin Project*, by British writer Frederick Nolan, was published that tells the story of an assassin who creeps up on Patton's vehicle immediately after the accident and shoots a low-velocity projectile into the general's neck. It has been confirmed that Bazata read this book. However, two former Jedburghs who knew Bazata well, along with journalist Joy Billington of the *Washington Star*, claim that he confided to them about the Patton assassination as early as 1972, two years before the book was published.

★ ★ ★ ★

The strange death of George S. Patton should be reexamined by American military investigators. Although the trail is ice cold, technological advances could solve some of the puzzles.

There is no doubt that General Patton died a hero, and history certainly honors that to this day. But the tough old general did not go out on his own terms, and there are many unanswered questions surrounding his death. Those questions deserve to be addressed.

BILL O'REILLY
MARTIN DUGARD
MAY 2014

Postscript

———◆———

George Patton once stated that he wished to be buried with his men, and so he is. Many of the five thousand interred at the American Military Cemetery just outside Luxembourg City are Third Army soldiers who fell during the Battle of the Bulge. Patton's burial site became such a popular postwar attraction that the hordes of visitors made it impossible for grass to grow around his grave or those nearby. So on March 19, 1947, his body was exhumed and moved to the location where it now rests, in a solitary spot apart from the long rows of white crosses, at the very front of the cemetery. The location suggests that Patton is still leading his men.

★ ★ ★ ★

A devastated **Beatrice Patton** flew home to America the day after her husband's funeral. It was Christmas, but she had given herself over to grief and mourning. There would be no holiday for her.

In their thirty-five years together, she and George Patton endured countless separations as he waged war in Mexico, Africa, France, and Germany. In the letters he wrote during these long times away from her, she came to know his innermost thoughts and his deep love. George Patton had dyslexia, which makes spelling, reading, and writing a chore, so the very act of writing was as much a symbol of his love as the words themselves.

Patton's grave

But there would be no more letters from George Patton. As his body was lowered into the cold, wet ground of Luxembourg, Beatrice Patton's grief was almost overwhelming.

Her beloved Georgie was no more.

Beatrice Patton never remarried. Her grandson James Patton Totten, speaking in 2008, admitted that she hired several private detectives to look into her husband's death. Each of these investigations was unsuccessful in finding any hard evidence of an assassination.

A lifelong equestrienne, Beatrice suffered a ruptured aortic aneurysm while galloping across a field outside Hamilton, Massachusetts, eight years after her husband's death. Though Mrs. Patton immediately fell from the horse, she was dead before hitting the ground. As noted earlier, she had long made it clear that she wished to be buried with her husband. When the U.S. Army refused to allow her to be interred at the American Military Cemetery in Luxembourg, her children smuggled her ashes to Europe and sprinkled them atop the grave of George Patton.

★ ★ ★ ★

The hospital where Patton died remained a U.S. Army installation until July 1, 2013. At that time, the **130th Station Hospital**, or Nachrichten

Kaserne as it later became known, was closed and handed over to the German government. With the exception of a small ceremonial plaque that was hung outside the door, Room 110 was not treated with any fanfare after Patton's death, and was long used as a radiology lab. In the course of researching this book, a visit was paid to the facility to see this very special room. The place where Patton died was quite ordinary. Coincidentally, this visit occurred just hours before the decommissioning, making Martin Dugard the last American visitor to enter Patton's hospital room before it was handed over to the Germans.

★ ★ ★ ★

PFC Horace Woodring, driver of Patton's Cadillac at the time of the accident, returned home to Kentucky after the war. Gen. Dwight Eisenhower took the time to assure him personally that he had not been at fault in the auto accident that paralyzed the general. Nevertheless, Woodring was devastated by Patton's death. "I felt like a kid who had lost his father," he later remembered, "because that's how I felt about him. I had every admiration in the world for the man. I just thought he was the greatest." When Woodring's wife gave birth to a son, they gave him the middle name of Patton. Woodring and his family moved to Michigan in 1963, where he sold cars and rode snowmobiles to indulge his penchant for speed. Woodring died of heart disease in a Detroit hospital in November 2003. He was seventy-seven years old. Until the day he died, Woodring asserted that the accident that killed Patton was inexplicable.

★ ★ ★ ★

The hero of the Battle of Fort Driant, **Pvt. Robert W. Holmlund**, who won the Distinguished Service Cross, was promoted posthumously to staff sergeant. Strangely, he has become a historical mystery. Staff Sergeant Holmlund is not listed as being buried in any of the American military cemeteries in Europe; nor is he buried in Arlington National Cemetery.

★ ★ ★ ★

Capt. Jack Gerrie was sent home to Wisconsin for a thirty-day leave after the battle for Fort Driant. On his way back into Europe, he passed through a depot, to await transportation to his unit. While there, on December 29, 1944, Gerrie was killed when a captured German gun he was examining fired into his head.

★   ★   ★   ★

German generals **Ernst Maisel** and **Wilhelm Emanuel Burgdorf**, who came to Erwin Rommel's home bearing the field marshal's fatal suicide pill, lived two very different lives after that day. Maisel was promoted to lieutenant general (*Generalleutnant*) in the waning days of the war and placed in command of the Sixty-Eighth Infantry Division. He was captured by American forces on May 7, 1945, released two years later, and lived out his days in the mountains of German Bavaria, where he died on December 16, 1978, at the age of eighty-two.

Burgdorf was long dead by then. In fact, he had committed suicide five days before Maisel was taken prisoner. Called to Adolf Hitler's Berlin bunker during the final days of the war, Burgdorf witnessed the Führer's signing of his last will and testament. Three days later, Burgdorf shot himself in the head rather than be captured by Soviet troops.

★   ★   ★   ★

Just prior to Burgdorf's suicide, fellow bunker residents Joseph and Magda Goebbels chose a most grisly death. On May 1, 1945, **Magda Goebbels** medicated her six children with a drink containing morphine. She then cracked a vial of cyanide into their mouths as they slept, killing them one by one. She and her husband later went up out of the bunker, where she bit into a cyanide pill and Joseph Goebbels fired a bullet into the back of her head. Goebbels then killed himself with a pill and a simultaneous gunshot.

The other elite members of the Nazi Party died in similar fashion. SS leader **Heinrich Himmler**, who was captured by the British three weeks after fleeing Berlin, killed himself in prison with a hidden cyanide pill. **Hermann Goering**, the corpulent head of the Luftwaffe, was arrested by American troops on May 6, 1945. On September 30, 1946, he was sentenced to be hanged by the neck until dead. But Goering, who openly laughed and joked during the Nuremberg Trials, and declared that gruesome films showing Nazi concentration camp atrocities were faked, did not want to die a public death. With the unwitting help of Herbert Lee Stivers, a nineteen-year-old American army guard, a cyanide ampoule was smuggled into Goering's cell and he committed suicide. A local German girl who had caught Stivers's eye while he was off duty convinced him to carry "medicine" to Goering hidden inside a pen. Afterward, Stivers never saw the girl again. "I guess she used me," he lamented when Stivers finally admitted what had happened. He did so in 2005, sixty years after the fact, explaining that he was still bothered by a guilty conscience.

Goering's body was put on public display in Nuremberg before being cremated.

★ ★ ★ ★

Manfred Rommel, son of Erwin Rommel, returned to his post as a Luftwaffe antiaircraft gunner shortly after his father's forced suicide. He soon deserted and surrendered to French forces. After his release from captivity, he went to college and then entered politics, where he became mayor of Stuttgart and a leading liberal voice in postwar Germany. Magnanimous and much admired, he refused to run for national office, despite the widespread belief that he could have risen to chancellor. Rommel formed friendships with the sons of Field Marshal Bernard Law Montgomery and George S. Patton. He died on November 7, 2013, at the age of eighty-four.

★ ★ ★ ★

Gen. Dwight D. Eisenhower returned home a hero. He did not believe that a military officer should interest himself in politics. So despite widespread popular support for an Eisenhower presidential candidacy in 1948, he accepted a position as head of Columbia University, in New York City, rather than running for office. However, he soon changed his mind. He was elected president of the United States in 1952 and 1956, serving two terms. When doctors told him that his chain-smoking was a hazard to his health, Eisenhower quit the four-pack-a-day habit cold turkey. He died of heart failure on March 28, 1969. He was seventy-eight years old.

★ ★ ★ ★

Kay Summersby, Ike's Irish wartime consort, did not share in Eisenhower's success. She married and soon divorced, then became engaged for a short time to a man who mistakenly thought she was wealthy. After that, she wrote two tell-all books about her relationship with Eisenhower. There are unsubstantiated rumors that the two continued to meet secretly. Kay Summersby died of liver cancer in 1975, at her home in Southampton, New York.

★   ★   ★   ★

The life of **Jean Gordon**, Patton's wartime consort, ended on an even more tragic note. Shortly after the general's death, she and Beatrice Patton had a heated meeting in New York. The precise words that passed between them are unknown. Jean Gordon committed suicide on January 8, 1946, by gassing herself in a friend's apartment. No suicide note was entered into evidence by police. However, Patton family legend states that a message found at the scene read, "I will be with Uncle Georgie in heaven, and will have him all to myself before Beatrice arrives."

★   ★   ★   ★

Omar Bradley, the general with whom Patton sparred so often during the war, went on to serve for almost forty years in the army, rising to the rank of five-star general and serving as army chief of staff. He oversaw American forces in the Korean War, and later consulted with President Lyndon Johnson during the Vietnam War. He also served as a consultant on the movie *Patton*, which won the actor George C. Scott an Academy Award for his portrayal of the general. Bradley lived to be eighty-eight.

★   ★   ★   ★

Ironically, **Winston Churchill** enjoyed an even longer life. Though overweight, a heavy drinker, and rarely seen without a cigar, Britain's wartime prime minister lived to be ninety. He died on January 24, 1965, seventy years to the day after his father passed. Potsdam was the last great moment of World War II for Churchill. He flew home from Potsdam on July 25. The next day, he learned that he'd lost the general election in a landslide to Labour Party leader Clement Attlee, who was voted in by an electorate weary of all individuals associated with the grueling war effort. The election results were a shock to Churchill's Conservative Party, who thought his wartime exploits made him a shoo-in, but polls later show that the

British people believed Labour was better poised to rebuild the nation. The tables were turned in 1951, when Churchill was once again elected prime minister. He served from 1951 to 1955, whereupon he resigned, citing a series of strokes and his advanced age of eighty. In his later life, Churchill spoke candidly about the state of the world. His funeral was the largest such state ceremony in world history until that time, with delegates from 112 nations coming to pay their respects. As his casket was borne down the Thames aboard a barge, the dock cranes lining the waterway lowered their jibs in salute. He is buried in the Churchill family plot at St. Martin's Church in Bladon, next to his wife, Clementine. They were married for fifty-six years.

✶ ✶ ✶ ✶

Russian dictator **Joseph Stalin** ruled the Soviet Union for thirty years, dying at the age of seventy-four from a stroke and complications of heart disease brought on by years of heavy smoking. Ironically, his life might have been lengthened if doctors had reached him more quickly after his stroke, but Stalin's standing orders that his guards never enter his room worked against him. Though they thought it odd that he did not come down for breakfast or lunch on March 1, 1953, his guards refused to disobey his orders, thus delaying medical assistance. He died four days later. The official cause of death was a cerebral hemorrhage, but a subsequent examination of the body suggests that Stalin may have been murdered after someone slipped an odorless and tasteless rat poison named warfarin into his wine the evening before he collapsed. His body was embalmed, then placed in a mausoleum next to that of Vladimir Lenin, founder of the Soviet Union, where it was on public display in Moscow's Red Square until October 31, 1961. Stalin's remains were then removed and interred in the Kremlin Wall Necropolis. Lenin's body is still on display.

✶ ✶ ✶ ✶

Soviet marshal **Georgy Zhukov**, the Russian general who won the Battle of Berlin and later shared a review stand with George Patton, lived a tempestuous life after the war. Long viewed as a political threat by Joseph Stalin, he was stripped of his job as commander of Soviet ground forces in early 1946 and reassigned to a post far from Moscow, in Odessa. He was recalled to Moscow in 1953, and Stalin's death one month later allowed Zhukov once again to become a political force. Zhukov oversaw the arrest and execution of Lavrentiy Beria, the head of the NKVD, after which he became a close adviser to the new Russian leader Nikita Khrushchev. On his sixtieth birthday, in 1964, Zhukov was named a Hero of the Soviet Union. He died of a stroke in 1974; his ashes are interred in the Kremlin Wall Necropolis.

★ ★ ★ ★

Eleanor Roosevelt, the widow of American president Franklin Delano Roosevelt, moved to New York after her husband's death, where she lived for a time in suites at the Park Sheraton hotel while pursuing several prominent causes. She was one of the first delegates to the United Nations, where she oversaw the passing of a document known as the Universal Declaration of Human Rights, which promises basic freedoms to men and women throughout the world. Russia, quite notably, abstained from voting in its favor, due to a clause known as Article Thirteen, which asserts people's right to travel freely from one country to another. Eleanor traveled widely, and gave more than one hundred lectures each year. She died on November 7, 1962, from a combination of aplastic anemia and bone marrow tuberculosis. She was seventy-eight. Eleanor Roosevelt was laid to rest next to FDR at their family home in Hyde Park, New York.

★ ★ ★ ★

His time at the helm of the OSS marked the peak of **Wild Bill Donovan's** lifetime of adventure. He played a significant role in the birth of the Central Intelligence Agency, which was created by the National Security Act of 1947. However, President Truman was reluctant to allow him to lead the organization. Donovan returned to his law practice in New York, but once again left the law, in 1953, to assume the role of U.S. ambassador to Thailand, at the behest of President Dwight Eisenhower. Donovan's mental faculties soon began to slip, and he spent the last years of his life in a state of dementia. He died on February 8, 1959, at the Walter Reed Army Medical Center in Washington at the age of seventy-six. Wild Bill Donovan is buried in Arlington National Cemetery.

★ ★ ★ ★

Gen. George Marshall, the man who served as army chief of staff during the war, died in Washington, DC, in 1959 at the age of seventy-eight. In his lifetime, he served as general of the army (the most senior soldier in the U.S. Army), secretary of state, and secretary of defense; was *Time* magazine's Man of the Year; and won the Nobel Peace Prize in 1953. His most enduring legacy was the creation of the Marshall Plan, which allowed Europe to rebuild itself after World War II with financial assistance from the United States. President Harry Truman once said that Marshall was the greatest man of his generation.

★ ★ ★ ★

Bernard Law Montgomery was named First Viscount Montgomery of Alamein after the war, a title referring to his epic defeat of Field Marshal Erwin Rommel in the Egyptian desert. Montgomery served as Britain's chief of the Imperial General Staff from 1946 to 1948, and then held a number of other military positions until his retirement from the army in 1958, at the age of seventy-one. Outspoken as ever, he soon involved himself in a number of political issues, including supporting apartheid in South Africa, criticizing the 1967 legalization of homosexuality in Britain as "a charter for buggery," and publicly ridiculing American military policy in Vietnam. Montgomery continued his habit of second-guessing his superior officers from the Second World War, particularly Eisenhower, whom he derided in his eponymous 1958 memoir. Montgomery died in 1976, at age eighty-eight. He is buried in the Holy Cross churchyard in the southern English city of Binsted.

★ ★ ★ ★

Italian dictator **Benito Mussolini** preceded Adolf Hitler in death by just two days. Pro-Communist partisans captured him and his mistress near Lake Como, in the mountains of northern Italy, on April 27, 1945, as the two were attempting to flee to Switzerland. They were held overnight, then driven to a remote location and killed by a firing squad. Mussolini, at his request, was shot in the chest instead of the face. The first bullet did not kill him, so a second shot was fired at point-blank range. Their bodies were then driven into the city of Milan, where they were publicly displayed hanging upside down on meat hooks. The angry citizens of Milan then spat on, kicked, and threw rocks at the corpses. Adolf Hitler learned of Mussolini's fate while in his Berlin bunker; the news gave him further incentive to have his corpse burned.

* * * *

Miklós Horthy Jr., the target of SS commando Otto Skorzeny's Operation Mickey Mouse, spent the remainder of World War II as a German prisoner in the Dachau concentration camp. He was freed by Allied forces on May 5, 1945. Due to the Russian invasion of his Hungarian homeland, he spent the rest of his life in exile in Portugal with his father, **Miklós Horthy**, the longtime Hungarian regent.

* * * *

Otto Skorzeny was acquitted of war crimes at the 1947 Dachau Trials. While he was being held to determine if further charges could be filed, three former SS officers dressed as American MPs successfully helped him escape. For a time, he devoted himself to helping other former SS members escape from Germany. Skorzeny later worked with espionage agencies around the world in a number of clandestine activities. Ironically, among them was Mossad, the intelligence agency for the Jewish state of Israel. Skorzeny died of cancer in July 1975, at the age of sixty-seven.

* * * *

Maj. Hal McCown, who was the prisoner of Joachim Peiper at La Gleize, remained in the army until 1972. He went on to serve in Korea and Vietnam, and retired as a major general. McCown died in 1999. He is among a number of American junior officers during the Second World War who went on to lead the military during the Vietnam War years. Another was **Lt. Col. Creighton "Abe" Abrams**, who had a long and successful military career. He became a four-star general and chief of staff of the army during the Vietnam War. All three of his sons became general officers, and his three daughters all married military men. Abrams's lifelong fondness for cigars finally caught up with him in the 1970s, and he died of complications of lung cancer in 1974. He is buried in Arlington National Cemetery, next to his wife of thirty-eight years, Julia.

Other key Bastogne figures went on to long and successful army careers, and formed the backbone of the officer corps during the Vietnam War. **Lt. Col. Harry Kinnard**, who suggested that Gen. Tony McAuliffe formally reply "Nuts" to the German surrender order, commanded the First Air Cavalry Division in Vietnam, which fought in the legendary Battle of Ia Drang. This was immortalized in the book *We Were Soldiers Once . . . and Young* and the movie by the same name. Kinnard lived until 2009, when he passed away at the age of ninety-three. **Maj. William Desobry**, who so famously held the line in Noville, remained a German prisoner of war until the spring of 1945. He later rose to lieutenant general, and stayed in the army until 1975. He passed away in 1996. A street in Noville now bears his name. The Rue du Général Desobry is a pivotal crossroads on the way into Bastogne.

★ ★ ★ ★

Gen. Anthony McAuliffe, the hero of Bastogne, would never shake his connection with the "Nuts" response, which has gone down in history as one of warfare's great quotations. His military career continued until 1956, when he left the service and went on to a number of high-ranking civilian occupations. He died in 1975 at the age of seventy-seven. Before dying, he recounted his weariness about his claim to fame: "One evening a dear old Southern lady invited me to dinner. I had a delightful time talking to her and her charming guests. I was pleased because no mention was made the entire evening of the 'nuts' incident. As I prepared to depart and thanked my hostess for an enjoyable evening, she replied, 'Thank you and good night, General McNut.'"

★ ★ ★ ★

George Patton's oldest daughter, **Beatrice**, remained married to John Waters until her death on October 24, 1952. She gave birth to two sons, John and George Patton. Her sister, **Ruth Ellen**, married a career army officer, James Totten, who rose through the ranks to become a major general. They had two sons, Michael and James, both of whom continued the family lineage of service in the army. In her memoir, *The Button Box: A*

Daughter's Loving Memoir of Mrs. George S. Patton, Ruth Ellen wrote that at the moment of her father's death, she woke up and saw him standing at the foot of her bed in full uniform. "I sat up in bed—I could see him plainly. When he saw I was looking at him he gave me the sweetest smile I've ever seen." In the morning, she called her sister, Beatrice, who reported a similar occurrence. "She said she had been fast asleep when the phone by her bed rang. She picked it up and there was a lot of static, as if it were an overseas call, and she heard Georgie's voice ask, 'Little Bee, are you alright?'" But when young Beatrice Patton called the overseas operator, she was told that there had been no call.

Gen. George Patton's only son, **George Patton IV**, got the news at West Point, where he was midway through his senior year. His father was buried on his twenty-second birthday. George Junior was unable to leave West Point for the funeral. After his commissioning, he followed in his father's footsteps, and rose to the rank of major general. He served in the Korean War and also did several tours in the Vietnam War. Like his father, he spoke fluent French and was passionate about history. During his lifetime, Patton legally changed his name to avoid any confusion between him and his father, who had gone by George S. Patton Jr. even though his actual name was George S. Patton III. The younger Patton dropped the Roman numeral four so that he was simply George Patton. He died in 2004, at the age of eighty. General Patton and his wife, Joanne, had five children, among them their oldest son, George Patton V.

APPENDIX

Gen. George S. Patton's Speech to the U.S. Third Army

Southern England

June 5, 1944

Be seated.

Men, this stuff that some sources sling around about America wanting out of this war, not wanting to fight, is a crock of bullshit. Americans love to fight, traditionally. All real Americans love the sting and clash of battle.

You are here today for three reasons. First, because you are here to defend your homes and your loved ones. Second, you are here for your own self-respect, because you would not want to be anywhere else. Third, you are here because you are real men and all real men like to fight.

When you, here, every one of you, were kids, you all admired the champion marble player, the fastest runner, the toughest boxer, the big league ball players, and the All-American football players. Americans love a winner. Americans will not tolerate a loser.

Americans despise cowards.

Americans play to win all of the time. I wouldn't give a hoot in hell for a man who lost and laughed. That's why Americans have never lost nor will ever lose a war; for the very idea of losing is hateful to an American.

You are not all going to die. Only two percent of you right here today would die in a major battle. Death must not be feared. Death, in time, comes to all men. Yes, every man is scared in his first battle. If he says he's not, he's a liar. Some men are cowards but they fight the same as the brave men or they get the hell slammed out of them watching men fight who are just as scared as they are.

The real hero is the man who fights even though he is scared. Some men get over their fright in a minute under fire. For some, it takes an hour. For some, it takes days. But a real man will never let his fear of death overpower his honor, his sense of duty to his country, and his innate manhood. Battle is the most magnificent competition in which a human being can indulge. It brings out all that is best and it removes all that is base. Americans pride themselves on being He Men and they *are* He Men.

Remember that the enemy is just as frightened as you are, and probably more so. They are not supermen.

All through your Army careers, you men have bitched about what you call "chickenshit drilling." That, like everything else in this Army, has a definite purpose. That purpose is alertness. Alertness must be bred into every soldier. I don't give a f-ck for a man who's not always on his toes. You men are veterans or you wouldn't be here. You are ready for what's to come. A man must be alert at all times if he expects to stay alive. If you're not alert, sometime, a German son-of-an-asshole-bitch is going to sneak up behind you and beat you to death with a sock full of shit!

There are four hundred neatly marked graves somewhere in Sicily, all because one man went to sleep on the job. But they are German graves, because we caught the bastard asleep before they did.

An Army is a team. It lives, sleeps, eats, and fights as a team.

This individual heroic stuff is pure horse shit. The bilious bastards who write that kind of stuff for the *Saturday Evening Post* don't know any more about real fighting under fire than they know about f-cking! We have the finest food, the finest equipment, the best spirit, and the best men in the world. Why, by God, I actually pity those poor sons-of-bitches we're going up against. By God, I do.

My men don't surrender. I don't want to hear of any soldier under my command being captured unless he has been hit. Even if you are hit, you can still fight back. That's not just bullshit either. The kind of man that I want in my command is just like the lieutenant in Libya, who, with a Luger against his chest, jerked off his helmet, swept the gun aside with one hand, and busted the hell out of the Kraut with his helmet. Then he jumped on the gun and went out and killed another German before they knew what the hell was coming off. And, all of that time, this man had a bullet through a lung. There was a real man!

All of the real heroes are not storybook combat fighters, either. Every single man in this Army plays a vital role. Don't ever let up. Don't ever think that your job is unimportant. Every man has a job to do and he must do it. Every man is a vital link in the great chain.

What if every truck driver suddenly decided that he didn't like the whine of those shells overhead, turned yellow, and jumped headlong into a ditch? The cowardly bastard could say, "Hell, they won't miss me, just one man in thousands." But, what if every man thought that way? Where in the hell would we be now? What would our country, our loved ones, our homes, even the world, be like?

No, Goddamnit, Americans don't think like that. Every man does his job. Every man serves the whole. Every department, every unit, is important in the vast scheme of this war.

The ordnance men are needed to supply the guns and machinery of war to keep us rolling. The Quartermaster is needed to bring up food and clothes because where we are going there isn't a hell of a lot to steal. Every last man on K.P. has a job to do, even the one who heats our water to keep us from getting the "G.I. Shits."

Each man must not think only of himself, but also of his buddy fighting beside him. We don't want yellow cowards in this Army. They should be killed off like rats. If not, they will go home after this war and breed more cowards. The brave men will breed more brave men. Kill off the Goddamned cowards and we will have a nation of brave men.

One of the bravest men that I ever saw was a fellow on top of a telegraph pole in the midst of a furious firefight in Tunisia. I stopped and asked what the hell he was doing up there at a time like that. He answered, "Fixing the wire, Sir." I asked, "Isn't that a little unhealthy right about now?" He answered, "Yes, Sir, but the Goddamned wire has to be fixed." I asked, "Don't those planes strafing the road bother you?" And he answered, "No, Sir, but you sure as hell do!" Now, there was a real man. A real soldier. There was a man who devoted all he had to his duty, no matter how seemingly insignificant his duty might appear at the time, no matter how great the odds.

And you should have seen those trucks on the road to Tunisia. Those drivers were magnificent. All day and all night they rolled over those son-of-a-bitching roads, never stopping, never faltering from their course, with shells bursting all around them all of the time. We got through on good old American guts. Many of those men drove for over forty consecutive hours. These men weren't combat men, but they were soldiers with a job to do. They did it, and in one hell of a way they did it. They were part of a team.

Without team effort, without them, the fight would have been lost. All of the links in the chain pulled together and the chain became unbreakable.

Don't forget, you men don't know that I'm here. No mention of that fact is to be made in any letters. The world is not supposed to know what the hell happened to me. I'm not supposed to be commanding this Army. I'm not even supposed to be here in England. Let the first bastards to find out be the Goddamned Germans. Some day I want to see them raise up on their piss-soaked hind legs and howl, "Jesus Christ, it's the Goddamned Third Army again and that son-of-a-f-cking-bitch Patton."

We want to get the hell over there. The quicker we clean up this Goddamned mess, the quicker we can take a little jaunt against the purple-pissing Japs and clean out their nest, too. Before the Goddamned Marines get all of the credit.

Sure, we want to go home. We want this war over with. The quickest way to get it over with is to go get the bastards who started it. The quicker they are whipped, the quicker we can go home. The shortest way home is through Berlin and Tokyo. And when we get to Berlin I am personally going to shoot that paper hanging son-of-a-bitch Hitler. Just like I'd shoot a snake!

When a man is lying in a shell hole, if he just stays there all day, a German will get to him eventually. The hell with that idea. The hell with taking it. My men don't dig foxholes. I don't want them to. Foxholes only slow up an offensive. Keep moving. And don't give the enemy time to dig one either. We'll win this war, but we'll win it only by fighting and by showing the Germans that we've got more guts than they have; or ever will have.

We're not going to just shoot the sons-of-bitches, we're going to rip out their living Goddamned guts and use them to grease the treads of our tanks. We're going to murder those lousy Hun c-cksuckers by the bushel-f-cking-basket. War is a bloody, killing business. You've got to spill their blood, or they will spill yours. Rip them up the belly. Shoot them in the guts. When shells are hitting all around you and you wipe the dirt off your face and realize that instead of dirt it's the blood and guts of what once was your best friend beside you, you'll know what to do!

I don't want to get any messages saying, "I am holding my position." We are not holding a Goddamned thing. Let the Germans do that. We are advancing constantly and we are not interested in holding onto anything, except the enemy's balls. We are going to twist his balls and kick the living shit out of him all of the time.

Our basic plan of operation is to advance and to keep on advancing regardless of whether we have to go over, under, or through the enemy. We are going to go through him like crap through a goose; like shit through a tin horn!

From time to time there will be some complaints that we are pushing our people too hard. I don't give a good Goddamn about such complaints. I believe in the old and sound rule that an ounce of sweat will save a gallon of blood. The harder *we* push, the more Germans we will kill. The more Germans we kill, the fewer of our men will be killed. Pushing means fewer casualties. I want you all to remember that.

There is one great thing that you men will all be able to say after this war is over and you are home once again. You may be thankful that twenty years from now when you are sitting by the fireplace with your grandson on your knee and he asks you what you did in the great World War II, you *won't* have to cough, shift him to the other knee and say, "Well, your Granddaddy shoveled shit in Louisiana." No, Sir. You can look him straight in the eye and say, "Son, your Granddaddy rode with the Great Third Army and a Son-of-a-Goddamned-Bitch named Georgie Patton!"

That is all.

Sources

Researching this book was an adventure.

The journey began in the German town of Heidelberg, with a visit to the hospital room at Nachrichten Kaserne where Patton died. Shane Sharp, the base's public affairs officer, arranged for Major Aaron Northup to conduct a brief tour of the facility, allowing our first hands-on glimpse into the places visited by George S. Patton in the final years of his life.

After that simple and somewhat poignant beginning, the research careened all over Europe and through parts of America, as Hitler, Stalin, Churchill, Roosevelt, Eisenhower and many of the other influential figures that grace these pages demanded their own levels of in-depth investigation. Some of this was a straightforward dig into various archives, museums, and official U.S. Army battlefield histories. In particular, the Central Intelligence Agency, the presidential libraries of Franklin Roosevelt and Harry Truman, and the National Archives were of great assistance. This history is still close enough to the present time that two key figures in this book, Abe Baum and Manfred Rommel, passed away during the research process. As with many other figures in this book, their newspaper obituaries provided important background information. These are all standard sources for historical research. However, there were also several unexpected sources that helped bring the past to life.

Among them was the George S. Patton Memorial Museum at Chiriaco Summit in California's Mojave Desert, with its vast and diverse amount of Patton memorabilia, including several tanks displayed in the desert surrounding the museum. Also, the Topography of Terror Museum in Berlin offered a chilling look into Nazi Germany. It is built atop the former site of Gestapo headquarters, next to a small remaining section of the Berlin Wall. And, of course, the site of Patton's grave in Luxembourg was powerful in its elegant simplicity. Additional thanks go out to Eva Mozes Kor and Candles, the Holocaust Museum & Education Center, for providing unique insight into Auschwitz-Birkenau and Mengele's experiments, which she and her twin sister, Miriam, survived.

The city of Bastogne is not the commercial crossroads it was in 1944, but it pays homage to the Battle of the Bulge and its American defenders each year on the anniversary of the battle. The 101st Airborne's former barracks and site of General McAuliffe's headquarters is an operational military facility that sometimes opens its gates for tours. And while it is not to be found on any map, Fort Driant still exists in the hills above Metz, slowly being reclaimed by the forest. It is possible to walk the battlefield, following the path of Easy Company and Baker Company—though this is roundly discouraged by the locals due to the large amounts of unexploded ordnance. Open doorways and tunnels allow the adventurous to step inside Fort Driant's Wehrmacht gun emplacements and see for themselves the thickness of the fort's concrete walls.

Katerina Novikova, director of press relations at Moscow's Bolshoi Theater, was very helpful in passing along the ballet's program for the night in October 1944 when Olga Lepeshinskaya danced for Winston Churchill and Joseph Stalin. And Aleksandra Perisik-Green in the House of Commons Information Office was no less dogged in finding the meeting minutes for the day on which Churchill eulogized Franklin Roosevelt, allowing us to pinpoint the exact time that heartfelt speech began.

It is ironic that the people who make history are some of the most bold, courageous, and passionate people that have ever walked the earth, but that the actual writing of history is often so fact driven that all emotion is deflated from the telling of a person's life story. So it is interesting that most literature about George Patton breaks from this tradition and displays a subcurrent of deep empathy for the general. It says a great deal about the power of Patton's personality and the tragedy of his early demise.

There is a vast body of excellent literature about Patton, so there was no shortage of published resources. *War As I Knew It*, Patton's published journals, was a constant source of information and insight, as was *The Patton Papers*, which expanded his personal writings in a way that gave them context. Beyond the words of Patton himself, the writings of Carlo D'Este (the excellent *Patton: A Genius for War*), Martin Blumenson (*Patton* and *The Patton Papers*), Ladislas Farago (*The Last Days of Patton*), and Brian Sobel (*The Fighting Pattons*) were particularly helpful. Each of them writes of Patton as if they knew him (which was actually the case with Blumenson, who served as staff historian for Patton's Third Army). For specifics about the conspiracy theories surrounding Patton's death, the writing of Robert K. Wilcox (*Target: Patton*) was very helpful.

What follows is a list of sources that helped with the research for this book. It is lengthy but hardly exhaustive, because hundreds of sources were called upon.

World War II has been written about extensively, but Cornelius Ryan's *The Last Battle* and Rick Atkinson's *Guns at Last Light* are loaded with detail and action. *The Victors*, by Stephen E. Ambrose, takes the reader onto the battlefield through the eyes of ordinary soldiers, and in vivid fashion. For a look at the war from a command point of view, Omar Bradley's *A Soldier Story* is self-effacing and an easy read. While there are too many books detailing the war to list in this space, some that were very helpful in providing background nuance include *Darkness Visible: Memoir of a World War II Combat Photographer*, by Charles Eugene Sumners; *World War II in Numbers*, by Peter Doyle; *Patton, Montgomery, Rommel: Masters of War*, by Terry Brighton; *The Nuremberg Trials: The Nazis and Their Crimes Against Humanity*, by Paul Roland; and *The Battle for Western Europe, Fall 1944: An Operational Assessment*, by John A. Adams. *Wild Bill Donovan*, by Douglas Waller, proved to be the definitive source on the OSS chief; also useful on the topic were *The Jedburghs: The Secret History of the Allied Special Forces, France 1944*, by Will Irwin; and *OSS Against the Reich: The World War II Diaries of Colonel David K. E. Bruce*, by David Kirkpatrick Este Bruce.

Metz was written about in spectacular fashion by Anthony Kemp in *The Unknown Battle: Metz, 1944*, and Steven J. Zaloga with *Metz 1944* and *Lorraine 1944*. **The Battle of the Bulge** is another milestone of the war that has been covered at great length, but the books we relied on were Robert E. Merriam's *The Battle of the Bulge*; *Troy H. Middleton: A Biography*, by Frank J. Price; *Battle: The Story of the Bulge*, by John Toland; *11 Days in December: Christmas at the Bulge, 1944*, by Stanley Weintraub; *Alamo in the Ardennes*, by John C. McManus; *Against the Panzers: United States Infantry versus German Tanks, 1944–1945*, by Allyn R. Vannoy and Jay Karamales; *The Ardennes on Fire: The First Day of the German Assault*, by Timothy J. Thompson; *Fatal Crossroads: The Untold Story of the Malmedy Massacre at the Battle of the Bulge*, by Danny S. Parker; *The Ghost in General Patton's Third Army: The Memoirs of Eugene G. Schulz During His Service in the United States Army in World War II*, by Eugene G. Schulz; *Battle of the Bulge 1944 (2): Bastogne*, by Steven J. Zaloga; and the underrated *Once Upon a Time in War: The 99th Division in World War II*, by Robert E. Humphrey.

Adolf Hitler is modern history's best-known madman, so to step inside his world is frightening, to say the least. It helped to follow the research of other writers who had gone there already, including firsthand accounts by Otto Skorzeny (*Skorzeny's Special Missions: The Memoirs of Hitler's Most Daring Commando*) and Traudl Junge (*Hitler's Last Secretary: A Firsthand Account of Life with Hitler*). In addition, *Inside Hitler's Bunker: The Last Days of the Third Reich*, by Joachim Fest; *Hitler*, by Joachim Fest; *Hitler*, by Robin Cross; and *Hitler: A Biography*, by Ian Kershaw were all spectacular.

The Big Three Allied leaders were vital to telling this story properly, and their prominence ensured that a great amount of archival detail was available to document their movements and thoughts. Books of note were *The Lesser Terror: Soviet State Security, 1939–1953*, by Michael Parrish; *Joseph Stalin: A Biographical Companion*, by Helen Rappaport; *The FDR Years*, by William D. Pederson; *My Dear Mr. Stalin: The Complete Correspondence of Franklin D. Roosevelt and Joseph V. Stalin*, edited by Susan Butler; *No Ordinary Time: Franklin & Eleanor Roosevelt: The Home Front in World War II*, by Doris Kearns Goodwin; *Defending the West: The Truman-Churchill Correspondence, 1945–1960*, edited by G.

W. Sand; *The Last Thousand Days of the British Empire,* by Peter Clarke; and *The Road to Berlin,* volume 2 of *Stalin's War with Germany,* by John Erickson.

Thanks to these authors, and to those whose books are not mentioned but whose research aided in building this narrative.

Acknowledgments

My assistant Makeda Wubneh and literary agent Eric Simonoff were invaluable in helping me write *Killing Patton* with Marty Dugard, the best researcher I have ever known.

—BILL O'REILLY

Thanks to Eric Simonoff, the world's greatest agent. To Bill O'Reilly, a master storyteller and all-around great guy from whom I have learned so much. And, as always, to Callie: You are my sunshine.

—MARTIN DUGARD

Illustration Credits

Maps by Gene Thorp
Page xii: © Bettmann/CORBIS
Page 30: © Berliner/Verlag/Archiv/dpa/Corbis
Page 34: Archive Photos/Getty Images
Page 37: Popperfoto/Getty Images
Page 42: Hulton Archive/Getty Images
Page 44: AP Images
Page 46: © Hulton-Deutsch Collection/CORBIS
Page 52: National Archives
Page 55: Mondadori via Getty Images
Page 56: Mondadori via Getty Images
Page 63: Hulton Archive/Getty Images
Page 65: Time & Life Pictures/Getty Images
Page 86: Archive Photos/Getty Images
Page 96: top, © German Federal Archives/Bild 183-R65485/Kurt Alber; bottom, AP Images
Page 100: Gene Thorp
Page 113: © Corbis
Page 120: Archive Photos/Getty Images
Page 153: © 1949, 2014, *Stars and Stripes*
Page 156: AP Images
Page 162: Hulton Archive/Getty Images
Page 164: Archive Photos/Getty Images
Page 168: © Bettmann/CORBIS
Page 174: © Bettmann/CORBIS
Page 183: Premium Archive/Getty Images
Page 204: Archive Photos/Getty Images

Page 208: Courtesy of the *Weekly Standard*
Page 217: Courtesy of the Franklin D. Roosevelt Presidential Library Hyde Park, New York
Page 239: © Bettmann/CORBIS
Page 244: AP Images
Page 269: AP Images
Page 279: UIG via Getty images
Page 282: © Yergeny Khaldei/Corbis
Page 292: Time & Life Pictures/Getty Images
Page 293: © CORBIS
Page 303: Courtesy of the Department of Defense
Page 307: © CORBIS
Page 316: Walter Bibikow/JAI/Corbis

Index

Page numbers in *italics* refer to illustrations.